N

MW01673857

Beatrix Jungman

Alpha Editions

This edition published in 2022

ISBN: 9789356906198

Design and Setting By

Alpha Editions
www.alphaedis.com

Email - info@alphaedis.com

Contents

THE INVASION OF GREAT BRITAIN BY THE NORTHMEN

Norway.

PREFACE

IN preparing this volume it has been my aim to omit as few important events as possible without making the book a mere enumeration of names and dates. Above all, I have tried to be accurate. Among the works which I have used as sources, the first one to be mentioned is the great work of Snorre Sturlason: "The Heimskringla, or The Sagas of the Norse Kings," and I have used the English translation of the same by Samuel Laing, Esq., revised edition by Rasmus B. Anderson (Scribner & Welford, New York, 1889). I have also found much assistance in O. A. Överland's "Norges Historie." Among many other works used as sources or consulted, are: J. E. Sars's "Udsigt over den Norske Historie"; Jacob Aall's "Erindringer"; F. Winkel Horn's "History of the Literature of the Scandinavian North," translated by R. B. Anderson (S. C. Griggs & Co, Chicago, 1895). The Constitution of Norway, the most liberal Constitution of Europe, appeared to me to be an appropriate closing chapter in a History of Norway. This interesting document has been translated into English by the Honorable Knute Nelson, United States Senator from Minnesota, to whom I am under obligation for permission to use his translation.

S. S.

MINNEAPOLIS, MINN., 1899.

CHAPTER I
The Northmen

NORWAY (in the old Norse language *Noregr*, or *Nord-vegr*, *i.e.*, the North Way), according to archæological explorations, appears to have been inhabited long before the historical time. The antiquaries maintain that three populations have inhabited the North: a Mongolian race and a Celtic race, types of which are to be found in the Finns and the Laplanders in the far North, and, finally, a Caucasian race, which immigrated from the South and drove out the Celtic and Laplandic races, and from which the present inhabitants are descended. The Norwegians, or Northmen (Norsemen), belong to a North-Germanic branch of the Indo-European race; their nearest kindred are the Swedes, the Danes, and the Goths. The original home of the race is supposed to have been the mountain region of Balkh, in Western Asia, whence from time to time families and tribes migrated in different directions. It is not known when the ancestors of the Scandinavian peoples left the original home in Asia; but it is probable that their earliest settlements in Norway were made in the second century before the Christian era.

The first settlers probably knew little of agriculture, but made their living by fishing and hunting. In time, however, they commenced to clear away the timber that covered the land in the valleys and the sides of the mountains and to till the ground. At the earliest times of which the historical tales or *Sagas* tell us anything with regard to the social conditions, the land was divided among the free peasant-proprietors, or *bonde* class. Bonde, in English translation, is usually called peasant; but this is not an equivalent; for with the word peasant we associate the idea of inferior social condition to the landed aristocracy of the country, while these peasants or bondes were themselves the highest class in the country. The land owned by a peasant was called his *udal*. By udal-right the land was kept in the family, and it could not be alienated or forfeited from the kindred who were udal-born to it. The free peasants might own many thralls or slaves, who were unfree men. These were mostly prisoners captured by the vikings on their expeditions to foreign shores; the owners could trade them away, or sell them, or even kill them without paying any fine or *man-bote* to the king, as in the case of the killing of a free man. As a rule, however, the slaves were not badly treated, and they were sometimes made free and given the right to acquire land.

In early days Norway consisted of a great number of small states called *Fylkis*, each a little kingdom by itself. The free peasants in a Fylki held general assemblies called *Things*, where laws were made and justice administered. No public acts were undertaken without the deliberation of a Thing. The *Thing* was sacred, and a breach of peace at the *thing*-place was considered a great crime. At the Thing there was also a hallowed place for the judges, or "lag-men," who expounded and administered the laws made by the Thing. Almost every crime could be expiated by the payment of fines, even if the accused had killed a person. But if a man killed another secretly, he was declared an assassin and an outlaw, was deprived of all his property, and could be killed by any one who wished to do so. The fine or man-bote was heavier, the higher the rank of the person killed. For a thrall or slave no man-bote was paid.

The *Thing* or *Fylkis Thing* was not made up of representatives elected by the people, but was rather a primary assembly of the free udal-born peasant-proprietors of the district. There were leading men in the *fylki*, and each *fylki* had one or more chiefs, but they had to plead at the *Thing* like other free men. When there were several chiefs, they usually had the title of *herse*; but when the free men had agreed upon one chief, he was called *jarl* (earl), or king. The king was the commander in war, and usually performed judicial functions; but he supported himself from his own estates, and the free peasants paid no tax. The dignity of the king was usually inherited by his son, but if the heir was not to the liking of the peasants or people, they chose another. No man, however clear his right of succession, would think of assuming the title or power of a king except by the vote of a Thing. There he was presented to the people by a free peasant, and his right must be confirmed by the Thing before he could exert any act of kingly power. The king had a number of free men in his service, who had sworn allegiance to him, and who served him in war and in peace. They were armed men, kept in pay, and were called *hird-men* or court-men, because they were members of the king's *hird* or court. If they were brave and faithful, they were often given high positions of trust; some were made *lendermen* (liegemen), or managers of the king's estates.

CHAPTER II

The Religion of the Northmen

THE religion of the ancient Norwegians was of the same origin as that of all the other Germanic nations, and its main features will be given in this chapter.

In the beginning of time there were two worlds; in the south was Muspelheim, luminous and flaming, with Surt as a ruler. In the north was Niflheim, cold and dark, with the spring Hvergelmer, where the dragon Nidhugger dwells. Between these worlds was the yawning abyss Ginungagap. From the spring Hvergelmer ran icy streams into the Ginungagap. The hoar-frost from these streams was met by sparks from Muspelheim, and by the power of the heat the vapors were given life in the form of the Yotun or giant Ymer and the cow Audhumbla, on whose milk he lives. From Ymer descends the evil race of Yotuns or frost-giants. As the cow licked the briny hoar-frost, the large, handsome and powerful Bure came into being. His son was Bur, who married a daughter of a Yotun and became the father of *Odin*, Vile, and Ve. Odin became the father of the kind and fair *Æsir*, the gods who rule heaven and earth.

Bur's sons killed Ymer, and in his blood the whole race of Yotuns drowned except one couple, from whom new races of Yotuns or giants descended. Bur's sons dragged the body of Ymer into the middle of Ginungagap. Out of the trunk of the body they made the earth and of his blood the sea. His bones became the mountains, and of his hair they made trees. From the skull they made the heavens, which they elevated high above the earth and decorated with sparks from Muspelheim. But his brain was scattered in the air and became clouds. Around the earth they let the deep waters flow, and on the distant shores the escaped Yotuns took up their abode in Yotunheim and in Utgard. For protection against them the kind gods made from Ymer's eyebrows the fortification Midgard as a defence for the inner earth. But from heaven to earth they suspended the quivering bridge called Bifrost, or the rainbow.

The Yotun woman Night, black and dark as her race, met Delling (the Dawn) of the Æsir race, and with him became the mother of Day, who was bright and fair as his father. Odin placed mother and son in the heavens and bid them each in turn ride over the earth. Night rides ahead with her horse Hrimfaxe, from whose foaming bit the earth is every morning covered with dew. Day follows with his horse Skinfaxe, whose radiant mane spreads light and air over the earth.

A great number of maggots were bred in Ymer's body, and they became gnomes or dwarfs, little beings whom the gods gave human sense and appearance. They lived within the mountains and were skilful metal-workers, but they could not endure the light of day. Four dwarfs, the East, West, North, and South, were placed by the gods to carry the arch of heaven.

As yet there were no human beings on earth. Then, one day, the three gods, Odin, Hœner, and Lodur, were walking on the shore of the sea, where they found two trees, and from them they made the first man and the first woman, Ask and Embla (ash and elm). Odin gave them life, Hœner reason, Lodur blood and fair complexion. The gods gave them Midgard for a home, and from them the whole human race is descended.

The ever green ash tree Ygdrasil is the finest of all trees. It shoots up from three roots. One of them is in the well Hvergelmer in Niflheim, and on this the dragon Nidhugger is gnawing. The other root is in Yotunheim, in the wise Yotun Mimer's fountain. One of Odin's eyes, which he pledged for a drink of the fountain, is kept here. Whoever drinks of this fountain becomes wise. The third root is in heaven, at the Urdar well, where the gods hold their Thing or court. To this place they ride daily over the bridge Bifrost. Here also the three Norns abide, the maidens Urd, Verdande, and Skuld (past, present, and future). They pour water from the well over the roots of the tree. The Norns distribute life and govern fate, and nothing can change their decision.

The dwelling in heaven of the *Æsir* or gods is called Asgard. In its middle was the field of Ida, the gathering place of the gods, with Odin's throne, Lidskialv, from which he views the whole world. Odin is the highest and the oldest of the gods, and all the others honor him as their father. Odin's hall is Valhalla. The ceiling of this hall is made of spears, it is covered with shields, and its benches are ornamented with coats of mail. To this place Odin invites all who have fallen in battle, and he is therefore called Valfather, *i.e.*, the father of the fallen. The invited fallen heroes are called *Einherier*; their sport and pastime is to go out every day and fight and kill each other; but toward evening they awake to life again and ride home as friends to Valhalla, where they feast on pork of the barrow Særimner, and where Odin's maidens, the Valkyrias, fill their horns with mead. These Valkyrias were sent by Odin to all battles on earth, where they selected those who were to be slain and afterward become the honored guests at Valhalla. At Odin's side sit the two wolves, Gere and Freke, and on his shoulders the ravens Hugin and Munin. These ravens fly forth every morning and return with tidings from all parts of the world. Odin's horse is the swift, gray, eight-footed Sleipner. When he rides to battle he wears a golden helmet, a beautiful coat of mail, and carries the spear Gungner, which never fails. Odin is also the god of wisdom and poesy; in the morning of time he deposited one of his eyes in pledge for a drink of Mimer's fountain of wisdom, and he drank Suttung's mead in order to gain the gift of poesy. He has also taught men the art of writing Runes and all secret arts.

Thor, the son of Odin, is the strongest of all the gods. His dwelling is called Thrudvang. He rides across the heavens in a cart drawn by two rams. He is always at war with the Yotuns or evil giants, and in battle with them he uses his great hammer, Mjolner, which he hurls at the heads of his enemies. The earth trembles under the wheels of his cart, and men call the noise thunder. Thor's wife is Sif, whose hair is of gold.

Balder is a son of Odin and Frigg. He is so fair that his countenance emits beams of brightness. He is wise and gentle, and is therefore loved by all. His dwelling is Breidablik, where nothing impure exists. Nanna is his wife.

Njord comes from the race of the wise Vanir. He rules the wind, can calm the sea and stop fire, and he distributes wealth among men. His aid is invoked for success in navigation and fishing. His wife is Skade, daughter of a Yotun, and his dwelling is Noatun by the sea.

Frey, the son of Njord, rules rain and sunshine and the productiveness of the soil, and his aid is needed to get good crops, peace, and wealth. His dwelling is Alfheim. He sails in the magnificent ship "Skibladner," which was built for him by the dwarfs. His wife is the Yotun daughter Gerd, but in order to get her he had to give away his good sword, so that he will be unarmed in the coming final battle of the gods.

Tyr, Odin's son, is the god of courage and victory, whom brave men call upon in battle. He has only one hand, for the Fenris-Wolf bit off his right hand.

Brage, the long-bearded, is the god of eloquence and poetry. His wife is Idun, who has in her keeping the apples of which the gods eat to preserve their eternal youth.

Heimdal, the white god with teeth of gold, was in the beginning of time born by nine Yotun maidens, all sisters. He is the watchman of the gods. He is more wakeful than birds. He can see a hundred miles off, and he can hear the grass grow. His dwelling is Himinbjorg, which is situated where the Bifrost bridge reaches heaven. When he blows his Gjallar-horn it is heard throughout the world.

Among the other gods were Haad, son of Odin, blind but strong; the silent and strong Vidar; Vale, the archer; Ull, the fast ski-runner, and Forsete, the son of Balder, who settles disputes between gods and men.

Among the goddesses (or *asynier*), Frigg, Odin's wife, is the foremost. She knows the fate of everybody and shields many from danger. Her dwelling is Fensal. Next comes Freya, the goddess of love. She is the daughter of Njord and sister of Frey. She is also called Vanadis, or the goddess of the Vanir. She was married to Odd, and by him had a daughter, Noss. But Odd left her, and Freya weeps in her longing for him, and her tears are red gold. When she travels her wagon is drawn by two cats. The name of her dwelling is Folkvang. There were also a number of other goddesses, who were in the service of either Frigg or Freya.

Æger, the ruler of the turbulent and stormy sea, is a Yotun, but he is a friend of the gods. When they visit him his hall is lighted with shining gold. His wife is Ran, and their daughters are the waves.

In the beginning there was peace among gods and men. But the arrival of the Yotun women in Asgard undermined the happiness of the gods, and in heaven and on earth a struggle commenced which must last until both are destroyed. The Yotuns continually attack the inhabitants of Asgard, and it is only the mighty Thor who can hold them at bay. It is the evil Loke, who is the worst enemy of gods and men. He belongs to the Yotun race, but was early adopted among the gods. He was fair in looks, but wily and evil in spirit. He had three evil children—the Fenris-Wolf, the Midgard-Serpent, and Hel. The gods knew that this offspring of Loke would cause great trouble; therefore they tied the Fenris-Wolf, threw the serpent into the sea, and hurled Hel down into Niflheim, where she became the ruler of the dead. All who die from sickness or age are sent to her awful dwelling, Helheim.

The greatest sorrow which Loke caused the whole world was that by his deceit he caused the death of the lovely god, Balder. Then the gods took an awful revenge. They tied him to three stones, and over his head they fastened a venomous serpent, whose poison always was to drip upon his face. Loke's faithful wife, Sigyn, placed herself at his side and held a cup under the poisonous drip; but whenever the cup is full and she goes to empty it, the poison drips into Loke's face, and then he writhes in agony so that the whole world trembles. This is the cause of earthquakes.

There will come a time when these gods and the world shall perish in *Ragnarokk*, which means the perdition of the gods. They will have many warnings. Corruption and wickedness will be common in the world. For three years there will be winter without sun. The sun and the moon will be swallowed up by the wolves of the Yotuns, and the bright stars will disappear. The earth will tremble, and the mountains will collapse, and all chains and ties are sundered. The Fenris-Wolf and Loke get loose, and the Midgard-Serpent leaves the ocean. The ship "Naglfar" carries the army of the Yotuns across the sea under the leadership of the Yotun *Rym*, and Loke advances at the head of the hosts from the abode of Hel. The heavens split, and the sons of Muspel come riding ahead, led by their chief Surt. As the hosts are rushing across the Bifrost, the bridge breaks behind them. All are hastening to the great battle-place, the plains of *Vigrid*, which is a hundred miles wide. Now Heimdal arises and blows his Gjallar-horn, all the gods are assembled, the ash Ygdrasil trembles, and everything in heaven and on earth is filled with terror. Gods and Einherier (the fallen heroes) arm themselves for the battle. In the front rides Odin with his golden helmet and beaming coat of mail and carrying his spear, Gungner. He meets the Fenris-Wolf, who swallows him, but Vidar avenges his father and kills the wolf. Thor crushes the head of the Midgard-Serpent, but is stifled to death by its venom. Frey is felled by Surt, and Loke and Heimdal kill each other. Finally Surt hurls his fire over the world, gods and men die, and the shrivelling earth sinks into the abyss.

But the world shall arise again and the dead come to life. From above comes the all-powerful one, he who rules everything, and whose name no one dares utter. All those who were virtuous and pure of heart will gather in *Gimle* in everlasting happiness, while the evil ones will go to Naastrand at the well Hvergelmer to tie tortured by Nidhugger. A new earth, green and beautiful, shall rise from the ocean. The gods awake to new life and join *Vidar* and *Vale*, and the sons of Thor, Mode and Magne, who have survived the great destruction and who have been given their father's hammer, because there is to be no more war. All the gods assemble on the field of Ida, where Asgard was located. And from *Liv* and *Livthraser*, who hid themselves in Ygdrasil during the burning of the world, a new human race shall descend.

CHAPTER III

The Viking Age

IT is but natural that the ancient Norwegians should become warlike and brave men, since their firm religious belief was that those who died of sickness or old age would sink down into the dark abode of Hel (Helheim), and that only the brave men who fell in battle would be invited to the feasts in Odin's Hall. Sometimes the earls or kings would make war on their neighbors, either for conquest or for revenge. But a time came when the countries of the north with their poorly developed resources became overpopulated, and the warriors had to seek better fields abroad. The viking cruises commenced, and for a long time the Norwegians continued to harry the coasts of Europe.

At first the viking expeditions were nothing but piracy, carried on for a livelihood. The name Viking is supposed to be derived from the word *vik*, a cove or inlet on the coast, in which they would harbor with their ships and lie in wait for merchants sailing by. Soon these expeditions assumed a wider range and a wilder character, and historians of the time paint the horrors spread by the vikings in dark colors. In the English churches they had a day of prayer each week to invoke the aid of heaven against the harrying Northmen. In France the following formula was inserted in the church prayer: "*A furore Norman norum libera nos, o Domine!*" (Free us, O Lord, from the fury of the Northmen!)

Gradually the viking life assumed a nobler form. There appear to be three stages or periods in the viking age. In the first one the vikings make casual visits with single ships to the shores of England, Ireland, France or Flanders, and when they have plundered a town or a convent they return to their ships and sail away. In the second period their cruises assume a more regular character, and indicate some definite plan, as they take possession of certain points, where they winter, and from where they command the surrounding country. During the third period they no longer confine themselves to seeking booty, but act as real conquerors, take possession of the conquered territory and rule it.

In the latter part of the eighth century the vikings first found their way across the North Sea to the islands north of Scotland. In 787 they landed for the first time on the British coast. In that year it is recorded in the English annals that Norwegians came in three ships and committed great ravages on the coasts of Wessex. Six years later they attacked Northumberland, where they caused even greater ruin. They especially plundered churches and cloisters. Soon they extended their plundering expeditions to the northern coast of France, where the powerful emperor Charlemagne was then the ruler. They made only small progress as long as he lived, but during the reigns of his weak successors they made havoc along the coasts of France, and also forced the Straits of Gibraltar and made unwelcome visits to the countries on the Mediterranean. Some of the French kings knew no better remedy than to pay the vikings great sums of money to keep them away from the country. Thus King Charles the Baldheaded paid in the year 846 a sum of 7,000 pounds of silver, and in 877 a further sum of 5,000 pounds, for this purpose.

The Northmen, by their viking expeditions, early took possession of the Orkneys, the Shetland Islands, the Hebrides and the Faroe Islands. In going westward to these islands they were sometimes driven out of their course, and thus Nadodd, who was on his way to the Faroe Islands, was driven far to the north and northwest and found a large uninhabited country, which was afterward called Iceland.

The vikings often came to Ireland, and about the year 837 they succeeded, under the leadership of the chieftain Thorgeisl, in establishing a kingdom at Dublin, which they strongly fortified. Thorgeisl appears to have ruled in Ireland until about 846, when he was drowned. A more permanent kingdom was established by Olaf the White, who took possession of Dublin and the surrounding country in 852. The dominion in Dublin of the Norwegians is supposed to have lasted for three and a half centuries.

As to the influence of the Northmen on the development of the countries visited by them during the later Viking periods, the eminent English writer Samuel Laing, the translator of the "Heimskringla," or the Sagas of the Norse kings, says:

"All that men hope for of good government and future improvement in their physical and moral condition—all that civilized men enjoy at this day of civil, religious and political liberty—the British constitution, representative legislation, the trial by jury, security of property, freedom of mind and person, the influence of public opinion over the conduct of public affairs, the Reformation, the liberty of the press, the spirit of the age—all that is or has been of value to man in modern times as a member of society, either in Europe or in the New World, may be traced to the spark left burning upon our shores by these northern barbarians."

CHAPTER IV

The Yngling Family—Halfdan the Swarthy

THE authentic history begins with Halfdan the Swarthy, or Halfdan the Black, who reigned from about the year 821 to about 860. The Icelander Snorre Sturlason, who, in the twelfth century, wrote the "Heimskringla," or the Sagas of the Norse Kings, gives a long line of preceding kings of the Yngling race, the royal family to which Halfdan the Swarthy belonged; but that part of the Saga belongs to mythology rather than to history.

According to tradition the Yngling family were descendants of Fiolner, the son of the god Frey. One of the surnames of the god was Yngve, from which the family derived the name Ynglings. Their original home is said to have been Upsala in Sweden, but they were driven away on account of their cruelty. One of them, whose name was Olaf, emigrated with his followers to Vermeland, which he made habitable by cleaning away a great deal of the timber. Hence he was called Olaf the Tree-feller (Tre-telgja). His son, Halfdan Whiteleg (Hvitbein), conquered Romerike and other Norwegian districts, and Halfdan's son also became king of Vestfold, or the country west of the Folden, the bay now called the Christiania Fjord. Vestfold now became the most important part of the country. In the neighborhood of the present town of Laurvik a famous temple was founded in Skirings-sal, where the kings often resided, and which soon became a popular trading place.

Halfdan Whiteleg's grandson, Gudrod the Hunter, made war on Harald Redbeard, who was king of Agder, the southwestern part of Norway. He killed Harald and his son Gyrd, and took a great booty. He afterward married Harald's daughter, Asa.

Gudrod's son, Halfdan, surnamed the Swarthy, was only a year old when his father was killed, and his mother Asa then returned with him to Agder, where he grew up and became stout and strong. At the age of eighteen he became king in Agder, and soon afterward went to Vestfold, where he divided that kingdom with his brother Olaf. Halfdan increased his possessions, both by marriage and by warfare, until he ruled over the whole country around the Christiania Fjord, Thoten, Land, Hadeland, Romerike and Sogn. King Halfdan was a wise man, a lover of truth and justice. He made good laws, which he observed himself and compelled others to observe. He fixed certain mulcts, or penalties, for all crimes committed. His code of laws, called the Eidsiva Law, was adopted at a common Thing at

Eidsvold, where about a thousand years later the present constitution of Norway was adopted.

Halfdan became the ancestor of the royal race of Norway, his son, Harald the Fairhaired, being the first king of united Norway. According to tradition, when Queen Ragnhild was with child she dreamed that she was standing in her herb-garden, and she took a thorn out of her chemise, and while she was holding it in her hand it grew into a great tree, one end of which struck roots into the earth, while the other raised itself in the air until she could hardly see the top or the end of its widely spread branches. The lower part of the tree was red with blood, but the stem was beautifully green, and the branches white as snow, and they spread over all Norway, and even much more. This dream was years afterward interpreted as having foretold the destiny of Ragnhild's son.

One day in the spring of 860, when Halfdan the Swarthy was driving home from a feast across the Randsfjord, he broke through the ice and was drowned. He was so popular that when his body was found the leading men in each *Fylki* demanded to have him buried with them, believing that it would bring prosperity to the district. They at last agreed to divide the body into four parts, which were buried in four different districts. The trunk of the body was buried in a mound at Stein, Ringerike, where a little hill is still called Halfdan's Mound.

CHAPTER V

Harald the Fairhaired (860-930)—Norway United

HARALD was only ten years old when he succeeded his father. Many of the chiefs thought that it would be an easy matter now to divide the country between them, but Guthorm, a brother of Harald's mother, who was at the head of the government and commander of the army, soon subdued them.

When Harald had become old enough to marry, he sent his men to a girl named Gyda, a daughter of King Erik of Hordaland, who was brought up as a foster-child in the house of a rich *Bonde* in Valders. Harald had heard of her as a very beautiful though proud girl. When the men delivered their message, she answered that she would not marry a king who had no greater kingdom than a few *Fylkis* (districts), and she added that she thought it strange "that no king here in Norway will make the whole country subject to him, in the same way as Gorm the Old did in Denmark, or Erik at Upsala." When the messengers returned to the king, they advised him to punish her for her haughty words, but Harald said she had spoken well, and he made the solemn vow not to cut or comb his hair until he had subdued the whole of Norway and had become the sole king.

Harald immediately gathered an army and went northward over the Dovre Mountain, and after several battles conquered the whole of Trondelag, the common name of all the districts about the Throndhjem (Drontheim) Fjord. Here he procured ships, sailed southward along the coast and conquered one district after another in the western part of the country. Finally, the remaining kings gathered their men and ships and met Harald in naval battle in Hafrsfjord, a little inlet in Jæderen, near the present city of Stavanger. The battle was fierce and long, but Harald finally gained the day. After this battle, which occurred in 872, King Harald met no opposition, and was acknowledged as king of the whole of Norway. Shortly after the battle the king attended a feast given by Ragnvald, the Earl of More (Morejarl), and the latter cut the king's hair, which had not been cut or combed for ten years, and gave him the surname, the Fairhaired. Harald shortly afterward married Gyda.

King Harald deprived the peasant-proprietors of their allodium or udal-right, and compelled them to pay land dues of their possessions. Over every *Fylki* or district he placed an earl *(jarl)*, who was to administer justice and collect the taxes, of which he retained one-third as salary. In case of war the earl was to serve the king with sixty warriors. Each earl had under him four *herses*, each of whom had a royal estate of twenty marks annual income to manage, and was bound to support twenty men-at-arms.

Many of the proud peasants objected to the rule of Harald and to the payment of taxes. They wanted to be independent, as before, and left the country. Many of them settled on the Faroe Islands and the Scotch islands, and in the summer they would make viking cruises and harry the coasts of Norway to revenge themselves on the king. To stop this Harald sailed westward one summer with a fleet, fought the vikings and took possession of Shetland and the Orkney Islands, and placed an earl in charge of them. Many of the fleeing Northmen then sailed northward with their goods and men and settled in *Iceland*, where they established a free state, which existed for nearly 400 years.

Earl Ragnvald (Morejarl) was King Harald's dearest friend, and the king had great regard for him, but he did not allow that to excuse a crime committed by his son. Ragnvald had a son by the name of Rolf, who was so stout and strong that no horse could carry him, and therefore he was called Gange-Rolf, or Rolf the Walker. He went early on viking cruises to the shores of the Baltic Sea. One summer, on his return from one of his expeditions, he made *strand-hug* in Viken. (Strand-hug was a foray for cattle to provision the viking ships.) Harald had declared this a great crime, and when he heard what Rolf had done, he called an extra session of the Thing, and had Rolf declared an outlaw in all Norway. Gange-Rolf, however, did not remain in Norway, but sailed westward to the Sudreys, the present Hebrides, and afterward joined the army of vikings, which, in the year 885, went to France and plundered the country around Paris and the province of Bourgogne. The Frenchmen made a compromise with the vikings, and for some years they spared the French coasts, but later Gange-Rolf returned with a great number of vikings, and finally compelled the French king, Charles the Simple, by the peace of Saint-Clair-sur-Epte to cede to him and his successors a large province, which he peopled with Northmen, and which, therefore, was afterward called Normandy. The French king also promised to let him marry his daughter Gizela if he would adopt Christianity. This Rolf agreed to, and he was baptized in the year 912, being christened Robert. He ruled his new country well, and died in the year 931. From him descended the mighty earls of Normandy, who in time conquered the kingdoms of England and Naples.

King Harald had many sons, and as they grew up they created a great deal of disturbance in the country. They had come from such different stock on the maternal side, and had been brought up so far from each other by rich peasants in different parts of the country, that brotherly feelings were little known to them. They became jealous of each other, and also jealous of the many mighty earls. They drove some of the earls from their estates, and even killed some of them. Thus two of the brothers set out one spring with a great force to attack Ragnvald, Earl of More, surrounded his house and burned him with sixty of his men.

Hoping to avoid further domestic disturbances, Harald called together a *Thing* at the Eidsiva Thing-place (the present Eidsvold), and summoned to it all the people of the Uplands. Here he gave to all his sons the title of king, and proclaimed a law that his descendants in the male line should each succeed to the title and dignity of king; but his descendants by the female side were to become only earls. He divided the country among his sons, but his dearest son, Erik, who was his son by the Danish Princess Ragnhild, and thus of royal birth on both sides, was to be acknowledged as their overlord. This the other brothers did not like, and the result was bloody conflicts. Erik first killed Ragnvald Rettilbeine, the ruler in Hadeland, because he was said to be a sorcerer. Next he attacked his brother Biorn, who generally lived at the trading-place Tunsberg, and who was called Biorn Farmand, or Biorn the Merchant, because he cared little for war, but more for trading expeditions. As he refused to pay tribute to Erik, the latter attacked and killed him, and plundered his house. King Biorn lies buried in the Seaman's Mound (Farmandshaugen) at Sæheim (in the present Sem's parish) in Jarlsberg. Halfdan the Black, who ruled in Throndhjem, resolved to avenge his brother Biorn's death, and collected a great force of men and ships. Erik sought the aid of his father Harald, who also equipped a fleet and took up a position at Rein-plain on the north side of the Throndhjem Fjord; but now friends of both interceded in order to bring about a reconciliation. In Halfdan's army there was a clever man called Guthorm Sindre, who had formerly been in the service of Harald, and was a great friend of both. He was a great skald (poet), and had once composed songs about the father and the son, for which they had then offered him a reward. He would take nothing at the time, but was given the promise that, some day or other, they should grant him any request he should make. He now went before King Harald with words of peace, and made the request that the kings should become reconciled. And the Saga adds: "So highly did the king esteem him that, in consequence of his request, they were reconciled."

When Harald the Fairhaired was eighty years old, he became very weak and unable to bear the burden of the government. Then he brought his son Erik to his royal high-seat and gave him the power and the command over the whole land (930). Three years later King Harald died of old age. He was buried under a mound at Hauge, near Haugesund in Ryfylke. The gravestone is still to be seen. At the grave a large monument in memory of Harald was erected in 1872, one thousand years after the battle of Hafrsfjord.

CHAPTER VI

Birth of Haakon the Good—Erik Blood-Axe (930-935)

WHEN Harald the Fairhaired was nearly seventy years old, he begat a son by Thora Moster-stang (Moster-pole). She was so called because she was tall, and her family came from the island of Moster. She was very handsome, and was descended from good people, but was called the king's servant-girl, for at that time, as the Saga says, "many were subject to service to the king who were of good birth, both men and women." Sigurd Ladejarl, or Earl of Lade (near Throndhjem), was a friend of Thora's family, and when she was about to be confined he brought her in his ship from Moster northward to Sæheim, where King Harald was then living. They spent the night at the shore south of the Alv-island, and here Thora bore her child, on a stone near the ship's gangway. It was a male child, and Earl Sigurd baptized him in heathen fashion, and called him Haakon after his own father. The boy soon grew handsome, large in size, and very like his father King Harald. When the king felt that he was not going to live much longer, he sent Haakon over to England to be brought up by the English king, Athelstan, the grandson of Alfred the Great. King Athelstan had Haakon baptized and brought up in the Christian faith, and in good habits and all sorts of exercises, and it is said he loved Haakon above all his relations. He gave him a sword, of which the hilt and handle were gold; but the blade was still better, for with it Haakon cut a millstone to the centre eye. The sword was thereafter called Kvernbite (millstone cutter), and Haakon carried it to his dying day.

As stated, Erik was proclaimed king by his father in 930. Erik had early gone out on viking expeditions, and his daring enterprises had given him the surname Blood-Axe. He was handsome and manly-looking, but morally weak. He was hated during his father's lifetime, because he had killed his brother Biorn the Merchant; but still more hated was his cruel and treacherous queen, Gunhild. She enticed him into killing several of his brothers, and it began to be the common belief that Gunhild and Erik were going to remove all his brothers, in order to secure the whole of the kingdom for themselves and their children. This plan, however, was frustrated by Haakon, the youngest son of Harald.

When Haakon, Athelstan's foster-son, heard of his father's death, he immediately prepared to leave England, and was given men and ships by King Athelstan. He sailed north to Tröndelagen, where he found the mighty Sigurd, Earl of Lade, who had been his mother's friend and his guardian in early childhood. Sigurd received him well, and Haakon promised him great power if he became king. They assembled a great meeting of the peasants, where Earl Sigurd made a speech and advised the people to make Haakon their king. Thereupon Haakon arose and made a speech, which greatly pleased the peasants. They said to each other that it looked as if Harald the Fairhaired had come back and had become young again. Haakon promised, in case they would make him their king, to give them back the udal-right (allodium), which Harald had taken from them. His speech was so well received that the people cheered wildly, and with great enthusiasm they proclaimed him their king. He immediately started southward, and the other districts followed the example of Tröndelagen and swore allegiance to Haakon.

Erik made a desperate attempt to raise an army, but not succeeding, he had to leave the country with his wife Gunhild, his children, and a few followers (935). For some time he harried the coasts of Scotland and England as a viking, until finally he accepted a portion of Northumberland from King Athelstan on the condition that he was to defend the country against Norwegian and Danish vikings. Erik remained in England under shifting conditions, until he was killed in a battle in 954. After his death Queen Gunhild had a poem written in his honor, the so-called Eriksmál, of which a beautiful fragment still exists. Shortly after Erik's death Queen Gunhild went to Denmark with her sons, and was well received by the Danish king, Harald Bluetooth (Blaatand), the son of Gorm the Old. The children of Erik Blood-Axe and Gunhild were: Gamle, Guthorm, Harald, Ragnfred, Ragnhild, Erling, Gudrod, and Sigurd Sleva. All the boys were handsome and of manly appearance, but in character they resembled their mother.

CHAPTER VII

Haakon the Good (935-961)

HAAKON did a great deal to improve the internal conditions of the country. He regulated the judicial districts, and gave the Gulathings-law for the western district, with common Thing-place at Gula (in Ytre Sogn), and the Frostathings-law for the northern district, with common Thing-place at Frosten (peninsula in Throndhjems-fjord). Much was done for the defence of the country against enemies. The whole coast was divided into *Skibredes*, or ship districts, each of which was to build, equip, man, and provision a ship for use in case of war. In order to inform the inhabitants of the approach of an enemy, King Haakon built *Varder*, or signal fires, on the highest mountains at proper distances from each other. By the successive lighting of these signal fires the news of war could be carried from the southernmost signal-place to the northern end of Halogaland in seven days. Warning was also to be sent around from house to house by *Budstikke* as a signal for the people to assemble. The *Budstikke* was a stick of wood like a very heavy cane, with a spike at the end of it. If the bearer of the message found nobody at home, he would stick the cane on the side of the door, and the owner of the house would, on his arrival home, immediately despatch it to the next house.

King Haakon, who had been brought up in the Christian faith, resolved to introduce Christianity in Norway, but when he took the preliminary steps he found no support from his otherwise faithful friend, Earl Sigurd of Lade, who was an ardent adherent of the Asa-faith. Fearing to offend the earl, Haakon postponed his effort for a time, until he thought he had gained sufficient popularity in the country. He then sent to England for a bishop and other teachers, and announced that it was his intention to have the whole people embrace the Christian religion. When he made this announcement to the assembled peasants at Throndhjem, they declined to commit themselves, and asked to have this very important matter referred to the Frosta-thing, where it could be legally settled.

At the Frosta-thing, where a great number of people were assembled, King Haakon made an earnest speech, in which he said that it was his command and his prayer to all, rich and poor, young and all, that they should forsake the old heathen gods, be baptized, and believe in the one living God, Jesus Christ, the son of the Virgin Mary, abstain from work every seventh day, Sunday, and fast every Friday. A great murmur ran through the crowd of peasants, who complained that the king wanted to deprive them of their work and their old faith, and the mighty peasant,

Asbiorn of Medalhus, arose and made a speech to the king, in which he said that they had had great faith in him when they chose him for their king, but now they had made up their minds to part with him and choose another if they were not left free to retain the religion they believed in. And the king was told that he must accept one of these conditions before the meeting was concluded. The king felt that there was no escape but to yield to the peasants, and Earl Sigurd of Lade, who had all the time been near the king, arose and said: "King Haakon is willing to acquiesce in your wishes, peasants. Never will he give up your friendship." Encouraged by this the peasants afterward made the king participate in their heathen sacrifices, and the king was obliged to give up the attempt to introduce Christianity in Norway.

King Haakon soon afterward had to meet other demands upon him, when the southern parts of the country were attacked by the sons of his brother Erik, who, after their mother, were called the Gunhild-sons. Several times Haakon defeated the invaders, and after one great battle they stayed away for six years. Finally, in the twenty-sixth year of Haakon's reign, while he and his men were enjoying a feast at Fitje on the island Stord in Hordaland, the enemy appeared again with a great naval force. Although greatly outnumbered by the enemy, Haakon's men won the battle, and the aggressors were obliged to flee to their ships; but when Haakon pursued them without his coat of mail, he was hit in the armpit by a deadly arrow and received a wound from which he died, after being brought, shortly after the battle, to "Haakon's Rock," where he had been born. Before he died he requested his friends to send a ship after the sons of Gunhild, with the message asking them to return and assume the government, giving due respect to his adherents. He himself had no sons, and his daughter Thora could not, according to the law, succeed to the throne. Haakon was deeply mourned by friends and foes, and all said that Norway would never again get such a good king. The poet Eyvind Skaldaspiller composed a poem in his honor, the Haakonarmaal, in which he praised his virtues and described his reception in Odin's Valhalla.

CHAPTER VIII

Harald Grayfell and his Brothers (961-970)

THE Gunhild-sons (or Eriks-sons) immediately returned to Norway when they received the message that Haakon the Good had named them as heirs to the throne. The oldest one, Harald Grayfell (Graafeld, so named after having once worn a gray fur robe), was considered as chief king, but their mother Gunhild was in fact the chief ruler. They were penurious and cruel, and soon became widely hated. There were many chiefs in the country at that time. Trygve Olafson, a grandson of Harald the Fairhaired, ruled in Viken, or the country around the Christiania Fjord; his cousin Gudrod, son of Biorn the Merchant, was chief in Westfold, and Earl Sigurd of Lade ruled the country around Throndhjem. Gunhild's sons at first resided mostly in the middle of the country, but soon laid plans to obtain more power. By great promises they bribed Griotgard, a brother of Earl Sigurd, to send them word when there might be a favorable opportunity to attack and kill the earl. This plan succeeded. Having been notified by Griotgard that Earl Sigurd was at a feast at Oglo in Stjoradal and had but few men with him, King Harald Grayfell and his brother Erling surrounded the house at night, set fire to the building, and burned the earl and all his men.

When the people heard of Earl Sigurd's death, there was a great uprising. They gathered a large fleet, and, after having proclaimed Sigurd's son, Haakon, as their earl and commander-in-chief, they steered out of the Throndhjem Fjord, intent upon taking vengeance. When Gunhild's sons heard of this, they fled southward to Raumsdal and South More. Some time afterward the Gunhild-sons attacked and murdered Trygve Olafson, king in Viken, and Gudrod Biornson, king in Westfold. Harald Grayfell hastened to Trygve Olafson's home, hoping to be able to exterminate the whole race; but Trygve's widow, Astrid, had fled with her foster-father, Thorolf Lusarskeg.

Gunhild's sons collected a great army in Viken and sailed northward, collecting men and ships on the way from every district for the purpose of fighting Earl Haakon. When Earl Haakon heard of this, he also collected men and fitted out ships, but when he ascertained the size of the approaching fleet, he sailed with a few men south to Denmark, where he was well received by King Harald Bluetooth (964). Gunhild's sons brought their army north to Throndhjem, and subdued the country and collected taxes, of which they had received none while Earl Haakon was there.

In Denmark Earl Haakon laid some deep plans to obtain power again. A nephew of King Harald Bluetooth, called Gold-Harald, had returned home and demanded half of the kingdom. As the king had no desire to yield to his demand, but still feared Gold-Harald's influence with the people, Earl Haakon advised him to get Norway for his nephew instead. He was to invite the Norwegian king, Harald Grayfell, on a friendly visit to Denmark, and then have Gold-Harald kill him. Afterward it would be easy to take Norway on account of the very hard times prevailing there, and the great unpopularity of the Gunhild-sons. The plan was followed; but when Gold-Harald had killed Harald Grayfell, he was in turn attacked and killed by Earl Haakon. Soon after King Harald Bluetooth sailed for Norway with 720 ships. He had with him Earl Haakon, Harald Grenske, a son of King Gudrod, and many other great men who had fled from their udal estates in Norway on account of Gunhild's sons. They won the country without resistance, and King Harald installed Haakon as earl of the northern and western parts of the country. The earl was to pay certain taxes to the king and help him with armed men in case of war. The king retained for himself the country around Viken, and left Harald Grenske there as his representative.

The two surviving brothers, Gudrod and Ragnfred, fled with their mother, Gunhild, to the Orkneys.

CHAPTER IX

Earl Haakon (970-995)

EARL HAAKON subdued all those parts of the country belonging to his dominion, and remained all winter (970) in Throndhjem. As he proceeded along the coast he ordered that in all his dominions the heathen temples and sacrifices should be restored, and continued as of old. The people thought they soon had proof that the gods were pleased with Haakon's action, for, according to the saga, "the first winter that Haakon ruled over Norway the herrings set in everywhere through the fjords to the land, and the seasons ripened to a good crop all that had been sown," while for several years previously dearth and hard times had prevailed.

Earl Haakon waited for an opportunity to repudiate his obligations to the Danish king, and it came in time. In 973, when Otto II. became emperor of Germany, King Harald Bluetooth prepared himself for war in order to resist the emperor's claim to sovereignty over Denmark, and in 975 he ordered Earl Haakon to come to his aid with all the forces it was possible to raise. Haakon complied with the request, and for a time successfully fought the Germans. But when he had boarded his ships and prepared to sail homeward, the emperor returned for a second attack, and soon compelled the Danish king to make peace. King Harald Bluetooth agreed to introduce Christianity both in Denmark and in Norway. He sent for Earl Haakon and made him accept baptism and promise to introduce Christianity in Norway. Priests were sent with him to help him with this work. Haakon set sail with the priests on board; but no sooner did he get a favorable wind than he put the priests ashore, and sailed away. From now on he considered himself the sworn enemy of the Danes. He steered through the Sound, and harried the coasts on both sides. At the coast of East Gautland he made a great heathen sacrifice. Thereupon he burned his ships and marched through the country with his men. He defeated Earl Ottar, the ruler in Gautland, and continued his march through Smaaland and West Gautland to Norway. He again took up his residence in Throndhjem.

King Harald Bluetooth was greatly incensed at Earl Haakon's action, and decided to take an awful revenge. He collected a great fleet, which he brought to Norway. He burned and destroyed the settlements and killed a great number of people wherever he came. In Lærdal in Sogn, it is said that only five dwellings were left unburned. The inhabitants fled to the woods with such movable goods as they could save. As soon, however, as it was reported that Earl Haakon was coming southward with a fleet, King Harald lost his courage, set sail, and returned to Denmark.

When Harald Bluetooth died (985), his son Svein, who afterward was given the surname Tjuguskeg (Fork-beard), became king of Denmark. He instigated the Joms-vikings to make war on Earl Haakon. These vikings were Danes, who lived at Jomsborg, Pomerania, on the island Wollin or Jom, at the mouth of the river Oder. They were very powerful and warlike, and had very strict laws. No one could join their company who was older than fifty or younger than eighteen years, and no woman was permitted to enter their burgh. They considered it a disgrace to show fear or to complain of pain. Earl Sigvald (Sigvalde Jarl), a son of King Strut-Harald of Scania (Skaane, in the southern part of Sweden), was chief of the Joms-vikings at this time. King Svein of Denmark invited these vikings to a great feast in memory of his father, and as Earl Sigvald's father had fallen about the same time, he suggested that they should also drink his "funeral-ale." The Joms-vikings came to the festival with their bravest men, forty ships of them from Vendland (Pomerania), and twenty ships from Scania. All the guests drank a great deal, and there was great gayety in the hall. According to old custom on such occasions they made solemn vows, in emptying the drinking-horns. King Svein, in drinking to his father's memory, made the solemn vow, that before three winters were past he would go with his army to England and conquer King Ethelred. The guests also drank Christ's health, and a bowl to the memory of Saint Michael. Thereafter Earl Sigvald drank to his father's memory, and made a vow, that before three winters came to an end he would go to Norway and either kill Earl Haakon or chase him out of the country, and the other Joms-vikings vowed that they would go with Earl Sigvald to Norway and share in the fight. The next morning, when they had slept off their drink, they thought they had promised rather much, and, in order to find Earl Haakon unprepared, they sailed away on their expedition at once.

When Earl Erik, the son of Haakon, who was then in Raumarike, heard of the festival and of the vows of the Joms-vikings, he immediately gathered his men, and went to the Uplands, and thence over the mountains to Throndhjem, and joined his father, Earl Haakon. They immediately sent warnings around, and sent messages to North More and South More, and to Raumsdal, and also north to Namdal and Halogaland, summoning all the country to furnish men and ships. Earl Haakon went with an army to South More, and Erik was to follow with what army he could collect from the north.

Meanwhile, the Joms-vikings sailed slowly northward, plundering the coasts. Christmas night they were at Jæderen. At Hjorungavaag (on the island Hareidland in South More) they met Earl Haakon and his sons Erik,

Svein, Sigurd and Erling. The earl had 180 ships and boats, fully manned and equipped, and the Joms-vikings had 60 ships. A bloody and fierce battle followed, probably the greatest that had ever taken place in Norway. At first the advantage was on the side of the Joms-vikings, and Earl Haakon was hardly pressed. So many spears were thrown against him that his armor was split asunder, and he threw it off. It is said that Earl Haakon then sacrificed his young son Erling to the gods in order to gain victory. A great hailstorm arose, and the Joms-vikings were defeated, but only after a most desperate fight. Earl Sigvald turned and fled with some of his ships; but many of his men preferred to fall in battle. Haavard the Hewer (Huggende) stood on his knees and fought, after both his feet had been cut off. One of the champions, Bue the Thick (Digre), received a terrible cut that took away his under-lip and chin, and, seeing that resistance was in vain, he took a chest full of gold in each hand and shouted: "Overboard, all Bue's men," and jumped into the sea. After the battle the dead were ransacked by Haakon's men, and the booty brought together to be divided; and there were twenty-five ships of the Joms-vikings in the booty.

While Earl Haakon ruled over Norway there were good crops in the land and peace internally among the peasants. The earl, for a long time, was therefore well liked; but later he became proud and much given to debauchery. According to the saga, he would go so far as to have the daughters of people of high station brought home to him, and after keeping them a week or two send them home in shame. The people therefore began to murmur loudly, and finally they rose against him. Early in the year 995 Earl Haakon was at a feast at Medalhus in Gauldal. There was a mighty peasant in the neighborhood, by name Orm Lyrgja, who had a wife called Gudrun, a daughter of Bergthor of Lundar. She was called the Lundar-sun, because she was so beautiful. The earl sent his slaves to Orm, with the errand that they were to bring Gudrun to the earl. Orm first invited the slaves to take supper, and while they were eating and drinking he sent word around to all his neighbors, and soon had so many gathered at his house that he could refuse to let his wife be taken away. The slaves departed with many threats; but Orm sent out messages to all the neighboring country, and soon a large body of armed men were marching toward Medalhus where Haakon was. With a single thrall (slave) called Kark, who had been with him since boyhood, Earl Haakon fled across the Gaula River, rode his horse into a hole, and left his cloak behind on the ice, in order to make his pursuers believe that he had been drowned. Then he went to the estate of Rimul, where one of the earl's mistresses, Thora, lived, and asked her to hide him for a few days until the army of the peasants had dispersed. They went to a swine-sty, where Kark dug a deep hole and covered it with boards. The earl and Kark went into the hole, and Thora covered it, and threw earth and manure over it, and drove the swine upon the top of it.

Olaf Trygvason had just then arrived in the country, and when the peasants heard he was of the family of Harald the Fairhaired, they flocked around him and hailed him as their king. Then they all set about hunting for Earl Haakon. At Rimul they looked everywhere for him without finding him. Then Olaf held a House-Thing or council out in the yard, and stood upon a great stone which lay beside the swine-sty, and made a speech to the people, in which he promised rewards and honors to the man who should kill the earl. This speech was heard by the earl and the thrall Kark.

"Why art thou so pale," asked the earl, "and now again black as earth? Thou hast not the intention to betray me?"

"By no means," replied Kark.

"We were both born on the same night," said the earl, "and the time will be short between our deaths."

King Olaf went away in the evening. When night came the earl kept himself awake; but Kark slept, and was disturbed in his sleep. The earl woke him, and asked him what he had been dreaming.

Kark answered: "I was at Lade, and Olaf Trygvason was laying a golden ring about my neck."

The earl then said: "It will be a bloody ring Olaf will lay about thy neck if he catches thee. Take care of that! From me thou shalt enjoy all that is good, therefore betray me not."

Then they both kept awake, evidently mistrusting each other. But toward morning the earl dropped asleep. Then Kark killed him, and cut off his head, and hastened to Olaf Trygvason with it, but Olaf had the faithless thrall decapitated. Earl Haakon was fifty-eight years old at his death, in February, 995.

CHAPTER X

The Youth of Olaf Trygvason

WHEN the Gunhild-sons had killed Trygve Olafson, king in Viken (the grandson of Harald the Fairhaired), in 963, Trygve's widow Astrid fled with her foster-father, Thorolf Lusarskeg. Astrid was pregnant with a child of King Trygve, and she went to a lake and concealed herself on a small island with a few followers. Here she gave birth to a boy, and she called him Olaf, after his grandfather. She remained there all summer, but when the nights became dark, and the days began to shorten and the weather to be cold, she travelled further with Thorolf and a few others until she reached Ofrustad, where her father, Erik Biodaskalle, lived, and they remained there during the winter. But in the spring spies were sent out by Gunhild to find the boy, and Astrid had to flee again with her son. She proceeded eastward, and at last came to her father's friend, Haakon the Old, in Sweden, where she and her son remained a long time and were well treated. When Gunhild heard that Astrid and her son Olaf were in Sweden, she sent ambassadors to the king of Sweden with the request that the king assist them in getting hold of Olaf Trygvason, to bring him back to Norway, where Gunhild would bring him up. Astrid then determined to go with her son to Gardarike, or Russia, where she had a brother, Sigurd Eriksson, who held a high position there. Olaf was then three years old. As they sailed out into the Baltic, however, they were captured by vikings from Esthonia, who made booty both of the people and their goods, killing some, and taking others as slaves. Thorolf, whom they considered too old for a slave, was killed. Olaf was separated from his mother, and an Esthonian took him and a son of Thorolf as his share of the booty. The boys were sold for a stout and good ram, and a third man, called Reas, afterward bought Olaf for a good cloak. Olaf remained with Reas in Esthonia for six years (967-972), was treated well, and was much beloved by the people.

Sigurd Eriksson, the brother of Astrid, happened to come to Esthonia to collect taxes for King Valdemar (or Vladimir), king in Novgorod, Russia. In the market-place he saw a very handsome boy, and as he could see that he was a foreigner, he asked him his name and family. The boy answered that his name was Olaf, that he was a son of Trygve Olafson, and that Astrid, a daughter of Erik Biodaskalle, was his mother. Sigurd thus discovered that the boy was his sister's son, and he bought him, and took him with him to Novgorod, He at first said nothing to the boy about their relationship, but treated him well. Olaf was then nine years old.

One day Olaf was in the market-place, where a great many people were assembled. There he saw and recognized Klerkon, who had killed his foster-father, Thorolf Lusarskeg, on the journey from Sweden. Olaf had a little axe in his hand, and with it he clove Klerkon's skull, and then he ran home and told his uncle Sigurd what he had done. Sigurd immediately took Olaf to Queen Allogia, told her what had happened, and begged her to protect the boy. The queen took a liking to the boy, paid the fine for the manslaughter he had committed, and induced King Valdemar to admit him to his court, where he was brought up as a king's son. Olaf remained with King Valdemar nine years (973-981).

At the age of eighteen Olaf was given ships by King Valdemar and set out on viking cruises. After a plundering visit to the island of Bornholm he came to Vendland (Pomerania), where he married Queen Geira, the daughter of King Burislav, and subdued the countries which had formerly belonged to her dominions, but had lately failed to pay her taxes. Every summer he made viking cruises, and in the winter he stayed with Queen Geira. Olaf had been three years in Vendland when Geira was taken sick and died. His grief was so great that he could not afterward stay in Vendland. He then provided himself with warships and made viking cruises to Denmark, England, Northumberland, Scotland, the Hebrides, the Isle of Man, and western France. On returning from France he was driven by a storm to the Scilly Isles, where he and all his men were baptized in the Christian faith. Afterward Olaf came to England, and married Princess Gyda, a daughter of the Irish king Olaf Kvaran. The English annals contain many references to Olaf Trygvason, and name him as chief of a fleet of nearly 400 ships which, in the year 991, harried the east coast of England and won a great battle, after which the Englishmen were compelled to pay him 10,000 pounds in silver. Three years later he again attacked the coast of England, and the English king, Ethelred, had to beg for peace and promise to pay him 16,000 pounds in silver. Olaf and his army went into winter quarters in Southampton. Soon afterward King Ethelred invited him to his home; Olaf accepted the invitation, and the two became good friends. During his stay with the king, Olaf was confirmed, and King Ethelred himself became his sponsor and gave him many precious gifts. Olaf, for his part, made a solemn vow that he would never again attack the coasts of England, a promise which he appears to have kept.

Early in the year 995 Olaf proceeded to Norway, and arrived at Throndhjem just when the peasants had risen against Earl Haakon. They made him their chief, and when the earl was dead, and his sons had fled, Olaf Trygvason became king of Norway.

CHAPTER XI

Olaf Trygvason (995-1000)

OLAF TRYGVASON was twenty-seven years old when he came to Norway. At a general Thing at Throndhjem the people elected him king of all Norway, as Harald the Fairhaired had been, and in return he promised to enforce law and justice. The following spring and summer Olaf travelled through the whole country, to the southernmost part of Viken, and everywhere he was hailed as king, even by the chiefs in the Uplands and in Viken, who, during the reign of Earl Haakon, had at least nominally acknowledged the suzerainty of the Danish king. In the Uplands the petty kings, who were descendants of Harald the Fairhaired, were allowed to retain their possessions on the old conditions.

Olaf had decided, before he left England, to introduce Christianity in Norway, and he found it advisable to commence this work in Viken, where he had many of his relatives and warmest friends. Here was the rich and influential Lodin, who, some time before, had married Olaf's mother Astrid. His mother's brothers and two brothers-in-law of Olaf were also mighty people in that part of the country. Another reason for starting the work here was that a good many had already adopted the Christian faith under the influence of missionaries from Germany and Denmark. During his stay in Viken, Olaf called his relatives together and informed them of his intention to convert the whole of Norway to the Christian faith. He would accomplish that, he said, or die in the attempt. But he promised to make his relatives great and mighty men if they would support him with all their power. This they agreed to do, and as the most powerful men among the people had now acceded to King Olaf's request, the others followed their example, and all the inhabitants of the east part of Viken allowed themselves to be baptized. Greater opposition was met in the north part of Viken (around "Folden"), where Christianity had not had so many former adherents. But Olaf would tolerate no opposition; those who opposed him he punished severely, killing some, mutilating others, and driving some into banishment. During that summer (996) and the following winter all Viken was made Christian.

The next spring King Olaf christianized Agder. He met no opposition until he came to Hordaland, where there were many mighty men. They met him fully armed at a public assembly, ready to resist; but after he had made his speech entreating them to accept Christianity, but adding that those who would not submit must expect punishment, their courage failed them, and all the people present were baptized before the assembly was dissolved.

King Olaf then went with his men to the *Gula-Thing*, where one of the chieftains asked of the king, as a sign of goodwill, that he give his sister Astrid in marriage to their relation, Erling Skialgson of Sole, whom they looked upon as one of the most hopeful men in the country. This the king readily acceded to, since Erling was a man of good birth and fine appearance. Erling Skialgson and Astrid were married in the summer, and the king, who was present at the wedding, at his departure invested Erling with all the land north of the Sogne Fjord and east to the Lidandisnes, on the same terms as Harald the Fairhaired had given land to his sons.

After having christianized the people of Sogn, South More, Raumsdal and North More, King Olaf, after a year's absence, returned to Throndhjem. At Lade he had the great heathen temple razed to the ground, took all the ornaments, and burned the temple with all the images. When the people heard of this they sent out war-tokens and collected a great force, with which they intended to attack the king. In the meantime Olaf sailed with his men out of the fjord along the coast northward, intending to proceed to Halogaland and baptize there. But when he came out to Bjarnaurar (Björnör), he heard from Halogaland that a force was assembled there to defend the country against the king. The chiefs of this force were Harek of Thiotta, Thorer Hiort from Vagar, and Eyvind Kinrifa. At the same time he learned that the peasants in Throndhjem had now dispersed. He therefore turned about and sailed in through the Throndhjem Fjord again.

In the fall King Olaf laid the foundation of the future city of Nidaros at the mouth of the river Nid. He built his royal residence at Skipakrok (the ships' creek), built a church further up, and laid out building lots for the people. The work was pushed forward with energy, so that Olaf could take up his residence there in the winter, and by Christmas the church was also ready.

At the beginning of the winter Olaf summoned the peasants to a Thing at Frosta, and they came in great numbers, but also well armed. When the Thing was called to order, the king began in a mild manner to preach Christianity; but the peasants soon objected, and the mighty Jernskegge (Ironbeard), who was their spokesman, said that the will of the people was now, as formerly, that the king should not break the laws. They wanted the king to offer sacrifice, as other kings before him had done. If he did not do as they wanted, they would kill him or banish him from the country. Seeing that the people were in earnest, and had a superior force present, King Olaf talked to them in a more conciliatory manner, promised to be present at their midwinter sacrifices, and said that they could then further discuss the proposed change of faith. This speech was well received, and the assembly dispersed.

When Yuletide came, Olaf invited all the mighty peasants from Strinden, Gaulardal, and Orkadal to a feast at Lade. They came, were entertained in the best possible manner the first evening, and toward morning became quite drunk. The next day he called a House-Thing, where his men were present in much greater number than the peasants. He made a speech, in which he said that at Frosta he had offered them Christianity, but instead of accepting it they had demanded that he should offer sacrifice to their gods, as other kings had done. "Now," he continued, "if I shall turn again to making sacrifice, then will I make the greatest of sacrifices that are in use, and I will sacrifice men. But I will not select slaves or malefactors for this, but will take the greatest men only to be offered to the gods." Thereupon he selected eleven of the principal men, and all these, he said, he would offer in sacrifice to the gods for peace and a fruitful season, and ordered them to be laid hold of immediately. As the peasants saw that resistance was useless, they all submitted to the king's demands. He spared their lives on the condition that they should be baptized, take an oath to support the true faith, and renounce all sacrifices to the heathen gods. They were then baptized, and had to send their sons, brothers or other near relations as hostages. Later on, King Olaf came with his men to Mærin, where the people were assembled. He promised to go into their temple to look at their ceremonies; but while there, he and his men knocked down and demolished the images of the gods, while the chief of the peasants, Jernskegge, was killed outside of the temple by one of the king's men. When the king came outside, he demanded that the peasants be baptized, or fight with him on the spot, and as their chief was dead, and there was a superior force against them, they yielded, were baptized, and gave hostages for their perseverance in the faith.

In this and similar ways King Olaf succeeded in christianizing, in name at least, practically the whole of Norway. Christianity was also introduced in Iceland, the Faroe Islands, and the Orkneys.

Queen Sigrid the Haughty (Storraade), widow of King Erik of Sweden, resided on her large estates in Gautland and wielded a great influence. Her son, Olaf the Swede, besides being king of Sweden, also ruled over Denmark, whence Svein Tjuguskeg had been expelled. Many were her wooers, but she had so far rejected all, and she even caused two of them, her foster-brother Harald Grenske and the Russian king Vsevolod, to be killed, by being burned in their lodgings, in order, as she said, to make petty kings quit courting her. Olaf Trygvason evidently thought that it would strengthen him if he could marry Sigrid, and sent messengers to her with a request for her hand. They were well received, and it was agreed that Olaf and Sigrid should meet at Konungahella, at the boundary line between Norway and Sweden, early in the spring. King Olaf sent Queen Sigrid as a gift the great gold ring he had taken from the heathen temple at Lade. She was greatly pleased with this ring, and had it passed around in her hall to be admired. When it came to her two goldsmiths they shook their heads, and upon being pressed, pronounced the ring false. The queen ordered the ring to be broken into pieces, and it was found to be copper inside. Sigrid became very angry, and said that Olaf would probably deceive her in more ways than this one.

Early in the spring Olaf met Queen Sigrid at the appointed place, and it seemed that they were coming to an agreement. But when Olaf insisted that Sigrid should become a Christian and be baptized, she answered: "I must not part from the faith which I have held, and my forefathers before me; but, on the other hand, I shall make no objection to your believing in the god that pleases you best." Then King Olaf became angry and struck her in the face with his glove, saying: "Why should I care to have thee, an old faded woman, and a heathen jade?" Greatly enraged Sigrid cried: "This may some day be thy death." Thus they parted. The king set off to Viken, and the queen returned to Gautland.

King Olaf unexpectedly met a new bride. The Danish king, Svein Tjuguskeg, had compelled his sister Thyra to marry King Burisleif of Vendland;[1] but Thyra had been with this heathen and dissolute husband only a week when she fled back to Denmark, and afterward, in order to avoid her brother, went to Norway, where she met King Olaf. "Thyra was a well-spoken woman," says the saga, "and the king had pleasure in her conversation." He also saw that she was a handsome woman, although she can not have been very young at that time, and the result was that they were married, much against the wish of Svein Tjuguskeg.

Shortly after this Sigrid the Haughty married Svein Tjuguskeg, who, by this relationship with King Olaf the Swede, recovered back his kingdom, Denmark. Their family connections also included the two sons of the late Earl Haakon, Erik, who married Svein Tjuguskeg's daughter Gyda, and Svein, who married Holmfrid, a sister of Olaf the Swede. Thus the chain was formed, which for a long time was to have influence on the destiny of Norway.

Olaf Trygvason and his wife, Thyra, spent the winter after their marriage at Nidaros (Throndhjem). Queen Thyra often complained, and wept bitterly over it, that she, who had great possessions in Vendland, had no property here suitable for a queen, and she entreated the king to go to Vendland and have her property there restored to her. But all King Olaf's friends advised him not to undertake such an expedition. It is told that on Palm Sunday the king was walking in the street, and met a man with a number of fine angelica roots, remarkably large for that early season. The king bought one, and brought it home to Queen Thyra, whom he found crying. He said to her: "See here, queen, is a great angelica stalk, which I give thee." But she threw it away and said: "A greater present my father, Harald Gormson, gave to my mother; and he was not afraid to go out of the country and take what was his; but thou darest not go across the Danish dominions for that brother of mine, King Svein." Then King Olaf sprang up, and answered with a loud oath: "Never did I fear thy brother, King Svein; and if we meet he shall give way before me!"

Shortly after Easter the king convoked a Thing in the town, and proclaimed to the people that in the summer he would go upon an expedition abroad, and announced how many ships and men he wanted from each district. The king had then just finished a ship which was larger and more magnificent than any other ship in the country. This ship was called the "Long Serpent" (Ormen lange). The crew was made up of picked men of great strength and courage, none of them more than sixty or less than twenty years of age. The only exception was Einar Thambaskelfer, who was only eighteen years old. Einar was unusually strong, and was considered the most skilful archer. He had a bow called Thamb, which he was wont to make quake; hence his name (Thambaskelfer, *i.e.*, Thamb-quaker). The king himself commanded the "Long Serpent." His half-brother, Thorkel Nefia, commanded the "Short Serpent," and his mother's brothers, Thorkel Dydril and Jostein, had the "Crane" (Tranen), and both these ships were well manned. King Olaf had sixty ships when he left Norway, and sailed southward through the Sound to Vendland. With him, on board the "Long Serpent," were Queen Thyra, his sister Ingibjorg, bishop Sigurd, and several priests. Many of his friends had joined him on the journey south along the Norwegian coast, among them his brother-in-law, Erling Skialgson of Sole, who had a large and well-equipped ship. When King Olaf arrived in Vendland, he was well received by King Burisleif, his claims to Queen Thyra's estates were peaceably settled, and he remained there a portion of the summer.

Sigrid the Haughty was Olaf Trygvason's bitterest enemy after their meeting at Konungahella, when he struck her in the face with his glove. She urged King Svein much to fight King Olaf, saying that he had the more reason to do so, as Olaf had married his sister Thyra without his leave. King Svein finally resolved to attack King Olaf. He sent messengers to his brother-in-law, King Olaf the Swede, and to Earl Erik, inviting them to join him with an army, so that they all together might attack King Olaf Trygvason. He also sent Earl Sigvald to Vendland to spy out Olaf Trygvason's movements, and by pretending friendship gain his confidence and lead him into a trap.

Between the island of Rügen and the mainland of the present Prussian province of Pomerania lies a little island called Greifswalder Oie, or Svolder, as it was called at that time. Here lay on the 9th of September, in the year 1000, a fleet of eighty ships. Sixty of them belonged to the Danish king Svein Tjuguskeg, fifteen to the Swedish king Olaf, and five to Earl Erik. They lay there waiting for King Olaf to pass by on his return home from Vendland.

With a light but favorable breeze the Norwegian fleet sailed out of the harbor, where it had been lying during the stay in Vendland. All the small vessels, which sailed faster, got out to sea before the others. Earl Sigvald with his ships remained near the king for a while, and then sailed ahead telling the king to sail in his keel-tracks, as he knew best where the water was deepest. The earl, who was informed of the presence of the Danish fleet, sailed close under the island of Svolder, and Olaf Trygvason with his remaining eleven large ships followed. Meanwhile the Danish king Svein, the Swedish king Olaf, and Earl Erik, gathered their forces and made ready for battle.

When Olaf Trygvason sailed in toward the island, the whole fleet of the enemy came out against him. When his chieftains saw this superior force they begged the king to proceed on his way, and not risk a battle against such odds. But the king, standing high on the quarter-deck of the "Long Serpent," replied: "Strike the sails; never shall men of mine think of flight. I never fled from battle. Let God dispose of my life, but flight I shall never take."

King Olaf ordered the ships to close up to each other. The "Long Serpent" lay in the middle of the line; on one side lay the "Little Serpent," and on the other the "Crane." King Olaf stood on the quarter-deck of the "Serpent," high over the others. He had a gilt shield, and a golden helmet, and over his armor he had a short red jacket, so that he was easily distinguished from the others. When he saw the enemy's ships drawing up for battle, he asked: "Who is the chief of the force right ahead of us?" The answer came that it was King Svein with the Danish army. The king said; "We are not afraid of these soft Danes, for there is no courage in them. But who are those on the right?" He was answered, that it was King Olaf with the Swedish forces. "Better it were," said King Olaf, "for these Swedes to stay at home licking their sacrificial vessels,[2] than to come under our weapons. But who owns the large ships on the other side of the Danes?" "That is Earl Erik, the son of Haakon," said his men. Then the king said: "He, methinks, has good reason for meeting us; and from these men we may expect the sharpest conflict, for they are Northmen like ourselves."

The battle commenced and became very severe, and many people were slain. King Svein made a violent attack on the "Long Serpent," but was soon compelled to retreat. Then Olaf the Swede came up with his fifteen ships, but he fared no better, and the king himself had a narrow escape from death. When Earl Erik came up with his ships the fight became most severe, and a great number of people fell. The men from the smaller ships soon began to seek refuge on board the "Long Serpent," and at last all King Olaf Trygvason's ships were cleared of men except the "Long Serpent." Then Earl Erik brought his ship up to the side of the "Serpent," and the fight went on with battle-axe and sword.

Einar Thambaskelfer stood at the mast of the "Serpent" and sent deadly arrows from his bow. He sent an arrow at Earl Erik, which hit the tiller-end just above the earl's head so hard that it entered the wood up to the arrow-shaft. The earl had hardly time to ask whose shot it was, when another arrow flew between his arm and his side, and clear through a board behind him. Again Einar drew his bow, when it was hit by an arrow from the enemy and broke in two. "What was it that broke with such a noise?" cried King Olaf. "Norway, king, from thy hands," answered Einar. "Not so," said the king, "take my bow and shoot," and the king threw his own bow to Einar. Einar took the bow, and drew it over the head of the arrow. "Too weak, too weak," said he, "is the bow of the king," and, throwing it aside, he took sword and shield, and fought desperately.

Finally, after a terrible combat, the earl's men boarded the "Serpent," and the few men who were left were killed or leaped overboard. King Olaf held his shield over his head when he threw himself in the water, and was drowned. Among the last men to leave the ship were Einar Thambaskelfer, who was captured in the water, and Thorkel Nefia, who swam ashore.

King Olaf Trygvason was thirty-six years old when he fell at Svolder. His widow, Queen Thyra, died shortly afterward from grief.

CHAPTER XII

The Discovery of America

DURING the reign of Earl Haakon a man from Jæderen, called Erik the Red, being obliged to leave Norway because he had killed a man, proceeded to the western part of Iceland. Here he committed a similar offence and was condemned at Thorsnes Thing to banishment. He had heard that a man called Gunbiorn, son of Ulf Krage, had some time ago been driven by the storm far westward and had seen a great country. Erik the Red fitted out a vessel and told his friends that he intended to find the country Gunbiorn had seen. He took with him a man by the name of Heriulf Bardson. They found the country (984), and on a visit later to Iceland Erik the Red gave such a fine description of the new country that it was called Greenland. A number of colonists returned with him to the new country, and the foundation of several settlements were laid. In the summer of 999 Leif Erikson, a son of Erik the Red, made a visit to Norway, and as he met King Olaf Trygvason he adopted Christianity, and passed the winter with the king. In the following spring King Olaf sent Leif Erikson, together with a priest and other teachers, to Greenland to proclaim Christianity there. Flourishing colonies, with churches, monasteries, and bishoprics, are known to have been maintained in Greenland until the end of the fourteenth century.

Biarne Heriulfson, a son of the above-named Heriulf Bardson, while sailing westward from Iceland in search of his father, met with stormy weather, northerly winds and fogs, and was driven out of his course. As he came to different shores, which, from the description he had received, could not be those of Greenland, he turned around, and, sailing in a northeasterly direction, finally arrived at his father's home in Greenland. When telling of his discovery he was much ridiculed for not having landed and examined the new countries. Leif Erikson bought Biarne's ship, and with a crew of thirty-five men set out, in the year 1000, to look for these lands. He came first to a land on his right as he sailed southward. It had great icy mountains in the interior and a shore of flat stones. He therefore named the country Helluland (from the Norse *helle*, a flat stone). He continued his course southward, and came to another country, which was level and covered with woods and had a low coast. He called this country Markland (outfield or woodland). The antiquaries consider Helluland to have been Newfoundland, and Markland some part of Nova Scotia. Leif and his party put to sea again with a northeast wind, and after two days' sailing made land, and came to an island lying on the north side of the mainland. They entered the channel between the island and a point projecting northeast from the mainland, and at last landed at a place where a river which came from a lake fell into the sea. They found the country very agreeable, and, resolving to winter there, erected some houses. Leif divided his people into two parties, to be employed in turns in exploring the country and working about the houses. One evening it happened that one of the exploring party, a German by birth, named Tyrker, was missing. They went out to search for him, and when they met him he told them he had been up the country, and had discovered vines and grapes, a fruit with which he was acquainted from his native country. They now occupied themselves in gathering grapes and cutting vines, and felling timber with which they loaded the vessel. Leif called the country Vinland. Toward spring they made ready and sailed away, and returned to Greenland.

In the year 1002 Leif Erikson's brother, Thorvald, fitted out a ship and sailed southward with thirty men, after consulting with Leif. They came to Vinland, to the houses put up by Leif, where they remained quietly all winter, and lived by fishing. In the spring Thorvald sent a party in the long-boat to explore the country to the south. They found the country beautiful and well wooded, but with little space between the woods and the sea, and the strand full of white sand. There were also many islands, and shallow water. They came back in the autumn to Leif's houses. The following spring Thorvald sailed with his vessel eastward, then northward along the land. Outside of a cape they met bad weather and were driven ashore and broke their keel. They remained there a long time to repair their vessel. Thorvald said to his men: "We will stick up the keel here upon the ness and call the place Keelness."[3] Then they sailed eastward along the country and landed on a headland, which Thorvald liked so well that he said he would like to make his home there. On going on board they saw three little hills on the sandy shore. They went up to them and found they were three canoes, made of skin, with three natives—or *Skrælings*, as the Northmen called them—under each canoe. They killed eight of them, while one made his escape in his canoe. Afterward a great number of the natives attacked Thorvald's party. They were repulsed, but Thorvald was wounded by an arrow and died. He was buried on the headland which he had said he liked so well. His men remained there during the winter, and in the spring returned to Greenland.

In the summer of 1006, an Icelander by the name of Thorfin Karlsefne came to Greenland, and, in the winter, married Gudrid, the widow of Thorstein, third brother of Leif Erikson. By her advice he resolved to undertake an expedition to Vinland and establish a colony there. In the spring (1007) they set out with three ships, 160 men, and all kinds of live stock, and sailed to Vinland. Some time after their arrival there Gudrid bore a son, who was named Snorre. The colonists occasionally traded with the *Skrælings*, giving them pieces of cloth and dairy products for their skins; but when they refused to sell them weapons, the *Skrælings* became hostile to the settlers and attacked them repeatedly. These constant hostilities so disheartened the settlers that they resolved to leave the country, and, after three years' sojourn in Vinland, Thorfin Karlsefne and his party returned to Greenland. Another expedition to Vinland was undertaken, shortly after their return, by Freydis, the illegitimate daughter of Erik the Red, her husband Thorvald, and two Norwegians named Helge and Finboge. This party quarrelled among themselves, and Freydis, who is described as a very bad woman, caused a great number of them to be murdered. The survivors returned to Greenland in the spring of 1013. The next summer, Thorfin Karlsefne went to Norway with his Vinland cargo and sold it to great advantage. He returned to Iceland and bought land there, and, according to the saga, many men of distinction are descended from him and his son Snorre, who was born in Vinland.[4]

CHAPTER XIII

The Earls Erik and Svein, Sons of Haakon (1000-1015)

AFTER the battle of Svolder, the three allied princes divided the kingdom of Norway between them. King Olaf the Swede got four districts in the Throndhjem country, and the districts of North More and South More and Raumsdal, and in the eastern part of the country he got Ranrike from the Gaut River to Svinesund. Earl Erik got four districts in the Throndhjem country, and Halogaland, Naumudal, the Fjord districts, Sogn, Hordaland, Rogaland, and North Agder, all the way to the Naze (Lindesnes, the southernmost point in Norway). The Danish king, Svein Tjuguskeg, retained Viken, which he had held before, and Raumarike and Hedemarken. After the division, the Swedish king gave his Norwegian possessions into the hands of his brother-in-law Svein, the brother of Earl Erik, on the same conditions as the sub-kings or earls held such possessions formerly from the chief king. At the same time the Danish king gave most of his possessions in Norway in fief to Earl Erik. Thus the two brothers together ruled over a larger territory than their father, Earl Haakon, had held; but they were not able to wield the same power. During his whole time, Earl Erik received no taxes from Rogaland, which Erling Skialgson ruled over with unlimited authority. The earls Erik and Svein were baptized, and adopted the Christian faith; but as long as they ruled in Norway they allowed every one to do as he pleased as to the manner of observing his Christianity. On the other hand, they upheld the old laws, and all the old rights and customs of the country. They were popular men and good rulers. Of the two brothers Earl Erik had most to say in all public matters.

The earls tried to gain the friendship of Olaf Trygvason's old friends, and in many cases they succeeded. The brave young Einar Thambaskelfer was won over by their giving him great fiefs in Orkadal, so that he became one of the most powerful and esteemed men in all the Throndhjem country. They also gave him their proud sister Bergliot in marriage. One mighty man, however, they tried in vain to conciliate. That was Erling Skialgson, the brother-in-law of Olaf Trygvason. He could not forgive Earl Erik for having joined the Swedes and Danes in an unexpected attack on Olaf Trygvason and causing his death. He managed to maintain a firm hold on the dominions his brother-in-law had given him. If the earls visited a neighborhood where they knew that Erling was staying, they always took with them a large armed force, and they never thought of visiting Erling on his estate, Sole. He had with him never less than ninety free men. If it was reported that the earls were in the neighborhood, he had two hundred men or more. He never went by water from one place to another except in a fully-manned ship of twenty benches of rowers. In the summer he used to make viking cruises in order to procure means with which to support his many men.

Erling was a good master. At home, on his estate, he always had thirty slaves besides the many servants engaged in work outside. He gave each of them a certain day's work; when one of them was through with that, he had the balance of the day at his own disposal. Each one received a piece of land to cultivate, and what grain he produced he could sell and use the proceeds toward buying himself free. The amount needed for this purpose was fixed by the earl, and it was so low that many bought their freedom at the end of a year, while all who were at all industrious could make themselves free within three years. He also assisted his men after they had become free. Some of them were given land to clear and cultivate, while others were shown how to conduct the herring-fisheries.

After the death, in England, of the Danish king, Svein Tjuguskeg, his son, Canute (Knut) the Mighty, sent word to Earl Erik in Norway (his brother-in-law) to come over and help him to conquer England. The earl immediately called together the mightiest peasants, and in their presence divided the country between his brother Svein and his son Haakon. As the latter was only seventeen years old, the earl appointed his brother-in-law, Einar Thambaskelfer, guardian for him. Thereupon Earl Erik set sail for England. He met King Canute there, and was with him when he captured London. He was given Northumberland to govern, and remained there until his death.

From the short joint reign of Earl Svein and Earl Haakon in Norway only one event of importance is known. As soon as Earl Erik had left the country, they effected a reconciliation with the mighty Erling Skialgson at Sole, who had never been able to forgive Earl Erik for the assault on Olaf Trygvason, but readily made peace with Svein and Haakon; and the new friendship was further cemented by Aslak, Erling's son, marrying Earl Svein's daughter Gunhild (or Sigrid, as the name is given in another place). One good reason why the earls sought to strengthen their power by an alliance with the powerful chieftain, Erling Skialgson, was no doubt the unexpected appearance of a most threatening enemy, the young pretender to the throne, Olaf, son of Harald Grenske.

CHAPTER XIV

The Youth of Olaf Haraldson

OLAF HARALDSON, after his death called Olaf the Saint, was the son of Harald Grenske and Aasta. Harald Grenske, who, as we have seen, at one time governed Viken under the suzerainty of the Danish king, was the grandson of Biorn the Merchant—who was killed by Erik Blood-Axe—and a great-grandson of Harald the Fairhaired. Olaf was born shortly after the death of his father. His mother Aasta was then staying at the home of her father, Gudbrand Kula, a mighty man in the Uplands. Soon afterward, Aasta was married again to Sigurd Syr, who was king in Ringerike and a descendant of Harald the Fairhaired, and in his house Olaf was brought up. When King Olaf Trygvason came to Ringerike to spread Christianity, he induced Sigurd Syr and his whole family to be baptized, and he acted as godfather at the baptism of little Olaf.

One day, when Olaf was ten years old, King Sigurd wanted to ride out, and, as there was nobody else about the house, he told his stepson Olaf to go and saddle his horse. Olaf did not refuse, but he went to the goats' pen, and put the king's saddle on the largest he-goat, led him up to the door, and went in and told King Sigurd that his horse was saddled. When King Sigurd came out and saw what Olaf had done, he said: "Easy it is to see that thou wilt little regard my orders; and thy mother will think it right that I do not order thee to do anything against thy own inclination. I see well enough that thou art far more proud than I am." Olaf answered little, but went his way laughing.

When Olaf grew up he became of medium height, but very stout and strong. He had light brown hair, and a broad face which was white and red. He had particularly fine eyes, which were beautiful, but piercing, so that one was afraid to look him in the face when he was angry. Olaf was very expert in all bodily exercises, understood well how to handle his bow, and was especially an expert in throwing his spear. He was well liked by his friends and acquaintances, was ambitious in his sports, and always strove to be the first.

Olaf was twelve years old when, for the first time, he went on board a ship of war (1007). His mother, Aasta, got Rane, who was called foster-father of kings, to command the ship and take Olaf under his charge. The men on board, however, gave Olaf the title of king. With two ships, Olaf first steered to Denmark and then to Sweden, where he harried the coasts and fought with vikings. Afterward he made cruises to Finland, Russia, and

Gotland. Later he turned westward to Friesland and England, where he took part in the fights between the Danes and the Anglo-Saxons. From the poems of the Skalds it appears that he took part in the battle of Hringmara (1010), and in the storming of Canterbury (1012). In company with Thorkel the Tall (a brother of Earl Sigvald) he entered the English king Ethelred's service, took part in his battles against the Danish vikings, and accompanied Ethelred on his flight to Normandy. From here he thought of making a pilgrimage to the Holy Land; but on the way he had, according to tradition, a remarkable dream. He thought he saw a tall and handsome man, who told him to return to Norway and take his Udal, adding "for thou shalt be king over thy country forever."

CHAPTER XV

Olaf the Saint (1015-1028)

LEAVING his long-ships (battleships) behind him at Northumberland, Olaf sailed, in the fall of 1015, with two merchant-ships and 120 well-armed men, across the North Sea to Norway. After a stormy voyage he landed on the west coast of Norway, near a small island called Sæla. King Olaf thought this was a good omen, because that word means luck. He sailed southward to Ulfasund, where he heard that Earl Haakon was south in Sogn, and was expected north with a single ship as soon as the wind was favorable. King Olaf then sailed further south, and when he came to Saudungssund he laid one of his vessels on each side of the sound, with a thick cable between them. Soon after Earl Haakon came rowing into the sound with a manned ship; they saw Olaf's ships, but thought they were only two merchant vessels, and rowed in between them. When the ship was over the cable, Olaf's men on each side wound it up with the windlass, so that Haakon's ship upset, and all his men plunged into the water. Most of them, however, were picked up and taken on board Olaf's ship; only a few were drowned. Among those saved was Earl Haakon. He was a very handsome boy of eighteen years, with fair, silken hair, bound about his head with a gold ornament. When Olaf saw him, he said: "True it is what has been said of your family: you are handsome people; but now your luck has deserted you." Haakon replied: "It is always so, that sometimes one is victorious, and sometimes another. I am little beyond childhood in years; besides, we did not expect any attack. It may turn out better with me another time." "But dost thou not fear that thou art now in such a condition that, hereafter, there will be neither victory nor defeat for thee?" asked the king. "That all depends upon thee," said the earl. Olaf then asked what he would give if he were allowed to go unhurt. The earl asked what he demanded. "Nothing," said the king, "except that thou shalt leave the country and take an oath that thou shalt never go into battle against me." Earl Haakon agreed to this, took the oath, and rowed away with his men. As soon as possible he sailed over to England, to his mother's brother, King Canute, who received him well. His father, Earl Erik, whom he afterward joined, considered his son's oath binding upon him also, and he therefore made no attempt to win back the lost kingdom, but remained in Northumberland until his death (1024).

King Olaf now went southward along the coast, holding Things with the peasants in many places. Many went willingly with him, while others, who were Earl Svein's relations or friends, refused him allegiance. He therefore decided first to apply to his relations, the kings in the Uplands, and see what support he could gain from them for his cause. He sailed east to Viken, set his ships on land, and proceeded with one hundred and twenty men up the country to Ringerike, to meet his stepfather, Sigurd Syr. The story of his reception at his mother's home, as detailed in Snorre Sturlason's *Heimskringla*, is very interesting, and gives a vivid picture of the life and customs at the home of a rich and mighty Norwegian in those days. The main portion of the description is here given.

As Olaf was approaching Sigurd Syr's home some of the servants ran ahead to the house. Olaf's mother, Aasta, was sitting in the room, and around her some of her girls. When the servants told her that King Olaf was coming, and that he might soon be expected, Aasta immediately got up, and ordered men and girls to put everything in the best order. She ordered four girls to bring out all that belonged to the decoration of the room, and put it in order with hangings and benches. Two men brought straw for the floor, two brought forward four-cornered tables and the drinking-jugs, two bore out victuals and placed the meat on the table, two she sent away from the house to procure in the greatest haste all that was needed, and two carried in the ale; and all the other serving men and girls went outside of the house. Messengers went to seek King Sigurd wherever he might be, and brought to him his dress-clothes, and his horse with gilt saddle, and his bridle which was gilt and set with precious stones. Four men she sent off in different directions to invite all the great people to a feast, which she was preparing as a rejoicing for her son's return. She made all who were in the house dress themselves with the best they had, and lent clothes to those who had none suitable.

King Sigurd Syr was in the field superintending the harvest work when the messengers came to him with the news, and told him all that Aasta was doing at the house. He had many people with him working in the field. He probably did not like the interruption of the work caused by his wife's message, but he dressed himself in the fine clothes sent him, mounted his horse, and rode home together with thirty well-dressed men whom he had sent for. As they rode up to the house, Olaf, under his banner, was seen coming up from the other side with one hundred and twenty men all well equipped. People were also gathered all around. King Sigurd saluted his stepson, and invited him and his men to come and drink with him. But Aasta went up and kissed her son, and invited him to stay with them, saying that all the land and people she could furnish would be at his service. King Olaf thanked her kindly for her invitation. Then she took him by the hand, and led him into the room to the high-seat, while King Sigurd got men to take care of their clothes, and see that the horses were cared for. Then Sigurd went in, and a great feast was had.

King Olaf had not been at the place many days before he called his stepfather, King Sigurd, his mother Aasta, and his foster-father Rane to a conference and consultation. He informed them that it was his intention to win back from the Danes and the Swedes the land of his forefathers or die in the attempt. He asked Sigurd to help him, and give him the best possible advice in the matter. King Sigurd thought the plan was very risky, but knew from experience that it would be useless to try to dissuade Olaf from it. He would, therefore, help him with goods and money; but he would not bind himself to anything more, before he knew the views and intentions of the other Upland kings.

In the Uplands there lived at that time many descendants from Harald the Fairhaired. They all bore the title of king, although their possessions were small. After the death of Olaf Trygvason they had acknowledged the suzerainty of the Danish king. One of them ruled over Raumarike, Hadeland and Thoten, another over Valders. In Gudbrandsdal there was a king named Gudrod, and in Hedemarken two brothers, Rorek and Ring, were the rulers. With these district-kings Sigurd Syr had a meeting in Hadeland which King Olaf also attended. Here Sigurd announced his stepson Olaf's purpose, and asked their aid to accomplish the plan. He also told of the many brave deeds which Olaf had performed on his war expeditions.

King Rorek then made a speech against the proposed change. The people, he said, had had many experiences. When King Haakon, Athelstan's foster-son, was king, all were content; but when Gunhild's sons ruled over the country, they became so hated for their tyranny that the people would rather have foreign kings, who usually left the people to themselves if only the taxes were paid. When Earl Haakon had succeeded in establishing himself firmly as a ruler with the help of the people, he became so hard and overbearing toward them that they could no longer tolerate him. They killed him, and raised to the kingly power Olaf Trygvason, who was udal-born to the kingdom, and in every way well qualified to be a chief. The whole country's wish was to make him supreme king, and raise again the kingdom which Harald the Fairhaired had established. But when King Olaf had become secure in his power, no man could manage his own affairs for him. With the small kings he was very hard, and collected even greater tribute than Harald the Fairhaired had done. A man was not even allowed to believe in what god he pleased. After Olaf Trygvason had been taken away, they had kept friendly with the Danish king, and had received great help from him in everything; they had been allowed to rule themselves, and had experienced no oppression. Rorek was, therefore, inclined to let well enough alone, and declined to take any part in the proposed plan. His brother Ring was of a different opinion. He said that even if he only could keep the same power and property that he held now, he would prefer to see one of his own race as supreme king rather than a foreign chief. And if Olaf succeeded in making himself supreme king, those of them would fare best who had best deserved his friendship. He believed Olaf to be an honorable man, and if they gave him aid now he would certainly show his gratitude afterward. He was in favor of giving Olaf all possible friendship and support. The others, one after the other, expressed the same opinion, and the result was that the most of them entered into a league with King Olaf. This league was confirmed by oath.

Thereafter the kings summoned a Thing, and here Olaf explained in a long speech what claims he had to the throne of Harald the Fairhaired. He requested the peasants to elect him king, and he promised them to uphold the old laws, and to defend the country. His speech was very well received. Then the different kings spoke in support of his request, and the result was that King Olaf was proclaimed king over the whole country according to the laws of the Uplands. The king thereupon proceeded through the Uplands accompanied by three hundred and sixty men, and from all directions the people flocked to him and hailed him as their king.

From the Uplands King Olaf hastened over the Dovre Mountain to the Throndhjem country. It was of importance to come there before the reports of his proceedings reached Earl Svein, who was about to celebrate Christmas at Steinker. At Medaldal, in Orkedal, he summoned the peasants to a Thing, where he requested them to accept him as king. They were without a leader and did not have sufficient strength to offer opposition to the king; so the result was that they took the oath of allegiance. At Griotar he met an army of about eight hundred men, which had been collected by Einar Thambaskelfer, but had been left without a leader while Einar went to Gauldal to get more men. Olaf offered the men peace and law, "the same as King Olaf Trygvason offered before me," and then presented them with two conditions—either to enter his service or fight him. The result was that they hailed him as their king. When Earl Svein heard of this, he fled from Steinker with a long-ship and proceeded to Frosta. After having reached Steinker, Olaf again summoned a Thing, and compelled the people to recognize him as their king. He thereupon sailed to Nidaros, where he made preparations to celebrate Christmas. Earl Svein and Einar Thambaskelfer meanwhile gathered an army of 2,400 men, with which they suddenly descended upon Nidaros. Olaf and his men barely escaped, and fled southward to the Uplands by the same way they had come. Earl Svein took the Christmas provisions which Olaf's party had been obliged to leave and then burned the town of Nidaros.

Olaf spent the winter in the Uplands, and in the spring gathered an army with which he intended to meet Earl Svein. The kings in Hedemarken furnished him with many armed men, and his stepfather, Sigurd Syr, joined him with a great force. During the winter he had built a ship, which was named "Karlshoved" (Carl's Head, possibly intended to represent the head of Charlemagne, whose name was held in great veneration). On the bow of the ship was a crowned head, which the king himself had carved. With a fine and well-equipped fleet Olaf set out from Viken, going first to Tunsberg.

Earl Svein in the meanwhile collected a great force in the north. Many of the chiefs were his relatives and friends, and were able to give him great assistance. His brother-in-law, Einar Thambaskelfer, was on his side, and with him many other lendermen (a sort of local governors); and among them were many who had taken oath of allegiance to King Olaf the winter before. Earl Svein sailed south along the coast, drawing men from every district. When they came to Rogaland, Erling Skialgson of Sole joined them with a considerable force. Svein's fleet is said to have consisted of forty-five ships, with probably upward of 2,500 men; Olaf hardly had half the number of ships, but his ships were considerably larger, so that the number of men was probably about the same. Toward the end of Easter he entered Viken with his fleet and put in at Nesiar (Nesje), a headland on the east side of the bay (near Fredriksværn).

On Palm Sunday, March 25, 1016, the two fleets met in battle. Before opening the battle Olaf had his ships tied together, his own ship, "Karlshoved," occupying a place in the centre. On this ship were one hundred and twenty men armed in coats of mail, French helmets, and white shields, on which was a gilt or painted cross. Olaf had a white banner on which the figure of a serpent was sewed. The king instructed his men to defend themselves with the shields in the beginning, and take care of their lances and arrows, so that they were not thrown away to no purpose. This advice was followed with good results. When the conflict had become exceedingly sharp, and the missiles began to be scarce on the earl's side, Olaf's men were well supplied, and their attack was very severe. Men fell in great numbers on both sides, but mostly on the earl's ships. King Olaf with the "Karlshoved" engaged Earl Svein's ship, and his men were soon preparing to enter it. The earl, seeing his defeat, ordered his ship cut loose from the others, and at the last moment his brother-in-law, Einar Thambaskelfer, succeeded in pulling the ship out of the line of battle from behind, using his own vessel as a tow-boat. When the earl's ship was gone, the flight became general. Some of the earl's men fled up the country, others surrendered on the king's mercy, but Earl Svein and his followers escaped out through the bay. Svein proceeded to Sweden to seek the aid of the Swedish king, while Erling Skialgson and some other chiefs sailed westward and returned to their homes. Earl Svein was well received by King Olaf the Swede, and it was agreed that next winter they should proceed with an armed force overland through Helsingland and Jemteland and down to the Throndhjem country, for the earl depended upon the faithful help of the people there. The summer was to be spent in viking expeditions in the Baltic. Svein made a cruise to Russia and plundered the coasts; in the fall he was taken sick there and died (1016).

King Olaf went north after the battle of Nesje, and settled down in Nidaros, where he rebuilt the royal residence and the church, and helped the merchants to rebuild the town. After the death of Earl Svein he was readily recognized by all the people in that part of the country as the rightful king. The Swedish king became very angry when he heard that he had lost the possessions in Norway which he had won by the battle of Svolder, and he threatened to take great revenge upon Olaf the Big, a nickname which he had given his Norwegian opponent on account of his stoutness. He sent tax-collectors into Norway, and when these were harshly treated, some of them even being killed, Olaf the Swede was highly enraged, and war between the two kings was threatened. King Olaf made preparations for an emergency, although he much preferred peace, and even wished to marry the Swedish king's daughter. He built fortifications on a headland in the river Glommen, near the falls of Sarpen, and around these fortifications he laid the foundation of the town of Borg or Sarpsborg. The people on both sides of the boundary were very much displeased with the feud between the kings, and on both sides the kings were urged to make peace. The Norwegian king was willing enough, and sent conciliatory messages to Olaf the Swede, but the latter rejected all overtures. Finally the matter was brought to a crisis at a general Thing assembled at the Swedish city of Upsala. Here the king at first also refused to hear the propositions for peace, when Thorgny Lagman (lawman, a kind of judge at the Thing) rose, and made the following speech: "The disposition of Swedish kings is different now from what I hear it was formerly. My grandfather, Thorgny, could well remember the Upsala king Erik Eymundson, and used to tell of him that when he was in his best years he went out every summer on expeditions, and conquered Finland and Karelen, Esthonia and Courland and many parts of the eastern country. Even at the present day the earth-bulwarks and other great works which he made are to be seen. And yet, he was not so proud that he would not listen to those who had something to say to him. Thorgny, my father, was a long time with King Biorn, and well knew his ways and manners. At that time the kingdom was in great power and suffered no losses. He, too, was sociable with his men. I also remember Erik the Victorious, and was with him on many a war expedition. He enlarged the Swedish dominion and bravely defended it, and with him also it was easy to talk about public affairs. But the king we now have allows no one to talk with him of anything but what he himself desires to hear. He wants to have Norway laid under him, which no Swedish king before him ever desired, and thereby causes many men to be alarmed. But now it is the will expressed by us peasants that thou, King Olaf, make peace with the king of Norway, and give him thy daughter Ingegerd in marriage. If thou wilt reconquer the countries on the Baltic which thy relations and ancestors had there, we will all go with thee. But if thou wilt not now consent to what we demand, we will no longer suffer law and peace to be disturbed, but will attack thee and kill thee. So our forefathers did when, at the Mora Thing, they drowned five kings in a morass because they were filled with the same insupportable pride thou hast shown toward us. Now tell us, in all haste, which of these two conditions thou wilt choose." The whole public approved, with clash of arms and shouts, the speech of Thorgny Lagman. Then the king rose and said he would do as the people desired. "All Swedish kings," he said, "have done so, and have allowed the peasants to rule in all according to their will." The murmur among the people then came to an end, and it was decided that the terms of peace offered by the Norwegian king were to be accepted, and that Ingegerd, the king's daughter, was to be married to King Olaf of Norway.

In the meanwhile King Olaf travelled through the country, and carefully investigated the manner in which Christianity was observed. Where he found the people lacking in Christian knowledge, he taught them and furnished them with Christian teachers. If he met with obstinate opposition, he acted with severity and cruelty. "If any there were," says the saga, "who would not renounce heathen ways, he took the matter so zealously that he drove some out of the country, mutilated others on hands or feet, or stung their eyes out; hanged some, slew some with the sword; but let none go unpunished who would not serve God." In this way he proceeded through the country, accompanied by three hundred and sixty armed men.

King Olaf soon found that Christianity was thriving less the further he proceeded into the interior. In the Uplands five small kings came together at Ringsaker, and under the leadership of King Rorek conspired to kill King Olaf. "But it happened here," says the saga, "as it usually does, that every one has some friend even among his enemies." Ketil Kalf of Ringenes, who was present at the meeting of the conspirators, went down after supper to the lake (Miösen), and boarded a little vessel which King Olaf had made him a present of after the battle at Nesje. He had forty well-armed men with him, and rowed in all haste down the lake. He arrived early in the morning at Eid (Eidsvold), where he found the king and told him of the intention of the small kings of Upland. King Olaf immediately gathered his men, sailed north to Ringsaker, surprised the conspirators, and captured them.

King Olaf now availed himself of the opportunity that chance had given him, to rid himself of royal rivals who, as descendants of Harald the Fairhaired, claimed under the law to have as much right to their possessions as any supreme king, and who had always been in the way of a national unity. King Olaf now, by one decisive act, secured the unity and independence of the country, and prepared the way for the victorious entrance of Christianity.

King Ring and two other kings were banished from Norway, under oath never to return. Rorek was a treacherous man and could not be depended upon, so the king ordered both his eyes put out, and afterward took him with him in that condition wherever he went. He ordered Gudrod Valley-king's tongue to be cut out, and of the lendermen and peasants who were implicated in the conspiracy some he banished from the country, some he mutilated, and with others he made peace. King Olaf took possession of the land that these kings had possessed. His stepfather, Sigurd Syr, who had had nothing to do with the conspiracy of the other small kings, died during the winter (1018), and now Olaf alone bore the title of King in Norway.

Shortly after his stepfather Sigurd Syr's death, Olaf went to visit his mother, Aasta, and on this occasion it is told that she took her boys (half-brothers of Olaf) to show them to the king. King Olaf took Guthorm on one knee and his brother Halfdan on the other. He made a wry face at the boys, and pretended to be angry, and they became frightened and ran away. Then Aasta brought in her youngest son, Harald, who was then three years old. The king made a wry face at him also, but the boy only stared back at him. The king then took hold of the boy's hair as if to pull it, but the boy in return pulled the king's whiskers. "Thou wilt probably be revengeful some day, my friend," said the king. The following day Olaf and Aasta were watching the boys at play down by the lake (at the Tyrifjord). Guthorm and Halfdan had built houses and barns and had little figures representing cattle and sheep. Little Harald was down by the water, where he had little chips of wood floating. The king asked him what they were, and Harald answered that they were warships. The king laughed, and said: "The time may come, kinsman, when thou wilt command ships." Then the king called Guthorm and Halfdan up to him, and asked them what they would like to have above all. "Fields," answered Guthorm. "And how large?" asked the king. "I would have that headland yonder sown with corn every summer," answered the boy. The headland included ten farms. "There would be a great deal of corn there," said the king. Turning to Halfdan, he asked what he would like best to have. "Cows," said Halfdan. "And how many?" asked the king. "So many that when they came to the lake to drink they would stand close together around the whole lake," was the answer. "You both take after your father in wanting a great husbandry," said the king. "But what wouldst thou have?" he asked Harald. "Men," replied the boy. "And how many?" "So many that in a single meal they would eat all of Halfdan's cows," was the answer. The king laughed, and said to Aasta: "Here, mother, thou art bringing up a king." "And more is not related of them on this occasion," says the saga; but the prophecy was fulfilled, for Harald, Sigurd's son, in time became king of Norway.

The Swedish king broke the promises he had given at the Upsala Thing, and did not send his daughter Ingegerd to the appointed meeting-place on the boundary, when King Olaf of Norway came to fetch his bride. Shortly afterward the Swedes revolted, and the Swedish king again had to make concessions, and promise to make peace with the king of Norway. The latter had, in the meanwhile, against the wishes of her father, married Astrid, a younger half-sister of Ingegerd. At the peace of Konungahella, where the kings finally met, this marriage was approved by the Swedish king, the boundary lines between the two countries were finally agreed upon, and friendly relations were established.

After the peace of Konungahella, King Olaf was able to pay more attention to the domestic affairs of the country. He went north, and in the fall came to Nidaros, where he prepared to take up his winter residence. He made careful inquiries as to the condition of Christianity, and learned to his regret that it was not observed at all up north, in Halogaland, and was not observed as it should be in Naumdal and the interior of the Throndhjem country. In the spring Olaf started on an expedition north to Naumdal, where he summoned the peasants to meet him, and at every Thing he was accepted as king. He had the laws read to the people, and threatened them with loss of life, limbs, and property, if they would not subject themselves to Christian law. They all promised to obey, and the rich men made great feasts for the king. Thus he proceeded north to Halogaland, where Harek of Thiotta, a mighty man of the family of Harald the Fairhaired, after having made a feast for the king, was made lenderman, and was given the same privileges he had enjoyed under former rulers. The king remained most of the summer in Halogaland, went to all the Things, and baptized all the people. Thorer Hund, who lived on the island Biarkey and was one of the most powerful men in that northern country, also became one of Olaf's lendermen. Toward the end of the summer King Olaf sailed back to Throndhjem.

During his stay at Nidaros the king ascertained that the people of the interior of the Throndhjem country were still offering sacrifices to the heathen gods for peace and a good season, and that Olver of Eggja, a mighty man in that neighborhood, presided over these sacrifice-feasts, although he had twice assured the king that the people were loyal Christians. Learning that they were preparing such a feast at Mæren, the king proceeded to that place one night with three hundred and sixty armed men, captured Olver of Eggja, and had him killed together with many others, and severely punished all the peasants who had taken a leading part in the sacrifices. In this way he brought the people back to the Christian faith, gave them teachers, and built and consecrated churches. The widow of Olver of Eggja, who was young and handsome, of good family, and rich, was given by the king in marriage to Kalf Arneson, a young favorite among the king's men. The king also gave him an office, and Kalf thus became a great chief.

In the summer of 1021 King Olaf proceeded to Mœre and Raumsdal. In the fall he left his ships in Raumsdal and proceeded to Gudbrandsdal. The mightiest man there was Dale-Gudbrand, who ruled over the valley districts there with the authority of a king, although he did not bear the title. When he heard that Olaf was approaching, he summoned all the men in the valley to a Thing, where they decided to resist the attempt to force Christianity upon them. A force of eight hundred men, under the leadership of Alf, the son of Gudbrand, was sent against Olaf, but a battle had scarcely begun when the peasants fled, and Alf was captured. Then the king was invited to hold a Thing with the peasants, so they could discuss the proposed change of faith. To the request of the king that the people should believe in the true God and be baptized, Dale-Gudbrand replied: "We do not understand of whom thou art speaking. Dost thou call him God whom neither thou nor any one else can see? But we have a god who can be seen every day, although he is not out to-day, because the weather is wet. I expect that fear will mix with your very blood when he comes into the Thing. Now, since thy God is so great, let him make it so that to-morrow we have a cloudy day but without rain, and then let us meet again." The next day when the Thing had assembled, the weather was such as Gudbrand had desired. Bishop Sigurd stood up in full vestments, with mitre on his head and crosier in his hand, and spoke to the peasants of the true faith, and of the many miracles that God had performed. On the third day the peasants came to the assembly carrying between them a great image of the god Thor, which they placed on the green. Dale-Gudbrand then said: "Where now, king, is thy god? I think he will now carry his head lower; and neither thou nor thy bishop are so bold to-day as on former days; for now our god, who rules over all, has come, and looks on you with an angry eye. And now I see well enough that you are terrified."

The king instructed one of his men, Kolbein Sterke (Kolbein the Strong), to strike the image with his club with all his might, if in the course of the king's speech it should happen that all the people looked in another direction. Then the king spoke to the people, saying: "Much hast thou talked to us this morning, and greatly hast thou wondered that thou canst not see our God. But I expect that he will soon come to us. Thou wouldst frighten us with thy god, who is both blind and deaf, and can neither save himself nor others, and cannot even move without being carried; but now I expect that he will soon come to grief. For turn your eyes toward the east. Behold our God advancing in great light!" The sun was just rising, and all turned to look. Immediately Kolbein struck the idol with his club, so that it burst into many pieces, and out of it ran rats as big as cats, snakes, and lizards, which had fattened on the good things that had daily been given to the god. At this the peasants became greatly terrified and fled. But the king ordered them together again, and urged them to abandon their worthless heathen gods, and finally he gave them the choice between accepting Christianity and fighting. Dale-Gudbrand then arose and said, that since their own god would not help them, they would have to believe in the king's God and serve him. Then Olaf caused all the people in the valley to be baptized, and gave them teachers. Gudbrand himself and his son were baptized by the bishop. Gudbrand built a church on his estate, and he and Olaf parted as friends.

With the same firm hand King Olaf established Christianity in Hedemarken and Raumarike. During his stay in Raumarike he assembled a great Thing at Eidsvold and proclaimed the Eidsiva law for all the Uplands.

King Olaf succeeded in having Christianity established by law throughout the whole of Norway. He built many churches and gave property to them, so that there was at least one priest in each Fylki. With the assistance of Bishop Grimkjell he had a church law adopted. He also improved the civil laws, and had a fourth *law-thing* established for Viken, the Borge-Thing, which had its own law, and was held at the city of Borg (now Sarpsborg). However, by his cruel way of introducing Christianity, and his relentless way of enforcing all laws, Olaf gradually made many enemies; he severely punished all who broke the laws, whether they were high or low, and one after the other among the chiefs became unfriendly to him. Among the most dangerous of these enemies were Erling Skialgson of Sole, Thorer Hund of Biarkey and Harek of Thiotta.

At this time Canute (Knut) the Great, called by some Canute the Old, a son of the Danish king, Svein Tjuguskeg, was king of England and Denmark. Canute claimed the hereditary right to all Norway, and his sister's son, Earl Haakon, who had held a part of it, appeared to him to have lost it in disgrace. Many of the discontented Norwegians went over to England, pretending various errands, and visited Canute the Great and Earl Haakon, who was staying with Canute. Every one who thus came was most hospitably received, and were given costly presents. The young earl listened with pleasure to the complaints of the discontented about King Olaf's tyranny, and to their appeals for a return of the former state of affairs. Haakon forgot the oath he had given to King Olaf, and begged his uncle Canute to try if King Olaf would not voluntarily surrender the kingdom or at least a part of it. King Canute then sent magnificently equipped messengers to Norway, bearing his letter and seal.

King Olaf had come down from the Uplands in the spring (1025) and was sojourning in Tunsberg, when the messengers of Canute the Great arrived and made known their errand. "King Canute considers all Norway as his property," they said, "his forefathers before him having possessed the kingdom; but as he offers peace to all countries, he will not invade Norway with an army if it can be avoided. But if King Olaf Haraldson wishes to remain king of Norway, he must come to King Canute, and receive the kingdom in fief from him, become his vassal, and pay the tribute which the earls before him have paid." To this King Olaf replied: "I have heard that the Danish king Gorm was considered a good and popular king, although he ruled over Denmark alone; but the kings who succeeded him were not satisfied with this. It has now come so far that King Canute rules over Denmark and England, and has also conquered a great part of Scotland. And still he lays claim to the kingdom I have inherited. I think he ought to be satisfied with what he has. Does he wish to rule over all the countries of the North? Will he eat up all the cabbage in England? He will have to do so before I show him any kind of vassalage. Bring him this answer: I will defend Norway with battle-axe and sword as long as life is given me, and will pay tribute to no man for my kingdom."

Later in the summer the discontented Norwegians in England were reinforced by Aslak and Skialg, the sons of Erling Skialgson of Sole, who, no doubt with their father's knowledge and consent, went over to England and were received by King Canute with open arms.

King Olaf understood the danger that was threatening him and took measures to protect himself. He had spies out to keep an eye on the movements of Canute, and in the fall he sent messengers eastward to Sweden to his brother-in-law, King Anund Jacob, who had succeeded his father, Olaf the Swede, as king of Sweden, and let him know King Canute's demands upon Norway, adding that, in his opinion, if Canute subdued Norway, King Anund would not long enjoy the Swedish dominions in peace. He therefore thought they ought to unite for their defence. King Anund received this message favorably, and promised to arrange a personal meeting with King Olaf in the near future.

In the autumn King Canute the Great came from England to Denmark, and remained there all winter with a large army. Believing that an offensive and defensive alliance between Norway and Sweden would be fraught with danger to his Danish kingdom, he sent messengers to the Swedish king, in order to win his friendship or at least secure his neutrality. But, although the messengers brought many costly presents for King Anund, they were very coolly received, and returned to King Canute with the information that he could not depend much upon the friendship of King Anund.

King Olaf spent the winter at Sarpsborg. Early in the spring he and King Anund met at Konungahella, on the Gaut River, where their alliance was concluded.

King Olaf set out with his men and raised a levy over the whole country. All the lendermen in the North followed him except Einar Thambaskelfer, who remained quietly on his great estate. Olaf sailed with his fleet south around Stadt, and many people from the districts around joined him. At Hordaland he heard that Erling Skialgson had left the country with a great force and several ships, and had sailed westward to England to Canute the Great. King Olaf proceeded eastward and then south to Denmark, where he first ravaged the coast of Seeland, and afterward met King Anund Jacob of Sweden, and with him harried the coast of Skåne (Scania, then a part of Denmark, now belonging to Sweden). They proclaimed to the people that they intended to conquer Denmark, and asked the support of the people for this purpose. Many men entered the service of the kings, and agreed to submit to them.

When King Canute heard in England that King Olaf had gone to Denmark with a plundering army, he collected a great force and a large fleet with which he proceeded to Denmark. Earl Haakon was second in command. King Olaf and King Anund now sailed eastward, and put up in Helgeaa, a short but wide river forming the outlet of a number of lakes near what was then the boundary between Sweden and Denmark. When they heard that King Canute was coming after them with his great force, they made preparations to receive him. They dammed up the lake at the head of the river, so that the water rose to a considerable height in the lake, while the river was quite low. Then the allies made their ships ready for battle. When Canute arrived, it was too late in the evening to begin the battle, and seeing the harbor empty, he entered it with as many ships as possible. Early in the morning the dam was broken, and the water rushed with great force down upon Canute's fleet. A good many people were drowned, and the ships were scattered, some of them in a considerably damaged condition.

However, when the fleet had again been collected, the allied kings perceived that it was of too formidable strength to be attacked, and so they withdrew. King Canute, after having vainly lain in wait for Olaf, and having no special desire for a war between Denmark and Sweden, sailed away and returned to England. King Olaf returned overland through Sweden to Norway.

In the following year (1028) Canute the Great returned with a large fleet to Norway. By a policy of general bribery he had won the friendship of a great many of the discontented chiefs. The saga says "that every man who came to him, and who he thought had the spirit of a man and would like his favor, got his hands full of gifts and money." He first landed in Agder, where he summoned a Thing and received the oath of allegiance from the peasants. King Olaf was then in Tunsberg. Canute sailed northward along the coast, and everywhere he was hailed as king. In Ekersund Erling Skialgson came to him with many people, and King Canute and Erling renewed their league of friendship. Canute then continued his journey until he came to Throndhjem, and landed at Nidaros. Here a Thing was summoned, at which King Canute was proclaimed king of all Norway. Thorer Hund and Harek of Thiotta were present, and the king divided Halogaland between them. The king made Earl Haakon governor-in-chief of all the land he had taken on this expedition. At the same time he appointed his son Hardeknut king of Denmark. He gave Einar Thambaskelfer great gifts, and restored to him the fiefs he had formerly held.

When King Olaf heard that King Canute had gone south to Denmark he sailed with a few ships, and as many men as would follow him, up along the coast. When he came north to Eikundasund (Ekersund), he heard that Erling Skialgson was ready to meet him with a great force. On the 21st of December the king sailed out of the harbor, and the wind being strong and favorable, he sailed past the place where Erling was with his fleet. Erling soon pursued him, but was separated from his main force, and when he overtook King Olaf he was met by the whole of the latter's force. A severe fight began, and many men fell on both sides; but finally Erling was the only man left on his ship. King Olaf who, with his men, had entered the ship, called out to him from the fore-deck: "Thou hast turned thy face straight against us to-day, Erling." "Face to face shall eagles fight," said Erling. The old man's courage and manly defence had awakened Olaf's sympathy, and the king asked him if he would enter his service. "That I will," said Erling. He took off his helmet, laid down his sword and shield, and went forward to the fore-deck. King Olaf, who half regretted his kindly feelings toward the conquered man, gently scratched his cheek with the edge of his battle-axe, saying: "The traitor to the king must be marked."

Immediately one of the king's men, Aslak Fitiarskalle, rushed up, and cleft Erling's skull with his axe, saying: "Thus we mark the traitor to the king." When the king saw the old chieftain lying dead at his feet he deeply regretted the ill-considered scorn he had uttered, and said to Aslak: "Ill luck was that stroke; for thou hast struck Norway out of my hands." Erling Skialgson was sixty-two years old at the time of his death, and the saga says that he was the greatest and worthiest man in Norway of all those who had no higher title.

Olaf continued his journey northward, but was soon pursued by Erling's sons, who had raised a great army. When he heard that Earl Haakon was also coming against him with an army from Throndhjem, he found himself compelled to flee from the country. He landed at Valdal and crossed the mountains to Gudbrandsdal and thence to Sweden, where he left his wife Astrid and his daughter Ulfhild. Olaf, with his son Magnus and a few faithful friends, travelled to Russia, where he was well received by his brother-in-law, King Jaroslav, who had married Ingegerd, the sister of the Swedish king, Anund Jacob.

CHAPTER XVI

The Battle of Stiklestad (1030)

IN the summer of 1029 Earl Haakon went to England to fetch his bride, Gunhild, a daughter of Canute's sister. Everything was satisfactorily arranged, but on his return voyage his vessel foundered, and all on board were lost.

One of King Olaf's best friends, Biorn Stallare,[5] believing that Olaf would not return to Norway, had been induced by great gifts and promises to give allegiance to Earl Haakon and King Canute; but when he heard that the earl had perished, so that the country was again without a chief, he greatly regretted that he had failed to be true to King Olaf, and it seemed to him that there was now some hope that Olaf might again become king if he came back to Norway. He therefore immediately journeyed east to Russia to Olaf, and told him of Earl Haakon's death, and brought him other news from Norway. When the king asked him how his friends had kept their fidelity toward him, Biorn answered that it had been different with different people. Then he fell at the king's feet, and said: "All is in your power, sire, and in God's. I have taken money from King Canute's men, and sworn them allegiance; but now I will follow thee, and not part from thee so long as we both live." The king answered: "Arise, Biorn; thou shalt be reconciled with me; but reconcile thy perjury with God. I must know that but few men in Norway have adhered to their fealty to me, when such a man as thou art could be false to me." Biorn named those who had principally bound themselves to be his enemies; among them were Erling's sons, Einar Thambaskelfer, Kalf Arneson, Thorer Hund and Harek of Thiotta.

Olaf now made preparations for his return to Norway, and shortly after Christmas started with two hundred and forty men. His young son, Magnus, was left behind with King Jaroslav in Russia. In Sweden, King Anund received his brother-in-law well, and gave him four hundred and eighty picked warriors to go with him. When it was reported in Norway that King Olaf had come from the east to Sweden, his friends gathered aid for him in Norway. The most distinguished man in this party was Harald Sigurdson, Olaf's half-brother, who was then quite young, but very stout and manly of growth. Many other brave men were there also; and they were in all seven hundred and twenty men, when they proceeded eastward through the Eid forest and Vermeland, and met Olaf in Sweden. Olaf's kinsman, Dag Ringson, collected an army of about 1,400 men, with which he joined King Olaf.

When King Olaf had crossed the mountain and was descending on the west side, where it declines toward the sea, and he could see the country for many miles, he became sad and rode by himself in silence for quite a while. Finally, Bishop Sigurd rode up to him, and asked him why he was so silent, and what he was thinking of. The king answered: "Strange things came into my mind a while ago. As I looked down the valley, it appeared to me that I was looking over all Norway. It then came into my mind how many happy days I have had in this country. My vision went further, until I looked over the whole wide world, both land and sea. I recognized places where I have been before; but I also saw places of which I had never heard, both inhabited and uninhabited, as far as the world goes." Then the bishop dismounted from his horse, kissed the king's foot, and said: "It is a holy man whom we are now following."

When King Olaf came down into Verdalen, he mustered his force, and he then had over 3,600 men. Among them were about six hundred who were heathens, and who refused to be baptized. These men were sent back, as Olaf would not have any heathens among his warriors.

In the evening Olaf's whole forces took up their night-quarter in one place, and lay down under their shields; the king lay long awake in prayer to God, and slept but little. Toward morning he slumbered for a while, and when he awoke, day was breaking. The king thought it too early to awaken the army, and asked where the bard Thormod Kolbrunarskald was. Thormod was near by, and asked what the king desired. The king said: "Sing us a song." Thormod arose and sang, so loud that the whole army could hear him, the old Biarkemaal.[6] Then the troops awoke, and, when the song was ended, the people thanked him for it, and the king gave him a fine gold ring.

The king now led his army further down the valley until he came to Stiklestad, where he placed his army in battle array against the peasants' army. The lendermen and peasants had collected a vast army; it is said to have numbered 14,400 men. When the armies were near together, Thorer Hund went forward in front of the banner with his troop, and called out: "Forward, forward, Bonde-men!" The peasants repeated this war-cry and shot their arrows and spears. The king's men now raised their battle-cry, and encouraged each other to advance, shouting: "Forward, forward, Christ-men! cross-men! king's-men!" King Olaf's army rushed down the hill upon the peasant army with a fierce assault, and for a moment drove it from its original position; but the chiefs urged their men forward, and forced them to advance again. The peasant army pushed forward from all quarters, and the battle became very severe. Those who stood in front hewed down with their swords; those who stood next thrust with their spears, while those in the rear shot arrows, cast spears, or threw stones, hand-axes, or pieces of timber. Many fell on both sides. When the ranks in front of the king's banner began to be thinned, he ordered the banner moved forward, and the king himself followed with a party of chosen men, and placed himself in the front rank. King Olaf fought most desperately. He hewed at Thorer Hund, and struck him across the shoulders; but the sword would not cut, and it was as if dust flew from Thorer's reindeer-skin coat. Then the king said to Biorn Stallare: "Do thou kill the dog on whom steel will not bite." (Thorer's surname Hund means dog.) Biorn turned the axe in his hand, and gave Thorer such a blow with the hammer of it on the shoulder that he staggered; but the next moment Thorer ran his spear through the body of Biorn, and killed him, saying: "Thus we hunt bears north in Finmark." (Biorn means bear.) Thorstein Knarrarsmid, one of Thorer Hund's followers, struck at King Olaf with his axe, and the blow hit his left leg above the knee. Fin Arneson immediately felled Thorstein; but the king, badly wounded, staggered toward a stone, threw down his sword and shield, and prayed God to help him. Then Thorer Hund struck at him with his spear, and the stroke went in under his mail-coat and into his abdomen. Still another wound was given the king on the left side of the neck, and these three wounds caused the death of King Olaf. He was then thirty-five years old.

The battle had lasted an hour and a half, and was now virtually ended. Dag Ringson and his men still fought desperately for a while, but they were soon overwhelmed by numbers and fatigue, and were obliged to retire. There was a valley through which many fled, and men lay scattered on both sides; many were severely wounded, and many so fatigued that they were unable to move. The peasants pursued them only a short way; for their leaders soon returned to the battlefield, where they had friends and relatives to care for.

It is said that Thorer Hund went to where King Olaf's body lay, laid it out on the ground, and spread a cloak over it. He told afterward that when he wiped the blood from the face it was very beautiful, and the cheeks were red. Some of the king's blood came on Thorer's wounded hand, and it healed so speedily that he did not need to dress it. This was told by Thorer himself when King Olaf's holiness came to be generally reported among the people; and Thorer Hund was among the first of the king's powerful opponents who endeavored to spread abroad the belief in Olaf's sanctity.

Harald Sigurdson, King Olaf's half-brother, was severely wounded at Stiklestad; but one of Olaf's men brought him to a peasant's house the night after the battle, and the peasant cared for Harald, and healed his wound in secret, and afterward gave him his son to attend him.

Some time after the battle, two young men were one day riding across the mountain to Jemteland in order to reach Sweden. One of them was a peasant's son from Verdalen, the other a young warrior, the last one of King Olaf's men who fled from the country. As they were passing over the ridge, the young man turned to his companion, and sang:

"The wounds were bleeding as I rode;
And down below the peasants strode,
Killing the wounded with the sword,
The followers of their rightful lord.
From wood to wood I crept along,
Unnoticed by the peasant-throng;
Who knows, I thought, a day may come
My name will yet be great at home."

It was Olaf's brother, Harald, who was setting out to try his luck in foreign countries, whence he was to return one day, rich in honors and goods.

CHAPTER XVII

King Svein Alfifuson (1030-1035)

WHEN King Canute the Great heard that Earl Haakon had been lost in a shipwreck on his way to Norway, he concluded to put his natural son Svein on the throne of Norway. Svein's mother was Ælfgifa, a daughter of an English chieftain in Northampton, but the Norwegians called her Alfifa and her son Svein Alfifuson. Svein had, a couple of years before, been appointed by King Canute to govern Jomsborg in Vendland; but after Earl Haakon's death King Canute sent word to him to proceed to Denmark and from there to Norway, to take that kingdom in charge and assume the title of king of Norway. With a number of men from Denmark, Svein proceeded to Norway together with his mother, Alfifa, and he was hailed as king at every Thing. He had come as far as Viken at the time the battle was fought at Stiklestad, where King Olaf fell. He continued his journey northward until, in the autumn, he came to the Throndhjem country; and there, as elsewhere, he was received as king.

Svein was very young and inexperienced, and it was his mother who had most to say in governmental affairs. Together with Bishop Sigurd and some Danes, whom she had brought with her from Denmark, she commenced to rule the country in a very arbitrary manner, and the people soon became greatly discontented. For a time the disaffection smouldered beneath the surface; but when the foreign rulers proceeded to introduce a new system of laws, fashioned in accordance with the development of the feudal system in the rest of Europe, there was a general uprising throughout the country.

Among the laws introduced in King Svein's name were the following: No man must leave the country without the king's permission; or if he did, his property fell to the king. Whoever killed a man should forfeit his land and movable property. At Christmas every man had to give the king a certain portion of the products of his farm. The peasants were obliged to build all the houses the king required on his farms. For every seven males over the age of five years one man was to be furnished for the service of war. Every ship that went out of the country should have storage reserved for the king in the middle of the ship. Several heavy taxes were provided. And to all this was added a provision that the testimony of one Dane should invalidate that of ten Norwegians.

When these laws were announced at the Thing in Throndhjem, loud murmurs were heard among the people. Those who had not taken part in the uprising against King Olaf said: "Now take your reward and friendship from Canute and his race, ye men of the interior of Throndhjem who fought against King Olaf, and deprived him of his kingdom. Ye were promised peace and justice, and now ye have got oppression and slavery for your great treachery." This was true, and the chiefs felt it well enough; but they were afraid of making open rebellion, as many of them had given King Canute their sons or other near relatives as hostages.

At this time the people began to talk much of King Olaf's sanctity. There were many rumors of miracles in connection with the dead king, and it gradually became the general opinion that a great mistake or rather a crime had been committed by the rebellion against King Olaf. People began to severely reproach those who had excited opposition to the king, and among those especially accused was Bishop Sigurd. He got so many enemies that he found it most advisable to leave the country, and proceeded to England to King Canute. When Bishop Sigurd had left, the people of Throndhjem sent word to Bishop Grimkell, desiring him to come to Throndhjem. King Olaf had sent Bishop Grimkell back to Norway when he went east to Russia, and since that time Grimkell had been in the Uplands. He now came north and visited Einar Thambaskelfer, who received him with open arms. Einar congratulated himself upon not having taken part in the strife against King Olaf, and was now one of the mighty men who looked upon the dead king as a saint. Einar and the bishop obtained King Svein's leave to exhume the body of Olaf. It is said that they found that the coffin had raised itself almost entirely to the surface of the earth, and when the coffin was opened they found that the king's face was red as if he had merely fallen asleep, and his hair and nails had grown as if he had lived all the time. Grimkell now declared that King Olaf was truly a holy man, and with the approbation of the king and the decision of the Thing Olaf was declared the saint of the nation. His body was transported into Clement's church, where a place was made for it near the high altar. The coffin was covered with costly cloth, and stood under a gold embroidered tent. People soon began to make pilgrimages to the shrine of Saint Olaf, and gradually a great number of churches were built and dedicated to him, not only in Norway, but also in other countries.

When King Svein had been three years in Norway, a young man, who called himself Trygve, and professed to be a son of Olaf Trygvason and Queen Gyda of England, came from the west with an armed force, intending to claim the throne of Norway. Svein called upon his chiefs to furnish him with men and ships in defence of the country, and an army was soon ready; but Einar Thambaskelfer, and Kalf Arneson, and some others refused to give aid. King Svein sailed south and met Trygve in battle in

Sognesund. In this battle Trygve fell, and many of his men with him; but some fled, and others received quarter.

After the battle in Sognesund King Svein returned to Throndhjem; but his stay there was not of long duration. He met the people at a Thing, and heard their complaints, but no understanding could be reached. Shortly afterward the situation became so strained that King Svein and his mother found it necessary to remove to the southern part of the country to spend the winter. During this winter Einar Thambaskelfer and Kalf Arneson had many consultations in Nidaros with the other chiefs, and the result was that in the spring a deputation of prominent chiefs, including Einar Thambaskelfer and Kalf Arneson, proceeded east to King Jaroslav in Russia to offer the throne of Norway to Magnus, the son of Olaf the Saint, who had been raised at King Jaroslav's court. They asked and received full forgiveness for having fought against Magnus's father at Stiklestad. They thereupon swore allegiance to Magnus, who, on the other hand, promised them under oath that he would be true and faithful to them all when he got the dominions and kingdom of Norway. Einar and Kalf were to act as his foster-fathers and counsellors. Magnus returned with them to Norway and was welcomed with great joy. At Oere-Thing he was proclaimed king over the whole land. When King Svein heard this news he tried to raise an army; but nobody would listen to him, and he and his mother were obliged to flee to Denmark. Here Svein died in the year 1036; his father Canute dying a short time before him.

CHAPTER XVIII
Magnus the Good (1035-1047)

MAGNUS was a natural child of Olaf the Saint, his mother being a girl by the name of Alfhild, who was usually called the king's slave-woman, although she was of good descent. She was a very handsome girl and lived in King Olaf's court. It is said that when Magnus was born she was very sick, and it was some time after the birth before it could be discovered whether the boy was alive. A priest, who was present, requested Sigvat the Skald (poet) to hasten to the king and tell him of the event; but Sigvat refused, as the king had strictly forbidden anybody to awaken him in the middle of the night. As the child was very weak, however, they decided to baptize it, and Sigvat the Skald named the boy Magnus. The next morning the king demanded to know why they had named the boy Magnus, since there was no such name in his family. Sigvat said: "I called him after King Carl Magnus (Emperor Charlemagne), who, I knew, had been the best man in the world." This satisfied the king.

Magnus was only eleven years old when he was proclaimed king at the Oere-Thing. In the beginning he allowed Kalf Arneson and Einar Thambaskelfer to take care of all government matters in his name; but he soon developed into a clever, intelligent young man with a great deal of independence. Hardeknut, who was then king of Denmark, was inclined to press his claims to Norway, which he had inherited from his father, Canute the Great, and collected an army. King Magnus also armed himself, and they were about to meet in battle at the Gaut River. However, the chiefs on both sides, who very much desired to avoid war, made overtures for peace, and the result was a friendly meeting between the kings at the Brenn Islands at the mouth of the Gaut River. They arranged for a brotherly union, under oath, to keep the peace with each other to the end of their lives; and if one of them should die without leaving a son, the survivor should succeed to both countries. Twelve of the principal men in each kingdom swore to the kings that this treaty should be observed.

After the conciliation at the Brenn Islands Magnus was in undisputed possession of his father's throne. During his stay in the southern part of the country he had come in contact with his father's former friends and faithful adherents, who had a great deal to say about the actions of the Throndhjem people toward King Olaf. Magnus listened with great eagerness to this talk, and, before he really understood it, he had become possessed of a bitter feeling against those men who had been his father's opponents. He especially began to dislike Kalf Arneson, who, according to common belief, had dealt King Olaf the last deadly blow at Stiklestad. One day the king was at a feast at the Haug estate in Verdalen. At the table he said to Einar Thambaskelfer: "Let us ride to-day over to Stiklestad. I wish to see the different reminders of the battle." Einar replied: "Well, I know little about how matters went there; but take Kalf with thee: he can give thee information about all that took place." When the tables were removed, the king made himself ready, and said to Kalf: "Thou must go with me to Stiklestad." After repeating this command the king went out. Kalf put on his riding clothes in all haste, and said to his foot-boy: "Ride immediately to Eggja, and order my house-servants to have all my property on board my ship before sunset."

The king and Kalf now rode over to Stiklestad. They alighted from their horses, and went to the place where the battle had been. "Where did the king fall?" asked Magnus. Kalf pointed with his spear, and said: "There he lay when he fell." The king further asked: "And where wast thou then, Kalf?" "Here, where I am now standing," answered Kalf. The king turned red as blood in the face, and said: "Then thy axe could well have reached him."

Kalf replied: "My axe did not come near him." Then he immediately went to his horse, and rode away with all his men, while the king returned to Haug. When Kalf reached home he found his ship ready, and immediately sailed for the Orkneys. The king confiscated the Eggja estate and other possessions which Kalf left behind him.

Magnus commenced to severely punish many of those who had borne arms against Saint Olaf. He drove some of them out of the country, took large sums of money from others, and had the cattle of others slaughtered for his use. Thorer Hund had escaped punishment by making a pilgrimage to Jerusalem shortly after Olaf's fall, and it is said that he never came back. Harek of Thiotta was killed with the king's consent by Asmund Grankelson, whose father had been killed by Harek. The people soon began to murmur, and the discontent spread throughout the country. In Sogn the people even gathered an armed force, and were determined to fight, if Magnus came into their district. When the young impetuous king heard of this, and made up his mind to punish the rebellious Sognings, his friends, who knew that the disaffection was widely spread through the country, decided to warn him of his danger. Twelve of his friends came together, and determined, by casting lots, which one of them should inform the king of the discontent of the people, and the lot fell upon Sigvat the Skald.

Sigvat then composed a poem, which he called "The Free-speaking Song" (*Bersöglisvísur*), in which he reminded the king of the promises he made when he was proclaimed king, and advised him to be guided by that respect for the laws and the rights of the people which his predecessors had shown. He blamed him for his severity, and warned him of the danger threatening him and his country.

Sigvat's song made a deep impression on the young king, and from now on he was an entirely changed man. He consulted the most prudent men, and revised the laws, repealing such of Svein Alfifuson's laws as were most obnoxious to the people. He codified the laws in a written book called "The Gray Goose" (*Graagaasen*).[7] It was only a short time before King Magnus became very popular, and was beloved by all the country people, who now called him Magnus the Good.

The Danish king, Hardeknut, who was also king of England, died of apoplexy at a wedding-feast at Lambeth, England, in June, 1042. This was the end of Danish rule in England. After the death of Hardeknut, his half-brother, Edward the Good, a son of the English king Ethelred and Queen Emma, was chosen king of England.

When King Magnus heard of Hardeknut's death, he immediately sent word to Denmark that he intended to claim the Danish throne in accordance with the agreement made between himself and Hardeknut at their meeting at the Gaut River. Shortly afterward King Magnus proceeded to Denmark with a fine fleet of seventy ships. He was well received, and at a Thing assembled at Viborg, Jutland (where the Danes always elected their king), he was proclaimed king of all the Danish dominions. He remained in Denmark during the summer (1042), and wherever he came he was received with enthusiasm. He divided the country into districts and appointed administrative officers, gave fiefs to influential men, and took all steps to secure himself in power. In the autumn he returned to Norway.

Among the Danes who swore allegiance to King Magnus was Svein, commonly called Svein Estridson, a son of Earl Ulf. His mother was Estrid (Astrid), a daughter of King Svein Tjuguskeg. She was a sister of Canute the Great by the father's side, and of the Swedish king Olaf by the mother's side, her mother being Queen Sigrid the Haughty. One day, as King Magnus was sitting in his high-seat with a large number of men around him, and with Svein Estridson sitting on a footstool before him, the king made a speech, in which he said that he had promised the Danes a chief who could defend and rule the country in the absence of the king. "And," he continued, "I know no better man fitted, in all respects, for this than Svein. I will therefore make him my earl, and give him the government of my Danish dominions while I am in Norway, just as King Canute the Great set his father, Earl Ulf, over Denmark while he was in England." Einar Thambaskelfer, who was with the king, was very ill-pleased with this appointment, as he put no faith in Svein, and said to the king: "Too great an earl, too great an earl, my foster-son!"

King Magnus had an early opportunity to regret his choice, for, the same winter in which Svein was given the administration of the government of Denmark as earl, he successfully courted the friendship of the most influential men, and assumed the title of King of Denmark. King Magnus heard this news, and at the same time that the people of Vendland had a large army with which they plundered in Denmark. He then gathered a large force, with which he sailed to Denmark. There he summoned the people to come to him, and drew together a great army in Jutland. Ordulf, the duke of Brunswick, who the year before had married Ulfhild, the daughter of King Olaf the Saint, and the half-sister of King Magnus,[8] also came to his aid with a great force. King Magnus met the Vends in battle at Lyrskog Heath in Schleswig and gained a great victory. It was generally reported in the army that King Magnus had a vision the night before the battle, in which Olaf the Saint had appeared and had given the king advice. "It is the common saying," says the saga, "that there never was so great a slaughter of men in the northern lands, since the time of Christianity, as took place among the Vendland people on Lyrskog Heath." This was on the 28th of September, 1043. King Magnus followed up his victory, and sailed to Vendland, attacked and captured the fortress of Jomsborg. A great many of the people of Vendland submitted to King Magnus, while others fled the country.

After this King Magnus turned his attention to Earl Svein. A battle was fought, and Svein had to flee to his relatives in Sweden. But as soon as Magnus went to Norway, Svein would return to Denmark and strengthen himself with the Danes, and Magnus had continual wars with his earl. Among the principal battles were those at Aaros (now Aarhus) and Helganes.

When King Magnus came back to Norway in the autumn of 1045, after one of his battles with Svein, he heard that his relative, Harald Sigurdson, had come to Sweden on his way to Norway, and that Harald and Svein had come to an understanding, and intended to endeavor to subdue both Denmark and Norway. King Magnus then ordered a general levy over all Norway, and he soon collected a great army with which to meet the intruder. The relatives and friends of both Harald and Magnus, however, said that it would be a great misfortune if there should be war between them, and the result was a friendly meeting, where Magnus gave Harald half of his kingdom. They were to rule together on equal terms; but whenever they were together in one place King Magnus was to be "the first man in seat, service and salutation." King Magnus died the following year (1047) on one of his expeditions to Denmark. Before his death King Magnus declared that Svein Estridson was to have Denmark, while Harald should rule over Norway.

CHAPTER XIX

Harald Haardraade (1047-1066)

HARALD, the son of Sigurd Syr and Astrid, now became the sole king of Norway. As we have seen, Harald fled from the country after the battle of Stiklestad (1030). He went to Russia to the court of King Jaroslav, who received him with kindness and made him a commander in the army. Harald remained in the service of King Jaroslav for three years, and then went with a body of men to Constantinople (called by the Northmen Miklagaard), where he soon became the captain or chief of the Varings. (The Varings were the bodyguard of the emperors, and the guard was composed mostly of Northmen.) With them he went on many expeditions, and always gained victories and a great deal of booty. He conducted expeditions against the Saracens in Africa (which the Varings called Serkland), where he gathered great wealth in gold, jewels, and other precious things. He also served in Sicily, where he won several battles. After having spent several years in these campaigns he returned to Constantinople, and then went to Jerusalem, and bathed in the river Jordan, according to the custom of other pilgrims. Thereafter he returned to Russia and was received in the most friendly way by King Jaroslav. He married the latter's daughter, Elisabeth, or Ellisif, as the Northmen called her.

When King Magnus died, Harald, as already stated, became sole king of Norway. But he also wanted Denmark, and called his men-at-arms together, and told them that he intended to go with an army to Viborg Thing and there proclaim himself king of Denmark, to which, he said, he had the hereditary right, as well as to Norway. The friends of the late King Magnus, however, did not like this, and Einar Thambaskelfer said that he considered it a greater duty to bring his foster son King Magnus's corpse to the grave, and lay it beside his father King Olaf's north in Throndhjem, than to be fighting abroad, and taking another king's dominions and property. He ended his speech with saying that he would rather follow King Magnus dead than any other king alive. The result was that King Harald returned to Norway with his army. For many years thereafter King Harald was at war with Svein Estridson (or Ulfson), but did not succeed in driving him away from Denmark.

Einar Thambaskelfer was the most powerful man in the Throndhjem country. There was but little friendship between him and King Harald, although Einar retained all the fiefs he had held under King Magnus. Einar had many large estates, and was married to Bergliot, a daughter of Earl Haakon. Their son Eindride was married to Sigrid, a daughter of Ketil Kalf and Gunhild, King Harald's sister's daughter. Einar was well versed in law, and often acted as spokesman for the peasants at the Things, when the king demanded more of the people than was his right. This happened more than once, for Harald's rule was quite severe. Therefore he was called Harald *Haardraade*, or Hard-ruler. Einar did not lack the boldness to assert his opinions at the Things, even in the presence of the king; and for this reason he was held in high esteem by the people, while the king came to hate him more after every such dispute. Einar, therefore, began to keep a number of men around him whenever the king was in the neighborhood. One day he came to the town (Nidaros) with eight or nine ships and nearly six hundred men. When Harald, who was standing in the doorway of his house, saw Einar going ashore, he exclaimed in verse: "Here I see Einar Thambaskelfer land with quite a force. In his haughtiness he probably expects even to fill the royal chair; for often has even an earl a smaller force of men with him. This Einar will some day deprive me of my kingdom, unless he himself has to kiss the thin lips of the axe."

One day there was a meeting, at which the king himself was present. A thief had been caught and was brought before the Thing. The man had been in the service of Einar, who had liked him very well. Einar well knew that the king would not let the man off, especially as Einar took an interest in him. He therefore let his men arm themselves, went to the Thing, and took the man away by force. The mutual friends of the king and Einar then intervened and tried to bring about a reconciliation, and they succeeded so far that a day was appointed for a meeting between them at the king's house at the river Nid. The king had the shutters for the smoke-hole in the roof closed so as to exclude the light. When Einar came into the yard with his people, he told his son Eindride to remain outside with the men, "for there is no danger here for me." Eindride remained standing outside the door. When Einar came into the room, he said: "Dark it is in the king's Thing-room." At this some men fell upon him with spears and swords. "Sharp are now the bites of the king's dogs," said Einar, and rushed toward the king, but was felled to the floor by the king's men. When Eindride heard the noise he drew his sword and rushed into the room; but he was instantly killed along with his father. The king then went with all his men to his ships, and rowed down the river, the peasants not having the courage to pursue him after having lost their leader. Einar's wife Bergliot, who came up from her home, and in vain urged the peasants to pursue the murderers, said: "Now we miss my kinsman, Haakon Ivarson: Einar's slayer would not be rowing out of the river if Ivar stood here on the river-bank."

Bergliot sent word to Haakon Ivarson (a son of Ivar the White, nephew of Earl Haakon the Great), who was a mighty man in the Uplands, and requested him to avenge the death of Einar and Eindride. Meanwhile

King Harald proceeded to his kinsman by marriage, Fin Arneson, who lived at Austraat in Yrjar, and persuaded him to first go to Nidaros and bring about a reconciliation with the peasants, and thereafter to proceed to the Uplands and reach an understanding with Haakon Ivarson, so that he would not oppose the king. In return for this the king promised to recall to the country Fin's brother Kalf, and restore to him the estates and dignities of which King Magnus had deprived him. To Haakon Ivarson, Fin was to offer any favor he might wish short of the kingdom. Fin successfully accomplished both of the missions intrusted to him. Haakon Ivarson said, as to the conditions of peace: "I will be reconciled with King Harald if he will give me in marriage his relation Ragnhild, King Magnus Olafson's daughter, with such dower as is suitable to her and she will be content with," and Fin agreed to this on behalf of the king.

The next Christmas Haakon went to King Harald to ask the fulfilment of the pledges given him. The king said that he, for his part, would adhere to the whole agreement; but as for Ragnhild it would be necessary for Haakon to ask her consent himself. When Haakon came to Ragnhild, and paid his addresses to her, she answered: "I have no fault to find with thee, for thou art a handsome man, expert in all exercises. But thou must remember I am a king's daughter, while thou art only a lenderman. Had my father, King Magnus, lived he would have found that no man less than a king was suitable for me; so it is not to be expected that I will marry one who has no princely rank." Haakon then went to the king and demanded that he be made an earl under the agreement made with Fin Arneson. This the king refused to do, saying that it had been the custom since the time of Saint Olaf to have only one earl in the country, and he could not take the title from Orm, who now held it. Haakon now understood that there was nothing to obtain from the king, and left in disgust. Fin Arneson became very angry, and told the king that he had broken his word.

Haakon shortly afterward left the country with a well-manned ship, and went to King Svein of Denmark, who received him well and made him commander of his coast defence against the vikings from Vendland, Kurland and other eastern countries.

It was not a long time before Fin Arneson fell out with the king. His brother Kalf, who had been on a viking cruise to the "Western" (British) countries ever since he had left Norway, was recalled by the king and given back his estates according to agreement. But shortly afterward, during an expedition to Denmark, the king sent Kalf ashore on the island Fyen with a small force of men, and commanded him to attack a much stronger Danish force, promising that he would soon make a landing with the others and come to their assistance. Kalf obeyed, and was attacked by a great force of the enemy, and he and many of his men were killed. A long while afterward, when the Danes had withdrawn, Harald landed and made a plundering expedition into the country. Later he composed some verses, in which he boasted of having caused the death of thirteen men, and Fin rightly supposed that his brother was one of them. Fin took this matter so much to heart that he left Norway and went to King Svein of Denmark, who gave him a friendly reception. He swore allegiance to King Svein, and was made earl of Halland (now a province of Sweden), where he remained for a long time and defended the country against the Northmen.

Haakon Ivarson showed great zeal in his position as commander of the Danish coast defence, being out with his warships both winter and summer, and was in high favor with King Svein, until he attacked and killed the king's nephew, Asmund, an ungovernable young man, who had been killing and plundering everywhere, both abroad and at home, and whom Haakon thought the king much desired to get rid of. The king sent Haakon a message that he had better leave the country. "Tell him," he said, "that I will do him no harm; but I cannot answer for all our relations." Haakon then proceeded north to his estates in Norway. During his stay in Denmark his relative, Earl Orm, had died. His many friends therefore gave themselves much trouble to bring about a reconciliation between him and King Harald, and in this they succeeded. Haakon was given the title of earl, with the same power that Earl Orm had had, and was married to Ragnhild, King Magnus's daughter. He swore to King Harald an oath of fidelity and pledged himself to render all the service he was liable to.

In the winter of 1061-62, King Harald resided at Nidaros, where he commenced building a large warship. He sent a message south to Denmark to King Svein, and challenged him to meet him in the spring at the Gaut River and fight, with the understanding that the one who gained the victory should have both kingdoms. King Svein accepted the challenge, but did not keep the appointment. King Harald, who had arrived at the place agreed upon, heard that Svein's forces lay in the south, partly at Fyen and partly about Seeland. Harald then sailed southward along Halland with one hundred and eighty of his ships, and brought up his fleet at the Nis-Aa (Nis River). Shortly afterward King Svein came upon them with a Danish fleet consisting of three hundred and sixty ships. King Harald held a war council, and many said that it would be better to fly than to fight with a fleet twice the size of their own. The king replied: "Sooner shall we all fall and lie dead one upon another than fly." King Harald drew up his ships in battle array, laying his great dragon ship in the middle. At his side lay Ulf Stallara, and on the other wing lay the ships of Earl Haakon Ivarson from the Uplands. At the extremity of the other side lay the Throndhjem chiefs. It was late in the day when the battle began, and it continued the whole night. The battle was very severe, and toward morning the greater part of the Danish fleet broke into flight. While Harald pursued some of the Danes, King Svein made his escape with the aid of Earl Haakon Ivarson, who, during the battle, had contributed more than any one else to the victory of the Norwegians.

King Harald sailed north to Viken with all the conquered ships after the battle of Nis River, and spent the winter at Oslo. Earl Haakon went to the Uplands and remained in his dominions there during the winter. In the spring, however, he gathered all his loose property and fled eastward; for he heard that King Harald had again become his enemy, mainly because Haakon had allowed King Svein to escape after the battle of Nis River. Haakon proceeded to King Steinkel of Sweden, who gave him the province of Vermeland to govern. When Haakon heard that King Harald had gone north to Throndhjem, he made a hurried expedition back to the Uplands and collected the taxes due him. The next summer King Harald in vain tried to collect taxes in the same places. Then King Harald gathered an army, with which he invaded Sweden, and defeated Haakon. Upon his return he severely punished the people of the Uplands for having been disloyal. He maimed some, killed others, and robbed many of all their property.

Year after year King Harald had made war on Denmark without coming nearer to King Svein's throne. It appears that finally the people in both counties became tired of this continual and wasteful warfare, and during the same winter that Earl Haakon had settled down in Vermeland, Sweden, there were many negotiations between leading men of both countries who wanted peace and demanded that their kings should come to an agreement. The result was a meeting of the two kings at the Gaut River, where peace was agreed upon. Harald was to have Norway, and Svein Denmark; the war should cease as it now stood, each retaining what he had got, and this peace should endure as long as they were kings. This peace was confirmed by oath, and the kings parted, having given each other hostages (1064).

In the year 1066, Earl Toste came from England and asked King Harald to aid him in an attempt to conquer England from his brother Harald Godwinson, who had been proclaimed king of England. Earl Toste had already been on a similar mission to Denmark, but King Svein Estridson had declared that he would be content if he could keep his own kingdom and defend that against the Northmen. King Harald Sigurdson looked upon the plan with more favor, and promised his help. He collected an army and sailed for England with a large fleet. Before he left Throndhjem he gave the reins of the government to his son Magnus, whom he had proclaimed king at the Oere-Thing. He took with him his younger son Olaf, the queen and two daughters. At first King Harald was very successful against the Englishmen, and after a great victory the citizens of York surrendered the city to him. In the evening he returned to his ships to spend the night. Later in the same evening, however, King Harald Godwinson arrived with a numerous army, and rode into the city with the goodwill and consent of the people of the castle. All the gates and walls were beset so that the Northmen could receive no report of their arrival, and the army remained all night in the town.

In the morning King Harald Sigurdson landed with a portion of his army, leaving the remainder behind with the ships. As they came across Stanford Bridge, they discovered a numerous army approaching. Earl Toste advised a speedy return to the ships to get more men and arms; but Harald Sigurdson did not wish to appear cowardly, and elected instead to send three messengers with their fastest horses back to the ships with an order to the men there to immediately come to their assistance. Harald then arranged his men in a line of battle, long but not deep. Then he turned both wings backward until they met together, so that the army formed a wide ring of the men standing shield to shield. Thus he would defend himself against the enemy's horsemen, from whom he expected a violent attack. Those in the first rank were ordered to set the spear-shaft on the ground, and the spear-point against the horseman's breast; those in the next rank were to direct the spear-point against the horse's breast. Inside the ring, the bowmen were to stand, and here he also selected a place for himself and Earl Toste, and a body of chosen men. Now the English king approached with his army, which was twice as large as that of the Northmen. While Harald was yet arranging his army, riding around on his black horse, twenty horsemen came riding up from the English army, and asked if Earl Toste was there. The earl himself answered: "Here you can find him." One of the horsemen, speaking for the English king, then offered the earl peace and a third of the kingdom if he would be reconciled with his brother. The earl said: "But if I accept this offer, what will he give King Harald Sigurdson for his trouble?" The horseman replied: "He will give him seven feet of English ground, or as much more as he may be taller than other men." "Then," said the earl, "return and tell King Harald to get ready for battle. Never shall the Northmen have a chance to say that Earl Toste left King Harald Sigurdson to join his enemy." Then the horsemen returned to the English army. King Harald Sigurdson said to Earl Toste: "Who was the man who spoke so well?" "That was my brother, King Harald Godwinson," said the earl. "Too late I learned that," said the king; "for he had come so near to our army that he never should have been able to report the felling of our men."

Now the battle began, the English horsemen advancing against the Northmen; but as long as the Northmen remained standing in a ring, shield to shield, and with the spears pointing out, the enemy could do nothing against them. But when the Northmen thought the enemy was retiring, they were imprudent enough to pursue the Englishmen, and thus break their own invincible ring. Then the Englishmen rode up from all sides, and made a terrible attack. Many people fell on both sides. King Harald Sigurdson was hit by an arrow in the throat and fell dead to the ground, and most of his men fell around him. Harald was fifty-one years old when he died (1066).

The town of Oslo (now a suburb of Christiania) was founded during the reign of King Harald Sigurdson. A church was built there and dedicated to the Virgin Mary. The shrine of the holy Halvard, lately discovered and acknowledged as a national saint, was placed in this church.

CHAPTER XX

Olaf Kyrre, the Quiet (1066-1093)

THE English king permitted King Harald Sigurdson's son Olaf to leave the country with the men he had left. Olaf proceeded to the Orkney Isles, where he remained during the winter (1066-67). The next summer he returned to Norway, where he was proclaimed king along with his brother, Magnus taking the northern and Olaf the eastern part of the country.

Shortly after the two brothers had assumed the government, the Danish king, Svein Estridson, gave notice that the peace between the Northmen and the Danes was at an end. The brothers hurriedly collected armies to defend the country, and Svein set out from the south with a Danish force. He met King Olaf on the coast of Halland, where an indecisive battle was fought. Soon afterward Magnus arrived with reinforcements from the north, but then negotiations were opened, and peace was concluded on the old conditions at Konungahella. The agreement here made was confirmed by Olaf taking King Svein's daughter Ingerid in marriage.

The following year King Magnus died at Nidaros, April 28, 1069, after being ill for some time. His son, Haakon, who was fostered by Thorer of Steig in Gudbrandsdal, being only an infant child, Olaf now became sole king of Norway.

After the short conflict with Denmark, Olaf had no wars. A long period of peace was something new in the history of the country, and the people therefore gave King Olaf the surname *Kyrre*, *i.e.*, the Quiet. He preserved law and order with firmness, and did a great deal to promote commerce and the prosperity of the towns. Before his time there were three towns in Viken (Tunsberg, Oslo, and Sarpsborg), and one in Throndhjem (Nidaros). King Olaf founded the merchant town of Bergen (then Björgvin), where many wealthy people settled down, and the place was soon regularly frequented by merchants from foreign countries. The other towns also made good progress.

In King Olaf's time there were held a greater number of general entertainments and hand-in-hand feasts than formerly. Already, during the heathen time, the Northmen used to arrange feasts by clubbing together. After the introduction of Christianity they were continued, but naturally changed their character. These feasts, which from the time of Olaf Kyrre were called guilds, had a partly religious character, and appear to have been regular meetings of fraternities, whose members were pledged to defend and help each other. The members were called guild-brethren and guild-sisters, and each guild was under the protection of a saint. The members were governed by strict laws, and in order to insure good and peaceful behavior, men of dignity, both clergymen and laymen, were present at the meetings. King Olaf built several guild-halls in different parts of the country, among them the great guild-hall in Nidaros. The guild-brethren built Margaret's church in Nidaros.

There are many stories of King Olaf's good works. Once when he sat in the great guild-hall in Nidaros, one of his men said to him: "It pleases us, king, to see you so happy." He answered: "Why should I not be happy when I see my subjects sitting happy and free in a guild consecrated to my uncle, the sainted King Olaf. In the days of my father these people were subjected to much terror and fear; the most of them concealed their gold and their precious things, but now I see glittering on his person what each one owns, and your freedom is my gladness."

At the Things, King Olaf did not speak much, preferring to let others speak for him. One who was often intrusted with this duty was his foster-brother Skule, who was a son of Earl Toste, and was usually called the king's foster-son. Skule, who had come over with him from England, was made commander of King Olaf's court-men and was given the king's cousin Gudrun in marriage. He was a dear friend of the king, who gave him fine estates near Konungahella, Oslo, and Nidaros. The principal one of these estates was Reine in Rissen, which became the seat of this afterward powerful family. Skule was the ancestor of King Inge Baardson and Duke Skule.

King Olaf made several changes in the rooms on the king's estates. The king had formerly had his high-seat on the middle of one of two long benches at the long walls of the house; but Olaf had the high-seat removed to a cross-bench at the short wall facing the entrance. Formerly the fire was in the middle of the floor between the long benches; but Olaf had the fireplace removed to one corner of the room, where he had a kind of a chimney-place built. He had the floors, which had formerly been without covering, covered with stone and strewed with juniper-tops. He introduced table-cups instead of the deer-horns out of which they formerly used to drink. Much unusual splendor and foreign fashions in the cut of clothes were also introduced. King Olaf doubled the number of attendants, so that he had one hundred and twenty courtmen-at-arms (*hird-men*), sixty "guests,"[9] and sixty house servants. He used the fashion, which was introduced from the courts of foreign kings, of letting his grand butler stand at the end of the table, and fill the cups for himself and the other distinguished guests who sat at the table. He had also torch-bearers, who held as many torches at the table as there were guests of distinction present.

King Olaf Kyrre was a devout Christian. A better order was introduced in the affairs of the church, and the country was divided into three bishoprics. Many churches were built, among the largest of which were the Christ Church in Bergen and the Christ Church in Nidaros.

King Olaf died on his estate, Haukby, in Ranrike, September 22, 1098. His body was brought north to Nidaros and buried in Christ Church. The saga says of King Olaf: "He was the most amiable king of his time, and Norway was much improved in riches and cultivation during his reign."

CHAPTER XXI

Magnus Barefoot (1093-1103)

IMMEDIATELY after the death of Olaf Kyrre, his son Magnus was proclaimed at Viken king of all Norway; but the Upland people chose his cousin Haakon, the foster-son of Thorer of Steig, as king. Haakon and Thorer went north to Throndhjem and summoned the Oere-Thing at Nidaros, and the people there proclaimed Haakon king of half of Norway, as his father had been. In order to win the goodwill of the Throndhjem people, Haakon relieved them of all harbor duties, did away with the Christmas gifts to the king, and gave them many other privileges. Thereafter he returned to the Uplands, where he gave the people the same privileges.

In the meanwhile King Magnus proceeded north to Nidaros, took possession of the king's house built by Harald Haardraade, and remained there the first part of the winter. When Haakon heard of this he also came up to Nidaros, and negotiations were opened for a settlement between the rival kings, Haakon offering to accept half the kingdom and let Magnus retain the other half. Magnus refused to acknowledge any rights of Haakon, and a conflict seemed imminent. However, one day, after having made quite a demonstration with his force, Magnus sailed southward, and Haakon also decided to go south, taking the inland route. While he was crossing the Dovre Mountain, he pursued a ptarmigan, which flew up beside him; and during this chase he was taken violently ill, and died on the mountain. His body was brought back to Nidaros, and all the people went to meet the body, as the saga says, "sorrowing, and the most of them weeping; for all the people loved him with sincere affection." Haakon, who was twenty-five years old at his death, was laid at rest in Christ Church (February, 1094).

Magnus Olafson was now sole king of Norway. A rebellion was started by some of the adherents of the late King Haakon, under the leadership of Thorer of Steig and the late Haakon's near friend, Svein, who aspired to become king. Svein was a Dane by birth, said to be of high family and a brave warrior. His father was one Harald Flette, of whom nothing is known. Several chiefs took part in this movement, among them the rich and powerful man, Skialg Erlingson from Jadaren, and Egil Aslakson of Aurland. The force proceeded from Gudbrandsdal down to Raumsdal, and afterward north to Throndhjem. King Magnus's liegeman and devoted friend, Sigurd Ulstreng, collected a force and met Thorer and Svein in battle, but suffered a bad defeat. He fled to King Magnus, who then collected an army, and proceeded north to Throndhjem. Magnus scattered the rebels, and captured Thorer of Steig and Egil Aslakson, and hanged them. Svein, Harald Flette's son, fled out to sea first, and then sailed to Denmark and remained there. King Magnus punished severely all who had been guilty of treason toward him, killing some and burning the houses of others.

King Magnus now had undisputed control of Norway, and devoted himself to the care of his country and his people. By his vigorous rule he maintained peace and order, and rooted out all vikings and lawless men. With his restless and ambitious disposition, however, he yearned for greater deeds and for fame in war. Wishing to retake the western countries, which had been dependencies of Norway under his ancestors, he set out with a great fleet, and first came to the Orkney Islands. There he took the two earls, Paul and Erlend, prisoners, and sent them to Norway, and placed his eight year old son Sigurd as chief of the islands, leaving some wise men with him as counsellors. Then King Magnus proceeded to the Southern Hebrides, where he harried the coasts and plundered wherever he came. Afterward he sailed to Wales and won a battle at Anglesey Sound, and took the Anglesey Isle. After this battle he returned north with his fleet, and came first to Scotland. He made a peace with the Scotch king, by which all the islands lying west of Scotland should belong to the king of Norway. King Magnus remained all the winter in the southern isles, and the next summer he returned with his fleet to Norway (1099).

During their long stay in the Western countries King Magnus and his men had adopted some of the habits and fashions of clothing of those countries. They wore short jackets and kilts without breeches. On account of this the king was called Magnus Barefoot or Bareleg.

A short time after his return to Norway, King Magnus became involved in war with the Swedish king, Inge Steinkelson. Magnus insisted that the Gaut River and Lake Venern should be considered the boundary between the countries, so that the Swedish district of Dalsland would belong to Norway. This war lasted for two years, and was generally unsuccessful for King Magnus. In the spring of 1100 there was a battle at Foxerne (at the Gaut River, between Kongself and Wenersborg), in which the Norwegians were overwhelmed by numbers, driven to flight, and many of them killed by the pursuing Swedes. King Magnus was easily known, for he was a stout man, had a red cloak over him, and bright yellow hair that fell over his shoulders. Ogmund Skoptason, who was also a tall and handsome man, rode at the side of the king. He saved the king by putting on the king's cloak. He started off in a little different direction, and the Swedes, supposing him to be the king, rode after him, while the king proceeded to his ships. Ogmund escaped with great difficulty, but succeeded at last in reaching the ships. King Magnus then sailed down the river and proceeded north to Viken.

The next summer a meeting of the kings was agreed upon at Konghelle on the Gaut River. The Danish king, Erik Eiegod, desired to have an archbishopric established for the northern countries, and it was important to have the other kings with him to execute this plan. By his mediation the meeting of the three kings was arranged, and they soon came to an understanding. Each should possess the dominions his forefathers had held before him, and each should make good to his own men the loss and manslaughter suffered by them. King Inge agreed to give King Magnus his daughter Margaret in marriage. This agreement was proclaimed to the people, and thus, within a short hour, the greatest enemies were made the best of friends.

Shortly afterward Margaret, King Inge's daughter, came to Norway with an honorable retinue, and her wedding with King Magnus was celebrated with great festivities. The Norwegians liked their new queen, whom they considered as a pledge of the peace with Sweden, and they therefore called her *Fridkolla*, *i.e.*, the peace-girl.

When Magnus had been nine years king of Norway, he again sailed westward with a great force. He first conquered the Isle of Man, and afterward proceeded to Ireland and conquered a great part of that country. He lay at Ulster, and was about ready to return to Norway, when he was suddenly attacked by an Irish army. King Magnus had a helmet on his head, a red shield on which there was a golden lion, and was girt with his costly sword, Legbit; in his hand he had a short spear, and over his shirt a red silk cloak. King Magnus received a wound, being pierced by a spear through both thighs above the knees. The king took hold of the shaft between his legs, broke the spear in two, and said: "This way we break spearshafts, boys; let us go briskly on; nothing ails me." A little later King Magnus was hit in the neck with an Irish axe, and this was his death-wound. Then those who were behind fled. Vidkun Jonson, from Biarkey (a great-grandson of Thorer Hund), instantly killed the man who had given the king his death-wound, and fled, after having received three wounds; but he brought the king's banner and the sword Legbit to the ships. Vidkun Jonson was the last man who fled. The Northmen who escaped sailed away immediately.

King Magnus was thirty years old when he fell.

CHAPTER XXII

Sigurd the Crusader (1103-1130), and his Brothers, Eystein and Olaf

IN the autumn the remnants of King Magnus's army and fleet left the island of Man, and with his thirteen year old son, Sigurd, returned to Norway. On their arrival in Norway, Sigurd and his two brothers, Eystein and Olaf, were proclaimed kings. Eystein, who was fourteen years old, was to have the northern, and Sigurd the southern, part of the country. Olaf was then four or five years old, and his third part of the country remained under the control of his two brothers.

When the three sons of Magnus Barefoot had been chosen kings of Norway, several of those who had been away taking part in the crusades returned home. They had made themselves renowned, and had many things to relate. Some had been to Jerusalem and some to Constantinople, and it was said that those who would enter the military service at Constantinople had the best of opportunities to earn great money. By these extraordinary tidings many of the Northmen were seized by a desire to make similar expeditions, and they asked of the two kings that one of them should place himself at the head of such an expedition. The kings agreed to this, and had the preparations made at their common expense. Many of the great men in the country took part in this enterprise, and when all was ready it was decided that Sigurd was to go with the crusade, while Eystein was to stay at home and govern the country for their joint account.

Four years after the fall of King Magnus (1107), King Sigurd sailed from Norway with sixty ships. He first visited the king of England, Henry I., and remained with him during the winter. In the spring he sailed with his fleet to Valland (the west of France), and in the fall came to Galicia, Spain, where he stayed the second winter. Along the coast he had several battles with the heathens. At the Straits of Gibraltar he defeated a large viking force, and on the island of Forminterra, east of Spain, he exterminated a band of Moorish brigands and took a great booty. After similar victories on the islands of Ivica and Minorca, he came to Sicily, where he was very well received by Duke Roger. It is stated in the saga that King Sigurd, during his stay in Sicily, conferred upon Duke Roger the title of king, though with what right he did so does not appear, nor is it mentioned by contemporary historians.

In the summer King Sigurd sailed to Palestine, and at Acre met Baldwin, king of Palestine, who received him particularly well, accompanied him to Jerusalem and showed him the holy sepulchre and other sacred places. They also rode to the river Jordan and bathed in it, and then returned to Jerusalem. King Baldwin and the patriarch of Jerusalem presented Sigurd with a splinter of the holy cross, with the condition that he, and twelve other men with him, should swear to promote Christianity with all their power, and erect an archbishop's seat in Norway if possible, and the splinter was to be kept where the holy king Olaf reposed. Thereupon King Sigurd with his fleet assisted King Baldwin in capturing the town of Sidon, Syria, and received his share of a great booty. He then proceeded to Constantinople, and was received in the grandest style by Emperor Alexius. After having stayed here for some time and enjoyed the great festivities given in his honor, King Sigurd made preparations for his return home. He gave the emperor all his ships, and the valuable dragon head which had adorned his own ship was set up in the Sophia church. The emperor gave him horses and guides to conduct him through his dominions. Leaving quite a number of his men, who went into the service of the emperor, King Sigurd started homeward on horseback through Bulgaria, Hungary and Germany. When in the midsummer of 1111 he came to Schleswig in Denmark, Earl Eilif gave him a magnificent reception. Here he also met the Danish king Nils, who had married his stepmother, Margaret Fridkolla. King Nils accompanied him north to Jutland, and gave him a ship provided with everything needful. He then returned to Norway, where he was joyfully received by his people. He had been absent three years and a half, and all agreed that no one had ever made a more honorable expedition from Norway. From this day he was given the surname *Jorsalfar*, *i.e.*, the Crusader.

While King Sigurd was attaining fame on his journeys far away from his country, King Eystein was occupied with peaceful achievements at home. A great deal was done for the real benefit of the country, and under his wise government Norway made progress in the same way that it had done in the time of his grandfather Olaf Kyrre. He improved the laws, built churches and monasteries, made harbors, and established beacon lights. On the mountain of Dovre he built cabins, where travellers could find shelter. In Bergen he built the monastery at Nordnes, Michael's Church, the Church of the Apostles, and the great king's hall. In Nidaros he built the Church of St. Nikolas. He also built a Church at Throndenes in Halogaland. King Eystein also extended the limits of the country, not by warfare and bloodshed, but by peaceful negotiations. Thus he gained the allegiance of the inhabitants of the Swedish province Jemteland, which was formerly a Norwegian province, but was taken by Sweden after the fall of Olaf Trygvason.

King Olaf was taken sick and died before he reached manhood, and it seems to have been only in name that he had any share in the government.

The relation between Eystein and Sigurd was not always the most cordial, and Sigurd was usually to blame for it. The winter of 1112-13 King Eystein spent most of the time at Sarpsborg. There lived at that time at Mikle-Dal in Aamord a rich and influential man called Olaf of Dal. He spent a good part of the winter at Sarpsborg with his daughter Borghild, a very handsome and accomplished girl. Borghild and King Eystein often met, and the king found great pleasure in conversing with her. The people began to talk about this friendship, and King Sigurd, who was then at Konghelle, also heard of the girl that his brother had taken a liking to. When Borghild heard it whispered that people talked ill of her intimacy with King Eystein, she took it much to heart. When Eystein had gone north she went to Sarpsborg, and, after suitable fasts, carried red-hot irons to prove her innocence, endured the test, and thus cleared herself from all offence. Sigurd then rode over to her home, where he remained all night, made Borghild his concubine and took her away with him. They had a son, who was called Magnus, and was immediately sent to Halogaland to be fostered by Vidkun Jonson of Biarkey.

The relation between the brothers remained strained as long as they both were kings, but it never came to a breach of peace. Occasionally they even peacefully met as each other's guests. On one of these occasions, when the two kings were feasting together at one of Eystein's estates, they had what was called a "man-measuring," or comparison of merits. The saga says that in the evening, when the people began to drink, the ale was not good, so that the guests were very quiet and still. Then said King Eystein: "Why are the people so silent? It is more proper in parties that people are merry, so let us find some jest over our ale that will amuse us; for surely, brother Sigurd, all will like to see us happy."

Sigurd replied, rather bluntly: "Do you talk as much as you please, but give me leave to be silent."

Eystein said: "It is a common custom over the ale-table for one person to compare himself with another, and now let us do so." Sigurd did not answer.

"I see," said Eystein, "that I will have to begin this amusement, and I will take thee, brother, to compare myself with; we are both kings, have equal property, and there is no difference in our birth."

Sigurd then said: "Dost thou remember that I could always throw thee when we wrestled, although thou art a year older?"

Eystein: "But I remember also that I was better at the games which require limberness."

Sigurd: "But how was it when we were swimming? I could duck thee whenever I wanted to."

Eystein: "But I could swim as far as thou, and could dive as well; and I could run on ice-legs[10] so well that nobody could beat me, while thou couldst no more do it than a cow."

Sigurd: "I consider it a more useful and suitable accomplishment for a chief to be an expert at his bow; but I think thou couldst hardly draw my bow, even with the help of the foot."

Eystein: "I am not as strong at the bow as thou art, but my aim is as good; and I can run on skis[11] much better than thou, and that is usually held a great accomplishment."

Sigurd: "It is much better for a chief who is to be the superior of other men that he is conspicuous in a crowd, and strong and powerful in weapons above other men."

Eystein: "It is just as well to be handsome, so as to be easily known from others on that account; and this behooves a chief, as a fair face and fine clothes go well together. I am also better versed in law than thou, and can speak better."

Sigurd: "It may be that thou hast learned more law-quirks than I, for I have had something else to do; neither will any one deny thee a smooth tongue. But many say that thy words are not to be trusted; that thy promises are not kept, and that thou talkest according to what those who are about thee say, which is not kingly."

Eystein: "Often I promise what people ask of me, as I like to have all be joyful about me, and it happens that conflicting interests afterward appear, which must be considered. But thou mostly promisest people what is evil, and no one is pleased because thy promises are kept."

Sigurd: "All say that the expedition I made out of the country was a princely expedition, while thou wert sitting at home like thy father's daughter."

Eystein: "Now thou hast touched the tender spot, and I would not have brought up this conversation if I had not known what to reply on this point. I think I equipped thee from home for this expedition like a sister."

Sigurd: "Thou must have heard that I was in many battles in the Saracen's land, and gained victory in all. I brought to this country many valuables, the like of which had never been seen here before. I became acquainted with great men, and was respected by them. I went to the Saviour's grave, and saw thee not there. I went to the river Jordan, in which the Lord was baptized, and I swam across, but I saw thee not there. On the edge of the river there is a bush of willows, and there I twisted a knot of willows, and said that this knot thou shouldst untie, brother, or take the curse thereto attached."

Then King Eystein said: "I have heard that thou hast had some battles abroad, but it was more useful for the country what I was doing here at home. North in Vaagen (Lofoten) I put up booths, so that the poor fishermen could find shelter; I also had a church built there, appointed a priest, and gave land for the support of the church; before that, they were nearly all heathens there. These people will remember that Eystein was king in Norway. Across the Dovre Mountain lay the road from Throndhjem. Formerly many froze to death, and all suffered hardships on the journey; but I built a mountain inn and endowed it with property. Those who hereafter travel there will remember that Eystein was king in Norway. Off Agdanes there were breakers and shoals and no harbor, so that many ships were wrecked; now there is a good harbor and good anchorage for the ships, and a church has also been built there. I had war-signals erected on the highest mountains, which is of benefit to all who live in the interior. I built the royal hall in Bergen and the Apostles' Church and a covered passage between them. The kings who succeed us will remember my name. I built St. Michael's Church at Nordnes (in Bergen) and the monastery Munkeliv at the same place. I improved the laws, brother, so that everybody could deal justly with his neighbor, and if the laws are upheld the government will be better. More by gentle words and wise dealings than by violence and breach of peace did I succeed in making the inhabitants of Jemteland subjects of this kingdom. All these things may be considered small matters, but they will benefit the people of the country more than the fact that thou hast butchered bluemen in Serkland for the devil and hurled them into hell. And if thou didst tie a knot for me, I will not untie it; but I think that if I had been inclined to tie a knot for thee, I could have tied such a knot that thou wouldst not have been king of Norway on thy return to this country with but a single ship."

This was the end of the "man-measuring." There was silence in the hall, and both kings were very angry. Several other incidents are recorded, which show the jealousy that existed between the kings. However, peace was preserved between them as long as they lived.

Six years after his brother Olaf's death, King Eystein was taken suddenly sick and died at the age of thirty-three, August 29, 1122. He was buried in Christ Church in Nidaros, and it is said that so many mourners had never stood over any man's grave in Norway since the death of King Magnus the Good.

Sigurd was now sole king of Norway and free from the restraint which the pacific disposition of the popular Eystein had placed upon him. Shortly after the death of Eystein, King Sigurd entered into an agreement with the Danish king Nils Sveinson, who had married his stepmother, Margaret Fridkolla. They agreed upon a joint invasion of Sweden. The real motive was probably to secure this kingdom, which was at the time torn by internal strifes, for Margaret's son Magnus Nilson; but the avowed purpose was to christianize the inhabitants of the Swedish province of Smaaland, where paganism still lingered. The two kings were to meet with their armies at Oeresund. King Sigurd collected a fleet of about three hundred and sixty ships and proceeded to the meeting-place; but through some mistake the Danish army had already returned home. King Sigurd held a council with his men, at which they spoke of King Nils' breach of faith and determined to take revenge by plundering his country. They first plundered the town of Tumartorp, and then sailed east to the merchant town Kalmar, which they attacked. They plundered in the province of Smaaland, compelled the people to accept Christianity, and imposed on the country a tribute of 1,800 cattle. After this King Sigurd returned to Norway with a great booty. This expedition was called the Kalmar levy, and was the only levy Sigurd carried out while he was sole king.

During the later years of his reign, King Sigurd was often violent and showed unmistakable signs of insanity. One Whit-Sunday he sat in his high-seat with Queen Malmfrid at his side, and in his hand he held the holy book, written in gilded letters, which he had brought with him from Constantinople. On the benches were seated many friends and guests. Then the king suddenly got one of his attacks. He rolled his eyes and looked all around him, and then said: "Many are the changes which may take place during a man's lifetime. Two things were dearer to me than anything else, namely, this book and the queen; and now it is quite different. The queen does not know herself how hideous she is; for a goat's horn is standing out of her head. And this book is good for nothing." Thereupon he threw the book on the fire which was burning on the floor, and gave the queen a blow with his fist between the eyes.

Before the king stood the young taper-bearer, Ottar Birting, who was on duty that day. He was of small stature, but of agreeable appearance, lively and bold. His surname Birting had been given him on account of his black hair and dark complexion. He sprang forward and snatched the book from the fire, held it out, and said: "Yes, sire, different were the days when you came with great state and splendor to Norway, and all your friends hastened to welcome you. Now days of sorrow have come over us; for to this holy festival many of your friends have come, and cannot be cheerful on account of your sad condition. Now, good king, follow my advice! Make peace first with the queen, whom you have so highly affronted, and then gladden by gentleness all your chiefs, friends, and servants." "What?" cried King Sigurd. "Dost thou dare to give me advice, thou black churl, thou great lump of a houseman's lad!" And he sprang up, drew his sword, and swung it, as if going to cut him down. But Ottar stood quiet and upright, and looked the king straight in his face. The king turned round the sword-blade, and gently touched Ottar on the shoulder with it. Then he sat down in silence on his high-seat. All were silent, for nobody dared to utter a word. In a little while the king had quieted down. He then rebuked his liegemen for not having stopped his insane acts, and thanked Ottar for what he had done. He concluded his speech by making Ottar a liegeman, and said: "Go thou now and sit among the lendermen, and be a servant no longer."

Ottar Birting became in later years one of the most celebrated men in Norway.

A few years before his death King Sigurd, in spite of the strong protest of Bishop Magne, discarded Queen Malmfrid, and married a beautiful and high-born woman, named Cecilia. The last winter of his life King Sigurd spent in Oslo. In the spring he was taken violently sick. His friends saw in this the punishment of Heaven for his improper marriage, and urged him to dissolve it; but he loved Cecilia too dearly to acquiesce in this. At last, she herself suggested a separation. "I did not know that thou, too, wouldst leave me like the others," said the king sadly. He grew gradually worse after this, and on March 26, 1130, he died, forty years old. His body was deposited in a vault in St. Halvard's Church. According to the saga, "the time of his reign was good for the country, for there was peace, and crops were good."

CHAPTER XXIII

Magnus the Blind and Harald Gille (1130-1136)

THE year before King Sigurd's death a young man named Harald Gille (or Gillekrist, *i.e.*, dedicated to Christ) came to Norway from Ireland with his mother, and declared that he was a son of King Magnus Barefoot. It is known that Magnus Barefoot had had a mistress in Ireland, and composed a verse once, in which he said he loved his Irish girl above all others. When the young man and his mother came to King Sigurd and told their story, the king told Harald that he would not deny him the opportunity to prove his birth by submitting to the ordeal by fire, but on condition that, if he should prove his descent, he should not claim the kingdom in the lifetime of King Sigurd, or of his son Magnus, and to this Harald Gille bound himself by oath. Harald agreed to the ordeal fixed by Sigurd, and walked over nine glowing plowshares with bare feet, attended by two bishops. Three days after the iron trial his feet were examined, and were found unburned. This ordeal was considered a divine judgment, and King Sigurd acknowledged Harald as his brother.

It became a source of danger to the country that Harald was acknowledged as a son of Magnus Barefoot; for at that time the law of royal inheritance was that every son of a king, the illegitimate as well as the legitimate, had a right to the kingdom. This encouraged many to proclaim themselves rightful heirs to the throne and to prove their rights by the ordeal of fire. The priests had the charge of such ordeals, and they probably had the result in their power.

Sigurd's son, Magnus, conceived a great hatred of Harald, and in this he had the sympathy of many of the leading men.

Immediately after the death of Sigurd, his son Magnus summoned a Thing at Oslo, and was there proclaimed king of all Norway, according to an oath which the people had formerly sworn to King Sigurd. Harald Gille was in Tunsberg when he heard of Sigurd's death. He broke his promise to the late king, summoned a Thing, and had his followers proclaim him king of half the country. Negotiations were opened with King Magnus, and, as the latter found he had fewer people, he was obliged to divide the kingdom with Harald.

For about three years the two kings kept the peace, although there was little friendship between them. They both passed the fourth winter at Nidaros, and invited each other as guests, but their people were always ready for a fight. In the spring King Magnus sailed southward with his fleet, and collected men from all districts, telling the people that he wanted to take the kingly dignity from Harald and give him such a part of the country as might be suitable. Harald proceeded from Throndhjem overland to the Uplands and Viken, and, when he heard what Magnus was doing, he also collected an army. At Fyrileif in Viken a battle was fought, and Magnus, who had a much superior force, won a decisive battle. Harald's army was put to flight, and he himself barely escaped to his ships. He sailed south to Denmark, and was well received by the Danish king, Erik Emune, who gave him the province of Halland in fief.

After the battle of Fyrileif (August 10, 1134), King Magnus proclaimed himself sole king of Norway. He showed great lenience toward Harald's men, and had the wounded taken care of equally with his own men. His leading men advised him to keep his army together in Viken, and remain there, in case Harald should return from the south; but he thought this was not necessary, allowed the men to return to their homes, and proceeded with his court-men to Bergen. It was not long before King Magnus had cause to regret that he had disregarded the advice of his friends. Harald had soon gathered a sufficient force to invade Norway, and, while he proceeded along the coast, a good many people joined him. He came to Bergen, where he met only nominal resistance, and King Magnus was taken prisoner. King Harald held a meeting with his counsellors, and here it was decided that Magnus should be deprived of his dominions and should no longer be called king. He was then delivered to the king's thralls, who put out both his eyes, cut off one foot, and otherwise mutilated him. Magnus, who after this was given the surname "the Blind," was brought north to Nidaros and entered the Nidarholm cloister.

When Harald Gille had been six years king of Norway, Sigurd Slembe came to the country, and claimed that he too was a son of Magnus Barefoot. Sigurd was in his childhood kept at his book, became a clergyman, and was consecrated a deacon. He showed early traces of a haughty, ungovernable spirit, and was therefore called Slembidjakn (*i.e.*, the bad deacon). When he heard that he was the son of Magnus Barefoot, he laid aside all clerical matters and set out on trading expeditions. In Denmark he claimed to have established his parentage by the iron ordeal in the presence of five bishops, and when he arrived in Bergen he requested Harald Gille to acknowledge him as his brother. King Harald, however, accused him of being an accomplice in a murder case, and attempted to capture him. Sigurd escaped and afterward arranged a conspiracy, in which many of Harald's court-men took part. On St. Lucia's night, December 13, 1136, they came to the house where Harald was sleeping with his mistress, Thora, Guthorm's daughter, killed the guardsmen outside, broke into the house, and killed the king in bed. Sigurd and his men then took a boat and rowed out in front of the king's house. It was then just beginning to be daylight. Standing in his boat Sigurd spoke to the men on the king's pier, avowed the killing of Harald, and requested them to choose him as chief according to his birth. But all replied with one voice, that they would never give obedience to a man who had murdered his own brother. "And if thou art not his brother, thou hast no claim by descent to be king." Thereupon they outlawed Sigurd and all his men. Sigurd and his men saw it was best for them to get away, and fled northward to North Hordaland.

King Harald Gille was thirty-two years old when he was slain. He was buried in the old Christ Church in Bergen. It was a few months before his death that pirates from Vendland, under their king, Rettibur, pillaged and burned the town of Konungahella (Konghelle). The town was afterward rebuilt, but never rose to the importance it had had before.

CHAPTER XXIV

Sigurd Mund, Eystein, and Inge Krokryg, the Sons of Harald Gille (1136-1161)

QUEEN INGERID, the widow of Harald Gille, immediately after her husband's death held a consultation with the liegemen and court-men, and they decided to send a fast sailing vessel to Throndhjem to request the people there to take Harald's son (with Thora, Guthorm's daughter), Sigurd, for king. Sigurd, who was then in his fourth year, was being fostered by Gyrd Baardson. The people of Throndhjem assembled at a Thing and proclaimed Sigurd king. Queen Ingerid herself proceeded to Viken, where her son with Harald, the one year old Inge, was fostered by Aamunde Gyrdson. A Borgar-Thing (Thing at Borg or Sarpsborg) was called, at which Inge was chosen king. "Thus," it is related in the saga, "almost the whole nation submitted to the brothers, and principally because their father was considered holy; and the country took the oath to them, that the kingly power should not go to any other man as long as any of King Harald's sons were alive." It was agreed that the chief liegemen should rule in the name of the brothers while they were in their infancy.

Sigurd Slembe proceeded north to Nidaros, and took Magnus the Blind out of the cloister in the hope that, by making common cause with him, he could secure a better following. In this he succeeded to some extent, many of King Magnus's old friends joining him. With quite a force they went south to the mouth of Raumsdal Fjord. Here Sigurd and Magnus divided their forces, Sigurd sailing westward to the Orkneys to seek aid. Magnus proceeded with his force through Raumsdal over to the Uplands, where he remained during the winter and collected an army. When it was rumored in Viken that Magnus the Blind had come to the Uplands, Thiostolf Aaleson and the other chiefs who were with King Inge gathered a great army and proceeded up to Lake Miosen, and met the forces of Magnus at Minne (1137). A great battle was fought, and Magnus was defeated. It is related that Thiostolf Aaleson carried the child-king, Inge, in his tucked-up cloak during the battle; but Thiostolf was hard pressed by fighting, and it was said that King Inge suffered an injury there, which he retained as long as he lived. His back was knotted into a hump, and one leg was shorter than the other. Hence he was afterward called Inge Krokryg, *i.e.*, Inge the Hunchback. Magnus fled eastward to Gautland, where he received aid from the Swedes, but being again defeated at Krokaskog he fled to Denmark.

Magnus the Blind was well received by the Danish king, Erik Emune, who collected a force and sailed north to Norway with two hundred and forty ships. Attacks were made at different places, and the town of Oslo was burned, including St. Halvard's Church; but King Erik soon returned to Denmark after having suffered great losses, and the expedition was pronounced a total failure.

Sigurd Slembe about this time returned from the West, and made cruises against the pirates in Vendland, and occasionally harried the coasts of Norway. In the fall of 1139 Sigurd Slembe and Magnus the Blind came up to Norway from Denmark with thirty ships manned by Danes and Northmen. They met the fleet of kings Sigurd and Inge at Holmengraa (the gray holm), where a battle was fought. After the first assault, the Danes fled home to Denmark with eighteen ships, and thus Sigurd had to fight against a greatly superior force. One after another of his ships was cleared. The blind and crippled Magnus lay in his bed and could do nothing to defend himself. When his ship was almost entirely bare of men, his old and faithful court-man, Reidar Griotgardson, took King Magnus in his arms and tried to leap over to another ship with him. But just then he was struck between his shoulders by a spear, which went through him and also killed King Magnus. Reidar fell backward on the deck and Magnus upon him. Everybody afterward spoke of how honorably he had followed his master and rightful sovereign. "Happy are they who are given such praise after death," adds the writer of the saga. Sigurd Slembe leaped overboard and would probably have escaped, if he had not been betrayed by one of his own men. He was captured and put to death with the most horrible tortures. The men who took upon themselves to kill him, and who had personal grievances to avenge, broke his shin-bones and arms with an axe-hammer. Then they stripped him and flogged him, broke his back, and finally hanged him. He bore the tortures with great fortitude. He never moved and never altered his voice, but spoke in a natural tone until he gave up the ghost, occasionally singing hymns. Sigurd's friends afterward came from Denmark for his body, took it with them and interred it in Mary Church in Aalborg.

When Sigurd was dead, it was acknowledged by all, both enemies and friends, that he was the most remarkable and most gifted man that had lived in Norway within memory of anybody living; "but in some respects he was an unlucky man," says the saga. Magnus the Blind was twenty-five years old when he fell. Thiostolf Aaleson transported his body to Oslo and buried it in St. Halvard's Church, beside King Sigurd, his father.

Norway now had peace for some years. About six years after Sigurd and Inge had been proclaimed kings, a third son of Harald Gille, named Eystein, came from Scotland accompanied by his mother, Biadok, and by three men of high standing. They immediately proceeded to Throndhjem, and at the Oere-Thing Eystein was chosen king and given a third of the country with his brothers, Sigurd and Inge. King Harald himself had spoken to his men about this son, so that Eystein did not have to resort to the ordeal of iron in order to prove his right. A fourth son of Harald Gille, Magnus, who was being fostered by the great chief Kyrpinga-Orm at Studla, was also given the title of king, so that for a short time there were nominally four kings; but Magnus was deformed, lived but a short time, and died in his bed.

Shortly after the death of Harald Gille, his widow, Queen Ingerid, had married the liegeman, Ottar Birting of Throndhjem, who thus became King Inge's stepfather and guardian, and who strengthened King Inge's government much during his childhood. King Sigurd was not very friendly to Ottar Birting, because, as he thought, Ottar always took King Inge's part. One evening Ottar was assassinated in Nidaros as he was going to the evening service. His relatives and friends accused King Sigurd of having instigated this deed and were much enraged against him. A peasant army under the leadership of King Eystein came to Nidaros and a conflict seemed inevitable. But King Sigurd then offered to clear himself by the ordeal of iron, and peace was made. King Sigurd hastened to the southern part of the country, and the ordeal was never heard of again. Many other things contributed to make Sigurd unpopular. As he grew up he became a very ungovernable and restless man. He was a stout and strong man, of a brisk appearance. He had light brown hair and quite a handsome face except that he had an ugly mouth. For that reason he was called Sigurd Mund (Mouth). His great immorality gave general offense to the people. He was not married, but had several illegitimate children.

In 1153 King Eystein made a cruise to the Orkneys. Some time after his return there was a quarrel between him and King Sigurd, because the latter had killed two of Eystein's court-men. A conference to settle this affair was arranged in the winter (1154-55) in the Uplands. They not only settled their difficulty, but privately arranged for a meeting of the three kings in Bergen next summer. It was said that their plan was to depose King Inge and give him two or three estates and a certain income, as he had not health to be a king. Their plan might possibly have succeeded if it had not been for King Inge's faithful man, Gregorius Dagson, who was then Inge's guardian and adviser. He made preparations for the meeting, and when Sigurd arrived in Bergen, King Inge had a superior force. After some hostile acts, King Sigurd was attacked in his lodgings by Gregorius Dagson and slain, June 10, 1155. Two or three days after King Eystein arrived from the east with thirty ships. He had along with him his brother's seven year old son Haakon, a son of King Sigurd. When he heard what had happened in Bergen, Eystein did not come up to the town, but anchored at Florevaag, while a reconciliation between the brothers was attempted. The result was that King Eystein returned to Viken and King Inge to Throndhjem, and they were in a way reconciled; but they did not meet each other.

About a year later, after several quarrels and provoking incidents, the two brothers met with hostile fleets at Fors, Ranrike, and made ready for battle. So many of King Eystein's ships left him, however, and joined King Inge that Eystein had no choice but flight. He was captured by his brother-in-law, Simon Skalp, who murdered him after having allowed him to hear mass (August 21, 1157). King Eystein was buried in Fors Church.

Inge was now sole king, but it was only a short time that he was in undisputed possession of the country. The adherents of the late kings, Eystein and Sigurd, chose the latter's son as their chief and gave him the title of king. He was then ten years old. He was afterward given the surname Herdebred, *i.e.*, the broad-shouldered. Haakon and his adherents were outlawed by King Inge, who took possession of all their estates, after they had sought refuge in Sweden. Gregorius Dagson was then in Konungahella, where the danger was greatest, and had with him a strong and fine body of men, with which he defended the country. He defeated Haakon's force in a decisive battle at Konungahella (1159). Later Haakon, who had strengthened his forces with a number of robbers and adventurers, harried the frontier districts in Viken. One day he came to the estate of Haldor Brynjolfson, a brother-in-law of Gregorius Dagson, set fire to the house and burned it. Haldor came out, but was instantly cut down together with his house-men; in all about twenty men were killed. Haldor's wife, Sigrid, Gregorius Dagson's sister, escaped to the forest in her night-dress; but the five year old Aamunde Gyrdson, a nephew of Gregorius, was carried away by Haakon's men.

When Gregorius Dagson heard of this he took it much to heart, and set out to avenge the outrage. On January 7, 1161, Gregorius caught sight of Haakon's force. There was a river, called Befia, between them, and in trying to cross it on the unsafe ice Gregorius fell through, and, while struggling to get ashore, was killed by an arrow shot by one of Haakon's men. When King Inge, who was then in Oslo, heard of Gregorius Dagson's death, he cried like a child, and, after having recovered himself, swore to attack Haakon, and either avenge his friend's death or die in the attempt. On the 3d of February, 1161, King Inge's spies brought him word that Haakon was coming toward the town (Oslo). The king ordered his men called together, and when they were drawn up in line they numbered nearly 4,800. When the night was well advanced, the spies came and informed the king that Haakon and his army were coming over the ice, which lay all the way from the town to the Hoved Isle. King Inge then led his army out on the ice, and drew it up in order of battle. The king and his brother Orm took their places under the banner in the centre. On the right wing, toward the nunnery, was Gudrod, the exiled king of the South Hebrides, and Jon Sveinson, a grandson of Bergthor Buk. On the left wing, toward Thrælaberg, stood the chiefs Simon Skalp and Gudbrand Skafhoggson, who was married to King Eystein Magnusson's daughter Maria. When Haakon and his army came near to King Inge's array, both sides raised a war shout. But then it appeared that there were traitors in Inge's army. Gudrod and Jon gave the enemy a signal, and when Haakon's men in consequence turned that way, Gudrod immediately fled with 1,800 men; and Jon, and a great body of men with him, ran over to Haakon's army and assisted them in the fight. When this news was told to King Inge, he said: "Such is the difference between my friends. Never would Gregorius have done so in his life." Some of Inge's men now advised him to mount a horse and ride up to Raumarike, where he could get help. But he refused to do so. "I have heard you often say, and I think truly, that it was of little use to my brother Eystein that he took to flight; and yet he was in many ways an abler man than I. I was in the second year of my age when I was chosen king of Norway, and I am now twenty-six. I have had misfortune and sorrow under my kingly dignity, rather than pleasure and peaceful days. I have had many battles; and it is my greatest luck that I have never fled, even when fighting against a superior force. God will dispose of my life, but I shall never betake myself to flight." As a result of the traitors' work Haakon gained a complete victory. When daylight came, King Inge was among the fallen. His brother Orm tried to continue the battle, but at last had to take flight. On the following day Orm was to have married Ragna, a daughter of Nikolas Mase and widow of King Eystein; but after the battle Orm fled to Svithiod, Sweden, where his brother Magnus was then king. Haakon and his men took possession of the town, and feasted on what had been prepared for the wedding. Those of Inge's friends who survived the battle fled in all directions. Only Kristina, Sigurd the Crusader's daughter, remained in town, for she had a promise to the late king to fulfil. She found King Inge's body, and had it laid in the stone wall of Halvard's Church, on the south side below the choir.

CHAPTER XXV
The Church

FROM the time of Olaf Kyrre (the Quiet) there were three bishops in Norway; one in Nidaros, one in Bergen, and one in Oslo. During the reign of Kings Eystein and Sigurd the Crusader a bishopric was also established in Stavanger. The bishops were chosen by the king, and the bishops appointed the priests.

For the last half century the Norwegian Church, as well as the Swedish, had been under the Danish archbishop at Lund. This arrangement appeared very unsatisfactory, as the Norwegian Church covered extended territory which called for special supervision. Since the time of Sigurd the Crusader there had been a constant desire to obtain an independent Norwegian archbishopric. Finally, during the reign of Harald Gille's sons, the pope sent Cardinal Nicholas Breakspear of Alba from Rome to Norway (1152). Cardinal Nicholas, who was an Englishman by birth and a very able and conscientious man, arrived in Nidaros, and seems to have immediately understood the situation. The saga says that he had taken offence at the brothers Sigurd and Eystein. The reason is not stated, but it was perhaps on account of their immoral life. "They were obliged to come to a reconciliation with him; on the other hand, he stood on the most affectionate terms with King Inge, whom he called his son." When an understanding had been arranged with the kings, the cardinal had John Birgerson consecrated archbishop of Throndhjem and gave him the consecrated vestment called pallium. He further settled that the archbishop's seat should be in Nidaros, in Christ Church, where King Olaf the Saint reposed. At the same time a new bishopric was established at Hamar, on Lake Miosen. Under the jurisdiction of the archbishopric at Nidaros were included the four other bishoprics of Norway, Oslo, Hamar, Stavanger, and Bergen, and those of the dependencies, Iceland, the Orkneys, the Faroes, Greenland, and the Hebrides with the Isle of Man.

The establishment of the archbishopric at Nidaros was probably the most important result of the mission of Cardinal Nicholas, but he also left other traces of his work. He changed the manner of choosing bishops, so that instead of being appointed by the king they were now to be elected by the canonical communities established at the cathedrals. The bishops after this exercised much greater authority than they had done before.

The saga says of Cardinal Nicholas that "he improved many of the customs of the Northmen while he was in the country. There never came a foreigner to Norway whom all men respected so highly, or who could govern the people so well as he did. After some time he returned to the South with many friendly presents, and declared ever afterward that he was the greatest friend of the people of Norway."

Cardinal Nicholas was, shortly after his return to Rome, elected pope and consecrated under the name of Adrian IV.

There were also several cloisters for monks in Norway at this time. They were generally quite wealthy, as many people would give all they had to the cloisters. There were at Throndhjem two cloisters, the Nidarholm and Elgeseter; in Bergen, Munkeliv, and a little further south Lyse Cloister, and near Oslo the Hoved Isle. At Gimsoe near Skien there was a convent for nuns.

CHAPTER XXVI

Haakon Herdebred (1161-1162)—Erling Skakke

AFTER the fall of King Inge in the battle at Oslo, Haakon Herdebred (the Broad-shouldered) took possession of the whole country. He distributed all the offices, in the towns and in the country, among his own friends. As he was only about fourteen years old, he could not, of course, be expected to attend personally to the affairs of the government; but his liegemen governed in his name.

Many of the adherents of the late King Inge refused to acknowledge King Haakon. Among them was the powerful and wily chieftain Erling Skakke. He was of a distinguished family, which resided on the Studla estate in Söndhordland. In his youth he had made a crusade to the Holy Land. On his way back through the Mediterranean he had a fight with pirates and was wounded in the neck, which compelled him afterward to carry his head on one side; hence his surname (*skakke*, wry). By the assistance of King Inge he obtained in marriage Kristina, a daughter of King Sigurd the Crusader and Queen Malmfrid. A year after their marriage she bore him a son, who was named Magnus.

Erling Skakke called together in Bergen all the chiefs who had been attached to King Inge, and all his court-men, and the house-men of the late Gregorius Dagson. When they met they discussed the situation, and resolved to keep up their party and to elect a king in opposition to Haakon. Erling proposed to make the boy Nicholas, a son of Simon Skalp and Harald Gille's daughter Maria, king; but the others objected to this, and, after some discussion, Erling was persuaded to do what had probably been his intention from the beginning, namely, to let his own son, Magnus, be proclaimed king, although this was against the law of the country, the boy not being of royal birth on his father's side. A Thing was held in the town, and here Magnus Erlingson, then five years old, was proclaimed king of the whole country.

Erling did not consider himself strong enough to immediately take up the fight with King Haakon. He therefore proceeded to Denmark, accompanied by his son and a large party. The Danish king, Valdemar the Great, received them hospitably and promised to furnish the necessary help to win and retain Norway, on condition that King Valdemar was to get that part of Norway which his ancestors, Harald Gormson and Svein Tjuguskeg, had possessed. With the help obtained in Denmark, Erling crossed over from Jutland to Agder, and thence sailed northward to Bergen, where he punished those who had given allegiance to Haakon. Then he returned along the coast, and attacked and defeated Haakon at Tunsberg. Haakon proceeded to Throndhjem, where he had most of his friends, and Erling returned to Bergen, after having reduced the whole of Viken in obedience to King Magnus.

In the spring King Haakon started southward with quite a fleet. By a stratagem Erling succeeded in surprising him, when his forces were divided, at Sekken, in Raumsdal, where a battle was fought. Haakon was defeated, and the young king himself was killed (1162). Haakon's body was buried in Raumsdal; but afterward his brother, King Sverre, had the body removed to Nidaros and laid in the stone wall in Christ Church south of the choir.

CHAPTER XXVII

Magnus Erlingson (1162-1184)—The Birchlegs

AFTER the battle of Sekken, Erling Skakke proceeded with King Magnus and the whole army up to Nidaros, where the Thing was convened, and Magnus was proclaimed king of all Norway. They remained there but a short time, however, for Erling did not put great faith in the Throndhjem people. Erling returned with his son to Bergen, and later in the fall went to Tunsberg, where he intended to stay during the winter.

Some of the late King Haakon's chiefs, who had not been present at the battle, among them Earl Sigurd of Reyr, refused to acknowledge King Magnus. They left their ships in Raumsdal and went over to Uplands, where they found many adherents. They chose for their king a young son of King Sigurd Mund, named Sigurd Markusfostre (*i.e.*, foster-son of Markus), who had been brought up by Markus of Skog, a friend and relative of Earl Sigurd. Quite an army was collected, but as the territory they held was small, their foraging became burdensome to the people, and there was considerable dissatisfaction. Erling Skakke took advantage of this, and when finally a battle was fought at Ree, near Tunsberg, he easily defeated Sigurd's adherents. Earl Sigurd fell in the battle (February, 1163). Sigurd Markusfostre and his foster-father were captured and killed in the fall of the same year.

The archbishop in Nidaros was at that time Eystein, a son of Erlend Himalde, who descended from a very influential family in the Throndhjem district. In the summer of 1164 Erling Skakke had a conference with Archbishop Eystein in Bergen, where all the bishops of the country were then assembled, together with the legate from Rome, Stephanus. The result of the conference was that Magnus was to be anointed and crowned as king by the archbishop, while on the other hand it was agreed that in the future the church—represented by the archbishop and the other bishops, together with twelve leading men from each bishopric selected by the bishop—was to decide at the death of a king which one of his heirs was to succeed him; and if the king left no heirs of whom the magnates approved, they were to elect a successor to the throne. In the presence of the papal legate, the bishops, and a great many other clergymen, King Magnus, who was then eight years old, was anointed and crowned by the archbishop. Magnus, Erling's son, was the first crowned king in Norway. By this solemn act Erling Skakke believed he had secured his son's dynasty on the throne, and he could now with greater safety turn his whole attention to internal and foreign enemies, as he felt convinced that the greater part of the people would rally around the anointed king.

When King Valdemar of Denmark heard that Erling Skakke had defeated Haakon Herdebred and Sigurd Markusfostre, and that his son Magnus had been crowned king of the whole country, he sent a message to Erling and reminded him of the agreement, by which Viken was to be ceded to the Danish king, if Magnus became king of Norway. Erling and his advisers showed no inclination to adhere to the agreement, and the messenger returned to Denmark without having accomplished anything. In the spring of 1165 King Valdemar sailed with a fleet north to Viken in order to take possession of the province. He tried peaceful proceedings; but he was so coolly received by the people of Viken that he returned to Denmark, preferring, as he said to his men, to use his army against the heathens of Vendland. The hostility between Norway and Denmark, however, lasted some time. Erling made a cruise to Jutland and defeated the Danes in a battle at Dyrsaa, and returned to Norway with a great booty. A second expedition of King Valdemar to Viken in the spring of 1168 became as indecisive as the first, so far as establishing any authority there; but he dealt the inhabitants of Viken a hurtful blow by forbidding them to trade with Denmark, at the same time forbidding the Danes to export grain to Norway.

While Erling Skakke was absent on an expedition to Denmark, a band of rebels was organized under the leadership of a new pretender, Olaf, a son of King Eystein Magnusson's daughter Maria, in her marriage with the chief Gudbrand Skafhoggson, who fell with King Inge in the battle at Oslo. Olaf was brought up by an influential man named Sigurd Agn-Hat. Probably from the latter's surname the adherents of Olaf were called Hat-Swains (Hættesveiner). The Hat-Swains proclaimed Olaf king, and went through the Uplands, and sometimes down to Viken, or east to the forest settlements. At Rydjokel, near Lake Oiern, they surprised Erling Skakke and his men early one morning, and in the fight that followed killed several of Erling's men and drove the remainder down to their ships. Because Olaf did not succeed in capturing Erling, although the odds were all in his favor, he was afterward called Olaf the Unlucky (Ugæva). The following spring the Hat-Swains met Erling in battle at Stanger, in the eastern part of Viken, where Erling won a decisive victory. Sigurd Agn-Hat and many others of Olaf's men fell here. Olaf escaped by flight, went south to Denmark, and spent the winter in Aalborg, where he died of sickness the following spring (1169).

The interruption of the navigation between Norway and Denmark under the decree of King Valdemar worked great hardship to the Norwegians, especially the inhabitants of Viken, and Erling Skakke was finally induced to open negotiations for peace. He spent a winter in Denmark, and in the following spring peace was finally concluded, the terms being that Viken should be under the sovereignty of the Danish king, but Erling was to hold it in fief as King Valdemar's vassal with the title of Earl. Erling returned to Norway, and the peace with Denmark was afterward well preserved.

Erling Skakke considered it a policy of necessity to remove any person who by reason of royal birth might become rivals of his son to the throne. King Sigurd Mund had left a daughter named Cecilia. As soon as she became old enough, he sent her to Vermeland and made her the mistress of Folkvid the lawman, knowing that the children from such a connection could not become dangerous rivals. About the same time one of the king's men discovered and brought to Erling a young man named Harald, who in all secrecy had been brought up in the Uplands. He was the son of Erling's own wife Kristina, and his father was the late King Sigurd Mund. An illicit intimacy between such near relatives as Kristina and Sigurd was, under the church laws of the time, considered one of the greatest sins, and everything had therefore been done to keep the matter secret, and Kristina had heretofore succeeded in concealing her guilt. When Erling saw the illegitimate son of his wife before him, he said very little, and those present understood that the young man was doomed. King Magnus, who had taken a liking to Harald, interceded in his favor; but his father answered: "Thou wouldst govern this kingdom but a short time in peace and safety, if thou wert to follow the counsels of the heart only." Earl Erling ordered Harald to be taken to Nordnes, where he was beheaded.

Erling Skakke, however, did not succeed in removing all pretenders. In the year 1174 there appeared on the scene a young man called Eystein, who claimed to be a son of King Eystein Haraldson. He was small of stature, and had a fine, soft face, and he was therefore generally called Eystein Meyla (Little Maiden). He first went on a visit to Gautland to Earl Birger Brosa, who was married to Eystein's aunt, Brigida, a daughter of Harald Gille. They received him well, and furnished him some assistance in men and money. Eystein then proceeded to Norway, and when he came to Viken many people flocked to him. His followers proclaimed him king, and he remained in Viken during the winter. His means of subsistence being soon exhausted, they commenced to rob and steal wherever there was an opportunity. They were not strong enough to remain long in any one place, but roamed about in mountains and forests. They suffered great hardships. Their clothes being worn out, they wound the bark of the birch-tree about their legs, and therefore the people called them Birkebeiner (*i.e.*, Birchlegs). During the two years which the Birchlegs spent in and about Viken (1174-76), they had three battles in regular array with the peasants, and were victorious in them all; but at Krokaskog they came near meeting a disaster in encountering a superior force, and they only saved themselves by a hasty flight.

In the third summer (1176), when Magnus had been king for thirteen years, the Birchlegs started on a more serious expedition. They procured ships and sailed along the coast gathering goods and men. After having passed out of Viken they proceeded with great speed northward to Nidaros, and no news preceded them until they reached the Throndhjem Fjord. Erling and his son Magnus, who were in Bergen, did not hear of their having sailed by. The Birchlegs easily overcame the opposition in Nidaros, and Eystein was proclaimed king by the Throndhjem people, who had never liked King Magnus. The Birchlegs afterward proceeded to Orkedal, where, upon reviewing the troops, they found that they had about 2,400 men. They then went to the Uplands, and on to Thoten and Hadeland, and from there to Ringerike, subduing the country wherever they came.

Earl Erling and King Magnus had remained in Bergen while the Birchlegs were in the North. Then they agreed that Erling should remain with a strong force in Bergen, in case the enemy should come down along the coast, while King Magnus, who was now twenty years old, was to go to Viken and take up his residence in Tunsberg, in order to protect that part of the country from possible enemies. King Magnus went to Tunsberg, where he and Orm, "King's-brother," had their Christmas festivities. In January, 1177, King Magnus with his army met the Birchlegs at Ree, and won a decisive victory over them. The whole body of the Birchlegs was scattered far and wide. Eystein fled into a peasant's house, and begged for his life; but the peasant killed him and brought his body to King Magnus at the Ramnes farm. All the Birchlegs took flight, as they had no hope of mercy from Erling Skakke or King Magnus. Some went to Thelemark, where they had their families, and others proceeded east across the frontier to Sweden. King Magnus's men pursued the fugitives for a time, and killed as many as they could overtake.

King Magnus then returned to Tunsberg, and gained great renown by this victory. It had heretofore been said by all that Erling, his father, was his best shield and support. But after gaining a victory over so strong and numerous a force with fewer men, King Magnus had shown that he could stand alone, and it was predicted that he would become a warrior as much greater than his father, Earl Erling, as he was younger.[12]

The defeated Birchlegs, who fled across the Swedish frontier, met in Vermeland a man who was especially qualified to take the leadership of this headless band. His name was Sverre, and he claimed to be a son of King

Sigurd Mund. He was at present staying with his sister Cecilia, who was the mistress of Folkvid lawman.

During the latter part of the reign of Harald Gille's sons a combmaker in Bergen by the name of Unas married a girl by the name of Gunhild. Unas was probably a Faroe Islander by birth; his brother Roe became bishop of the Faroe Islands in 1157. Gunhild belonged to a distinguished family in western Norway. Shortly after their marriage Gunhild bore a son, who was named Sverre, and everybody supposed that Unas was his father. Sverre remained in Bergen until he was five years old, when he was sent over to the Faroe Islands, to be brought up by Unas's brother Roe. He was educated for the priesthood and was in time ordained as deacon. When he was twenty-four years old, his mother disclosed to him the fact that Unas, who had died a short time ago, was not his father, but that he was the son of King Sigurd Mund. From that day Sverre became very thoughtful. It appeared to him to be too great a task to make war on King Magnus and Earl Erling; but, on the other hand, it did not seem manful to sit quietly as a poor peasant's son when he was the son of a king. He therefore gave up his clerical position and embarked for Norway. Here he was informed that his kinsman, Eystein Meyla, had accepted the title of king from the Birchlegs; but he did not consider it wise to enter into any dealings with him. Without making himself known, he spent some time in different parts of Norway, investigating the sentiment of the people. He made the acquaintance of Earl Erling and King Magnus, and often talked with them and their court-men, who found the young clergyman from the Faroe Islands a pleasant and entertaining companion, and by his cunning he learned from them many things which they would not have talked about if they had known who he was, or what plans he was nourishing. The next winter he went to Sweden, first to Earl Birger and then to his sister Cecilia in Vermeland, where he met the remnants of the Birchleg band. The Birchlegs told him of the fall of Eystein Meyla and urged him to become their chief. Sverre for a long time declined, as the whole band consisted of only seventy men, who were all in great poverty, some of them wounded and without clothes, and all almost unarmed. All his objections, however, were of no avail, and they finally compelled him to become their chief.

In the spring of 1177 Sverre set out with his seventy men to fight for the crown of Norway. He first went south toward Viken, and on the way he was joined by so many that, when he came to Saurboe, he had four hundred and twenty men. He held a Thing, and against his protest they proclaimed him king. Sverre soon discovered that a good many of his followers were but thieves and rascals, who were very much dissatisfied when he forbade them to rob and plunder the peasants. He started back toward Vermeland, and when he arrived at Eidskog and mustered his force, he found that it had again shrunk to seventy men. As he heard that the peasants of Thelemark, some of whom had served in the Birchleg bands under Eystein Meyla, were unfriendly to Earl Erling and King Magnus, he sent messages to them and promised to redress their grievances if they would join him. They were requested to meet him up north, where he was now going. Sverre well understood that, with his small force, he could not reach the Throndhjem country through the eastern, well-populated district, so he decided to proceed by unknown and almost impassable roads and make an unexpected invasion into the country. He passed through dense forests and wildernesses, through Dalarne and Jemteland, where he and his men underwent untold hardships. At times they had nothing to eat but sap, bark, and berries, dug up from under the snow. Finally, after many struggles, Sverre reached his destination early in June, 1177. His band had received some additions on his way through Jemteland, and he was now joined by eighty peasants from Thelemark, so that he had a force of about two hundred men. Outside of Nidaros he defeated and dispersed an army that was sent against him, and then marched into the town, where he met practically no opposition. He showed himself as a generous victor, and gave quarter to all who asked for it. After a few successful expeditions in the neighborhood he summoned the Oere-Thing, where he was proclaimed king of Norway (1177).

When King Magnus and Earl Erling heard what had been going on in Throndhjem, they gathered a large fleet and sailed northward along the coast. Sverre's force was so small that he did not dare to await their arrival, but left Nidaros with his men and proceeded across the mountains toward the southern part of the country. For two years he and his men now led a life of want and suffering, wandering from district to district, living most of the time in the forests and mountains, and subsisting on what they could obtain on their foraging expeditions into the settlements. They were pursued from time to time by King Magnus's men, and had many small battles with them. It was only by Sverre's great cunning, wisdom and perseverance that they got through some of the greatest dangers.

At last, in June, 1179, Sverre considered himself strong enough to meet Erling and Magnus, and in a battle at Kalveskindet, near Nidaros, he defeated their forces. Earl Erling fell in the battle, and King Magnus saved himself by flight. In the battle King Magnus suffered a considerable loss. Several of his prominent liegemen and sixty court-men were slain. Sverre captured most of the enemy's ships, among them the "Olafssuden," which King Magnus himself had commanded. Erling Skakke was buried outside the Christ Church, and Sverre, who seldom lost an opportunity to make a speech, held a funeral sermon over him.

The battle at Kalveskindet and the fall of Earl Erling brought a great change in the fortunes of Sverre and the Birchlegs. Sverre's power and influence grew rapidly, and in a short time the greater part of the people outside of King Magnus's immediate surroundings were willing to acknowledge him as king. Heretofore the name "Birchlegs" had been a contemptuous nickname; but now it became an honorable appellation, which everybody was proud to carry. King Magnus and Sverre seemed to have exchanged roles. Magnus, the anointed and crowned king, was now considered the usurper, while Sverre was considered the rightful king. Magnus's court-men and men-at-arms were soon looked upon as a band of adventurers, and they were called "Heklungs," because it was told of them that they had once robbed a beggar-woman, who had her few coins wrapped up in her cloak (*hekl*).

After the battle at Kalveskindet, King Sverre's men received pay for their services, and he distributed among them the honors and dignities which he had promised them. He appointed district officers throughout the whole of the Throndhjem country. Many prominent and high-born men of this part of the country soon came to him and offered their allegiance, and he therefore declared that Throndhjem should hereafter be considered his real home, and he called the people there his dearest subjects, remembering what loyalty they had always shown his father and his family.

King Magnus spent the year following his defeat mostly in Bergen, where he had many strong friends, among them Archbishop Eystein and Orm King's-Brother (a half-brother of Harald Gille's sons). Afterward he went to Viken, where he spent the winter and gathered an army for a new expedition against his rival. After a short stay at Nidaros, King Sverre made a levy throughout Throndhjem, and proceeded with a fleet south to Bergen; but when he arrived there Magnus had already gone to Viken. He therefore returned to Nidaros, but on his way north he installed officers in all the districts he passed. The winter of 1179-80 he spent in Nidaros.

In the spring King Magnus appeared outside of Nidaros with a force much more numerous than the one Sverre had been able to muster, and a bloody battle was fought on the plains of the Ilevolds. The battle resulted in a complete victory for Sverre. King Magnus and some of his chiefs saved themselves by flight and sailed south with a few ships.

King Magnus went first to Bergen, but soon after proceeded south to his kinsman, King Valdemar of Denmark, by whom he was well received. But Orm King's-Brother went to Viken, and Archbishop Eystein sailed over to England, where he remained for three years. From here he had Sverre declared under the ban of the church; but Sverre does not seem to have paid any attention to this step.

About a month after the battle at the Ilevolds, King Sverre appeared with his fleet outside of Bergen. Resistance was useless, and the inhabitants gave him a good reception. He remained in Bergen all winter (1180-81), and early in the spring quelled an uprising of peasants under the leadership of Jon Kutiza. Sverre promptly punished the rebels, and the peasants had to pay heavy fines. Later in the spring King Magnus and Orm King's-Brother came north with a strong fleet, and a battle was fought at Nordnes, near Bergen. A good many men fell on both sides; but Magnus was again defeated and compelled to save himself by flight. The Birchlegs captured eighteen of Magnus's ships and brought them into the town. They also took other rich booty, for Magnus was at that time well supplied with money and goods.

Magnus went to Stavanger, and it was but a short time before he was again ready to attack Sverre at Bergen. This time, however, Sverre wished to avoid a battle, and sailed with his ships north to Nidaros, where he proceeded to improve the fortifications of the town. Meanwhile Magnus remained in Bergen.

During Sverre's stay in Nidaros there came to him a young man named Erik, who claimed to be a son of King Sigurd Mund. He had been in many foreign lands, had been in the service of the emperor at Constantinople, and on a pilgrimage to the Holy Land, where he had bathed in the river Jordan. He now asked leave to prove his royal descent by the iron ordeal. After a consultation with his friends and chiefs, Sverre permitted him to undergo the ordeal upon the condition that he must not aspire to the crown. Sverre prescribed the oath to be taken by the young man in submitting to the ordeal to prove that he was the son of Sigurd Mund "and the brother of Sverre." In this way Sverre meant to obtain incidentally a confirmation of his own title. But Erik refused to undertake to establish the descent of anybody but himself, and omitted the additional words. He successfully underwent the ordeal, and King Sverre acknowledged him as his brother, and gave him a command in his royal guard.

The conflict between Sverre and Magnus continued for three years more. In 1181 King Sverre opened negotiations for a cessation of hostilities, offering first to share the kingdom with Magnus, and afterward proposing that they should reign alternately for three years each. Magnus, however, declined all offers, and the war was continued. During the years 1181 and 1182, King Magnus made three attacks on the Birchlegs at Nidaros with varying success. In the summer of 1183 Sverre sailed with a fleet down to Bergen, where he surprised and defeated the Heklungs, and compelled Magnus to flee east to Viken. The Birchlegs did not pursue the enemy very far, but returned to Bergen, and took possession of Magnus's whole fleet and a rich booty. Magnus's crown, sceptre and whole coronation outfit fell into Sverre's hands. Many men, who had heretofore been attached to Magnus, now joined King Sverre and swore him allegiance. Archbishop Eystein, who had just returned to the country after a three years' sojourn in England, was reconciled to King Sverre, and returned to his archbishopric in Nidaros. After a short stay in Bergen, and having installed district officers in Sogn, Hordaland, and Rogaland, Sverre returned with his whole army to Nidaros. Magnus again proceeded to Denmark, where the previous year King Knut VI. had succeeded his father, Valdemar the Great, on the throne.

Magnus made a final attempt to defeat Sverre in the summer of 1184, when he came up from Denmark with a large fleet. King Sverre had sailed into the Norefjord, a narrow arm of the Sognefjord, in order to punish the inhabitants of Sogn for having killed his prefect, Ivar Darre, and some other officers. Magnus sailed in after him with his greatly superior force, and a fierce battle was fought at Fimreite, June 15, 1184. The Birchlegs fought with great heroism, and a large number of men fell. The battle commenced in the afternoon. At sundown the first Heklungs turned to flee, and at midnight the battle was finished. The Heklungs had been completely routed. Two thousand men had fallen, among them King Magnus himself and the most prominent chieftains, the flower of the aristocracy of Gulathingslag and Viken. Among the slain were Harald, the son of King Inge; Orm King's-Brother and his son, Ivar Steig; Aasbiorn Jonson of Thiorn; Ragnvald, the son of Jon Hallkelson; Eindride Torve, Jon Kutiza's son, and many other prominent men.

King Magnus was twenty-eight years old at the time of his death, having borne the title of king for twenty-three years. His body was found two days after the battle, and was brought to Bergen, where it was buried with great ceremony.

CHAPTER XXVIII

Sverre Sigurdson (1184-1202)

AFTER the fall of Magnus Erlingson, King Sverre brought the whole country under his control, and no one dared to refuse him obedience. The same sagacity that he had shown in his struggles to gain the power, he also used in his efforts to maintain and strengthen it. He knew that he could expect nothing from the magnates of the powerful families, who resided on the largest estates throughout the country, and who looked with contempt upon the poor and lowly people that had constituted his following and helped him into power. He had to try to weaken the influence of this higher class and to look to the common people for his main support. The changes which King Sverre introduced in the domestic conditions of the country were in close coherence with the development of the country since the time of Harald the Fairhaired and Olaf the Saint. The kingdom of his predecessor had been upheld by the clergy and the aristocracy, the latter endeavoring to strengthen its power and dignity by united action, while the clergy tried to enforce the hierarchical principles of the time in the Church of Norway. King Sverre, on the other hand, depended upon the masses of the people, with their traditions and customs. For their benefit King Sverre appointed a new class of officers, who were called lawmen. They were to be learned in the law, and their duty was to see that the law was justly administered at the Things, and to aid the peasants in all legal matters. There had been a similar class of officers before, bearing the same title, but they had been elected at the Things, while from now on they were appointed by the king, especially for the benefit of the poorer classes, who themselves had little knowledge of the law, and often needed protection against the rich and powerful. Another class of officers whose functions were changed in such a manner as to greatly strengthen the king's power were the prefects (*Sysselmen*), whom the king appointed throughout the country. These prefects did not have the inherited dignity of the liegemen (*lendermen*), who were royal vassals and exercised independent authority, but were servants of the king and the representatives of his power. They supplanted the liegemen in their executive and judicial functions, and gradually transferred to the crown a great part of the power of the aristocracy.

Sverre was too shrewd to break entirely or too suddenly with the old influences, and where they had been loyal, he selected men from the high old families for his officers. This was especially the case in the Throndhjem country, where his party was strongest. But he found positions enough with which to reward the faithful men who had followed him through his struggles. Some were made chiefs in the army, and some were appointed prefects; some were given landed estates, and others were helped to rich marriages. Baard Guthormson of Rein was married to the king's own sister, Cecilia, after her marriage with Folkvid Lawman had been declared void. King Sverre himself married Margreta, a sister of the Swedish king, Knut Erikson. Before this marriage King Sverre had four children, namely, two sons, Sigurd (called Lavard) and Haakon, and two daughters, Cecilia and Ingeborg. With Queen Margreta he had only a daughter, Kristina.

The peace was not of long duration. The remnants of the Heklung party, which had been broken up by the battle in Norefjord, with several leading men, only waited for a favorable opportunity to start a revolt, and the opportunity soon offered itself. A monk, who called himself Jon and claimed to be a son of King Inge the Hunchback, left the cloister on the island near Oslo, and soon gathered about him a numerous band. He first went to Tunsberg, where, in September, 1185, he attacked and killed one of Sverre's prefects together with thirty men, and then summoned a Thing and was proclaimed king. The Birchlegs called this new party the Kuvlungs or Cowlmen, because their leader had worn a monk's hood or cowl. The Kuvlungs continued the rebellion for three years with varying success. They made several attacks on Bergen and Nidaros, and at times their strength was quite formidable. Finally their band was destroyed in Bergen, in December, 1188, and their leader was killed. After his death it appears to have been satisfactorily proven that Jon Kuvlung was not the son of King Inge the Hunchback, as he had claimed.

The rebellious spirit had become quite general, and King Sverre had many of these revolts to suppress. After the Kuvlung party had been broken up, a new band, called the Varbelgs (Wolf Skins), was organized by the chief, Simon Kaareson, who had brought from Denmark, as a pretender to the throne, a boy named Vikar, said to be a son of King Magnus Erlingson. This party was badly defeated in a battle near Tunsberg, where Simon Kaareson and the little Vikar were both killed. Another band, under the leadership of Thorleif Breidskegg, who claimed to be a son of King Eystein Haraldson, was next destroyed in Viken (1191). The next party that made war on King Sverre were the Oyskeggs (the Islanders), so called because they received considerable aid from the Orkney Islands, where Earl Harald favored them. Their leaders were Hallkel Jonson, who was married to King Magnus Erlingson's sister Ragnhild, and Olaf, a brother-in-law of Earl Harald of the Orkneys. They chose Sigurd, a son of King Magnus, as their king. The Oyskeggs developed a considerable strength in Viken, and from there made piratical expeditions to the Danish waters and the Baltic, and therefore boastingly called themselves the

Goldlegs (*Gullbeiner*). One of the men, whom King Sverre sent against them, Sigurd Jarlson (earl's son), an illegitimate son of Erling Skakke, turned traitor, and became one of the leaders of Sverre's enemies. In the fall of 1193 the Oyskeggs captured Bergen without much resistance, King Sverre being then in Throndhjem. In the spring King Sverre came south with a fleet, and a bloody battle was fought at Florevaag, near Bergen (April 3, 1194). The Oyskeggs were finally defeated, a great number of them, including Hallkel Jonson, Olaf (Earl Harald's brother-in-law), and Sigurd Magnusson, the pretender, being slain. King Sverre had thus gained a victory, but at great cost, for many of his best men had fallen, or died from the wounds they had received in the battle. Among the latter was Baard Guthormson of Rein.

While King Sverre was almost constantly engaged in quelling rebellion, he was also carrying on a hard struggle with the hierarchy. Archbishop Eystein had been obliged to make peace with King Sverre; but when Eystein died (1188), Bishop Erik of Stavanger, a man with strong hierarchical tendencies, became his successor. Archbishop Erik named as his own successor to the bishopric of Stavanger one of Sverre's bitter enemies, Nicholas Arneson, a half-brother of King Inge the Hunchback. King Sverre refused to recognize this selection, because he had not been consulted, and named another in his place. Finally, through the mediation of Queen Margreta, who was a relative of Nicholas Arneson, the matter was compromised, and Sverre consented to Nicholas being installed as bishop in Oslo. The fight between the king and the hierarchy was, however, continued in other matters. Archbishop Erik was constantly trying to extend the prerogatives of his office. He claimed the exclusive right to the control of all church property; he wanted the tribute to the church paid according to actual weight in silver instead of in current coin, whereby he would about double the tax, and, finally, he wanted to surround himself with a court and keep ninety men-at-arms in his service, while the law allowed only thirty men altogether, and only twelve of them armed. During his stay in Nidaros, in 1191-92, King Sverre summoned a Thing to have these matters settled. The law was read, and the case was decided in favor of the king. Archbishop Erik now found the surroundings too uncomfortable, and hurried away from the town, taking with him all the goods he could collect. He proceeded to Denmark, where he was cordially received by Archbishop Absalon. Shortly after his arrival in Denmark he prepared a letter to the pope, in which he complained of King Sverre's infringements on the rights of the Church. In response to this letter, Pope Celestinus III., on the 15th of June, 1194, declared King Sverre in the ban of the church. Before the papal bull reached Norway, however, King Sverre had compelled the bishops to crown him at Bergen, June 29, 1194. For some time King Sverre treated the papal bull with contempt, and even intimated that it was an invention of the bishops in Denmark; but later he sent ambassadors, under the leadership of Bishop Thore of Hamar, with a message to the Pope, in which he put matters in a different light from that given them by Archbishop Erik. The fate of these ambassadors is enveloped in mystery. They remained in Rome till the end of 1196, and then started for home. During their homeward journey they were suddenly taken sick in Denmark and died, having probably been poisoned. Some time afterward some Danes came to King Sverre with letters bearing the seal of the Pope, and which, they said, had been pawned with them by the ambassadors for a certain amount of money. Sverre redeemed the documents, which purported to revoke the ban against the king, and had them publicly read in the churches. Whether King Sverre knew that these documents were not genuine does not appear.

By the united efforts of King Sverre's enemies among the clergy and the aristocracy a rebellious band was organized in 1196, which was to become more dangerous than all the enemies he had heretofore had to fight. The principal leader of this movement was Bishop Nicholas Arneson, who was prepared to do anything to overthrow King Sverre. A favorable opportunity offered itself. The Byzantine emperor, Alexios Komnenos, had sent a Norwegian named Reidar the Messenger (*Sendemand*) to Norway to ask King Sverre to send him 1,200 good mercenaries for the service of the emperor. King Sverre replied that he had no troops to spare; but he was persuaded to allow Reidar to enlist such sons of peasants and traders as might wish to enter the service of the emperor. After Reidar had collected a considerable force, he was induced by Bishop Nicholas to enter into a league with him against King Sverre. At a fair in Halland he met Bishop Nicholas and Archbishop Erik, who had with them a large body of Norwegians, mostly from Viken. With them was also a young man named Inge, said to be a son of King Magnus Erlingson. The two armies united and proclaimed Inge king, and then made an invasion in Viken, where they were soon joined by Sigurd Jarlson, the former Oyskegg chief, and many other prominent men. The new rebel army was called *Baglers*, from the word *bagall*, a bishop's crosier, to signify that Bishop Nicholas was considered the real founder and chief leader of the party.

During the last six years of his life King Sverre had a continual war with the Baglers. His first encounter with them was in Saltoe Sound, in Viken. After an indecisive battle there he returned with his ships to Bergen and proceeded to Nidaros, where he spent the winter 1196-97. The Baglers meanwhile summoned the Borgar-Thing, where Inge was proclaimed king. The next year King Sverre gathered a strong force and proceeded to Viken, and defeated the Baglers at Oslo, July 26, 1197. After the battle Bishop Nicholas sent a messenger to King Sverre that he was willing to make peace; but Sverre, who knew how little Bishop Nicholas was to be depended upon, sent word back that he would only treat with him if he would come in person. Bishop Nicholas did not go to meet the king, but instead hastened with the chiefs and the remaining force of the Baglers overland to Nidaros, where the wooden citadel (blockhouse) "Zion" fell into their hands by the treason of its commander, Thorstein Kugad. They destroyed some of the fortifications and burned a number of Sverre's ships and took possession of the remainder. A part of the Bagler force went aboard the captured ships, and sailed southward under the leadership of Sigurd Jarlson. The others returned to Viken the same way they had come. King Sverre spent the following winter in Bergen, and in the spring (1198) sailed north and met the Baglers in battle at Thorsberg, near the mouth of the Throndhjem Fjord. After a hard fight the Birchlegs were defeated with great loss. The king then hastened back to Bergen, which had in the meantime been occupied by the Bagler chief Sigurd Jarlson. The latter, however, having, by a clever trick of one of the Birchlegs, been led to believe that King Sverre was approaching with a much superior force, left the town before Sverre arrived.

During the summer of 1198, which for a long time afterward was called the Bergen-summer, there was continual skirmishing in and about Bergen. On the night after August 10th the Baglers, led by Bishop Nicholas, rowed up to the landings with two ships full of wood. At the bishop's command they set fire to the town in three different places, and soon the greater part of it, including six churches, was laid in ashes. The Birchlegs had all they could do to save the wooden citadel (*Sverre's Borg*). The inhabitants of Bergen could never afterward forgive Bishop Nicholas and his party for the loss they suffered by this fire; but as heartily as they had heretofore hated the Birchlegs they now hated the Baglers. Sverre found his position untenable after the town had been burned, and proceeded with his men overland to Throndhjem. Meanwhile the Baglers, who had many ships, were masters on the coasts. Many deserted the king and supported the Baglers; but there were also some of their men who went over to Sverre. Among the latter was Thorstein Kugad, who had surrendered his garrison in Nidaros, and who now returned to Sverre and begged his pardon. This was given, and Thorstein became one of Sverre's useful men.

King Sverre spent the winter 1198-99 in Nidaros. His position was a desperate one. Outside of the Throndhjem country he had very little power, and the Baglers were masters at sea. Then, furthermore, a terrible blow was dealt Sverre, as Pope Innocent III., in October, 1198, issued his bull declaring Sverre to be in the ban of the Church, and laying the whole country under interdict, closing all churches and forbidding the administration of the sacraments wherever the people acknowledged King

Sverre. It is easily understood what horror such a papal bull would create at that time. Sverre did not lose courage, however, but called the Throndhjem people together and asked them to help him. They showed their usual loyalty, and with their help he set to work to build a new, strong fleet and to improve the fortifications of the town. In the spring the Baglers appeared in the Throndhjem Fjord with a strong fleet, and, after some skirmishing, the two fleets met in battle at Strindsö, June 18, 1199. It was a desperate fight, where no quarter was given. The result was a victory for King Sverre and the Birchlegs, who returned to town with most of the enemy's ships. The prisoners taken on this occasion were nearly all slain. Bishop Nicholas, who watched the beginning of the battle from a safe distance, fled with his ship when he saw that the Baglers were losing, and Sigurd Jarlson and Reidar the Messenger followed his example.

The Baglers who escaped from the battle of Strindsö proceeded to Denmark. Sverre, with his fleet, pursued them a part of the way, but gave up the chase and proceeded to Oslo, where he intended to go into winter-quarters. In January, 1200, the Baglers came up from Denmark with a number of small ships under the leadership of Reidar the Messenger and Inge Bagler-King. Some of them landed near Oslo and killed Sverre's kinsman, Earl Philip. Not feeling strong enough, however, to attack King Sverre's forces they withdrew during the night and sailed to Bergen. Afterward they made a sudden but unsuccessful attack on Nidaros, which was defended by an army of 1,800 peasants.

During the winter King Sverre attempted to make a levy of troops in Viken, intending to send home some of his Throndhjem people; but the inhabitants, who had never been greatly attached to King Sverre, murmured at this, and the result was a great uprising of the peasants in Viken and the Uplands. On the day secretly appointed, March 1st, Sverre's prefects at Tunsberg and several other places were killed, and a few days later a force many times as large as Sverre's marched against him from three different directions. On this occasion Sverre displayed a masterly leadership, and his men fought like heroes. During the day there were eight desperate encounters, and, in spite of the seemingly overwhelming force of the rebels, Sverre won the day. He afterward punished the peasants by exacting large fines in money and provisions.

Sverre had a few indecisive battles with the Baglers the same year, and spent the following winter in Bergen. In the spring of 1201 he called a new levy from the north, and, during the summer, sailed to Viken. Reidar the Messenger, with several chiefs and two hundred and forty men, had fortified himself on the *Slotsberg* (Castle Mountain) at Tunsberg, and defied any attack. King Sverre organized a regular siege, determined not to abandon it until he had conquered this dangerous enemy. Finally, when the

Baglers were nearly starved to death, Reidar and his little band surrendered to Sverre, who not only spared their lives, but gave them the best of treatment. He advised them not to eat much in the beginning; but several of them disregarded this advice and died. This remarkable siege had lasted for twenty weeks, or from the first week in September, 1201, to the fourth week in January, 1202.

At last King Sverre's physical strength succumbed to the hardships and cares which night and day he had had to endure. During his stay in Tunsberg he had been ailing, but, at first, his illness did not seem to be serious. When he left Tunsberg, however, he was obliged to keep his bed. He had his bed placed on the raised deck in the stern of his ship, and here also stood the bed of the Bagler chief, Reidar. During the journey the king found much pleasure in talking with the intelligent old chief, who could tell him of his crusades and other journeys in distant countries. They arrived in Bergen toward the end of February, and the king was carried to the royal residence, where his bed was placed in the large hall. When he understood that death was near, he called the priests and his trusted friends to him. He first let them read and seal a letter which he had prepared, to his son Haakon in Throndhjem, about the management of the affairs of the government after his death. Then he solemnly declared that he had only one son living, namely Haakon (his other son, Sigurd Lavard, having died the year before), so that if any one else should claim after his death to be his son he would be an impostor. Then he desired to be lifted into his high-seat, and seated there he received the last ointment. Afterward he said: "I have had more strife, disturbance, and adversity than quiet and peaceful days during my reign, and, so far as I can judge, many have been my maligners only from enmity toward me. God forgive them all, and judge between them and me in my whole cause." Soon after, on Saturday, March 9, 1202, King Sverre expired. His body was buried in the Christ Church, and on his tombstone was engraved the following epitaph: "Here lies one who was the ornament of kings, the support, picture and paragon of faith, honor and bravery, his country's defence, the vindication of justice, the delight of all his men." After his death even those who had been his enemies said that such a man as Sverre had not lived in Norway in their time.

CHAPTER XXIX

Haakon Sverreson (1202-1204), Guthorm Sigurdson (1204), and Inge Baardson (1204-1217)

AFTER Sverre's death his only son, Haakon, who was then twenty-eight or thirty years old, was proclaimed king of Norway. In the letter which Sverre wrote to his son on his death-bed, he advised him to make peace with the Church, and Haakon lost no time in calling the archbishop back to the country and in reconciling himself with the bishops. The clergy seemed to be very eager for peace, and each bishop returned to his bishopric, while the archbishop revoked the ban and the interdict without even taking time to obtain the consent of the pope. For this haste in making peace with the king the archbishop was afterward sharply reprimanded by the pope; but in the meanwhile the good relations between king and clergy had strengthened Haakon's position, and the people in general readily acknowledged him. The Bagler party gradually lost most of its support, and after their so-called king, Inge Magnusson, had been killed by one of his own men on an island in Lake Miosen (1202), the party was, for the time being, broken up. Some went to King Haakon and begged for mercy, the remainder fled either to Sweden or Denmark, and there was again peace in the country. The peace, however, did not last very long, this time probably on account of strained relations between the king and his stepmother, the queen-dowager Margreta. During the festivities in Bergen at Christmas, 1203, King Haakon was taken suddenly ill, and on January 1, 1204, he died, with all the symptoms of having been poisoned. It was the general opinion that Queen Margreta was the cause of his death. She was obliged to leave the country, and returned to her old home in Sweden. The death of King Haakon caused great sorrow, for he had been very popular; besides, it was generally supposed that he left no issue.

Two days after Haakon's death, a council was held by Bishop Martin and the chiefs of the Birchlegs, and it was decided to elect Haakon's nearest heir, his nephew, Guthorm Sigurdson, a son of Sigurd Lavard, as his successor, although he was only four years old. Haakon Galen, a son of Sverre's sister Cecilia and Folkvid Lawman, was to conduct the government under the title of earl. When this hasty election of a king was reported throughout the country, the Bagler party reorganized themselves under the leadership of Erling Steinvegg (Stonewall), who claimed to be a son of King Magnus Erlingson. This new pretender soon had a large following and also obtained substantial support from the Danish king, Valdemar II. Bishop Nicholas at first opposed him, as he wanted his own nephew, Philip, a grandson of Harald Gille's queen, Ingerid, elected king; but they finally came to an agreement, Erling promising to make Philip earl and to otherwise favor the bishop. With the aid of the bishop, Erling then proved his right to the throne by the ordeal of fire, the event taking place with great ceremony in Tunsberg in the presence of the Danish king and a large assemblage of people. King Valdemar made Erling a present of thirty-five fully equipped ships. The following day a Thing was summoned, and Erling was proclaimed king. He immediately appointed Philip as his earl. Both solemnly acknowledged the Danish king as their overlord and gave him hostages. The whole of Viken had soon acknowledged Erling as king, and the few Birchlegs who were there fled to the northern or western part of the country.

The child king, Guthorm Sigurdson, died suddenly in Nidaros, August 11, 1204, and there was a strong suspicion that he had been poisoned by Christina, the mistress of Haakon Galen. The Thing was immediately convened, and the people elected Inge Baardson of Rein as king. Inge was a younger half-brother of Haakon Galen, being a son of King Sverre's sister, Cecilia, and her husband, Baard of Rein. For some time there was again continual warfare between the Baglers and the Birchlegs. In the summer of 1205, King Inge and Earl Haakon made a cruise to Viken and had some encounters with the Baglers, and in the fall King Inge returned to Nidaros, while Earl Haakon went into winter-quarters in Bergen.

Shortly after Christmas it was reported in Nidaros that a body of warriors had come across the mountain from the south, and that they had the son of a king with them. It was feared that a new band of rebels was coming, and King Inge called all his men to arms. Two of his court-men, who were sent out to ascertain the object of the coming warriors, were met by some messengers, who had been sent ahead to inform King Inge of their errand. It was quite true that they had the son of a king with them, but he was as yet only a babe. It was learned that the approaching warriors were a number of good Birchlegs, and that the prince who was with them was the infant son of their late beloved master, King Haakon Sverreson.

During his visit in Sarpsborg, in 1203, King Haakon Sverreson had become enamored of a handsome girl of high birth, Inga of Varteig. She reciprocated his affection, and the intimacy that grew up between them was no secret to the king's friends. Soon after the king's death, Inga, who was then at the parsonage Folkisberg (in the present Eidsberg parish), gave birth to a son. The priest, Thrond, who well knew who the father was, baptized the boy and named him Haakon, after his father. Thrond kept the child at his home, but did all he could to keep the matter secret. Later he took Erlend of Huseby, a distant relative of King Haakon, into his confidence, and it was decided to get the child away from Viken, on account of the constant danger from the Baglers. Toward Christmas, 1205, when the boy was about a year and a half old, his mother, Inga of Varteig, the priest Thrond, and Erlend of Huseby started out on the dangerous journey. They arrived at Hamar Christmas eve, but were afraid to stay there long, and therefore continued their journey as soon as possible. They first came to Lillehammer, where a number of Birchlegs joined them, and then proceeded across the mountain to Oesterdalen, and thence north to Nidaros. During the journey across the mountain they suffered untold hardships on account of snow and cold, being often obliged to spend the night in the wilderness. Once the storm had become so severe that they did not know where they were. The royal child was then given to the two best ski-runners in the party, Thorstein Skevla and Skervald Skrukka, who started ahead of the others in order to find shelter if possible. They did not succeed in reaching any settlement that night, but struck a mountain hay-shed, where they made fire and prepared a couch for the child. The remainder of the party reached the place later in the night. In the morning the snow was so deep that it was only with the greatest difficulty that they could proceed. When they reached the settlements, however, they were well received, and many Birchlegs joined them on their journey northward.

When King Inge and his men heard of the journey of the royal child and of the hardships which the party had suffered, they all thanked God for having saved the child. The king and his whole court set out to meet the party at the blockhouse, and, on their arrival, he took the little boy in his arms and kissed him. The boy and his mother were given the best of care in Nidaros. The child became very popular with the old Birchlegs who had served under his father and his grandfather. They came often to see how he was getting along, and would sometimes playfully take him between them and stretch his arms and legs in order, as they said, to make him grow faster.

In the spring of 1206 Erling Steinvegg collected a fleet and proceeded north to Throndhjem, in order to attack King Inge in his stronghold in Nidaros. On Saturday, April 22, there were great festivities in Nidaros, for King Inge was celebrating the wedding of his sister Sigrid, daughter of Baard of Rein, to the liegeman, Thorgrim of Ljaanes. All the prominent men in the surrounding country had come to the wedding. There was much drinking during the night, and the king, as well as his chiefs and warriors, went to bed intoxicated. Toward morning the Baglers suddenly attacked the sleeping town and effected a general massacre. Many of the prominent Birchlegs, who had been with King Sverre in many of his battles, were killed by the Baglers on this occasion. King Inge, who was not at the royal residence, but was sleeping in the house of his mistress, was with some difficulty awakened by the latter's servants. He escaped to a neighboring roof, where he lay until the Baglers had passed the house; then he ran down to the docks and threw himself in the icy river in order to swim across. The strong current made this a very difficult task. Out in the stream he caught hold of the anchor cable of a ship, to which he clung for a while, but a man, who was keeping guard on board, pushed him off with a pole, and he was obliged to swim further. He finally reached the other shore, but was then so exhausted from cold and exertion that he would probably have succumbed, if one of his faithful men, Reidulf Baardsbrother, had not happened to come to his assistance. Reidulf took off his cloak and wrapped the king in it, and carried him on his back to Skyaas, where they obtained a horse and sled and escaped to Klæbu.

In the meanwhile the Baglers continued their dreadful work in Nidaros. They searched all the churches and killed those who had taken refuge there, and committed numerous acts of plunder and depredation. King Inge's half-brother, the seventeen year old Skule Baardson, escaped as by a miracle. He crept along the house walls and reached the river, where the chief, Jon Usle, and forty Birchlegs were just going across in some boats they had secured. They crossed in safety, and later proceeded to Klæbu, where Skule found the king with a hundred Birchlegs and peasants, who had gathered about him.

King Inge was greatly changed after the experiences of that awful night. The light-hearted and social young man became gloomy and melancholy. He never felt really at ease except on board his ship and in the solitude of his room. He was averse to seeing new faces, and only his nearest and dearest men were admitted to his presence.

King Inge soon returned to Nidaros with a force of Birchlegs, while the Baglers withdrew to Bergen with their large booty. Here they were soon afterward overtaken by Earl Haakon and the Birchlegs, who defeated them and took back the greater part of the spoil. Thus the two parties, from time to time, continued to surprise and attack each other with no other result than that the country suffered. Early in the year 1207 the Bagler king, Erling Steinvegg, died, and Bishop Nicholas at last succeeded in having his nephew, Philip, chosen as the third king of the Baglers.

In the summer of 1208 negotiations for peace were commenced. The manner in which the war had lately been conducted indicates that the strength of both parties was practically exhausted. The whole warfare was only a sort of hide-and-seek play, or a continual cruising back and forth between Bergen and Viken, in which they do not even seem to have tried to meet in decisive battle, but only to forestall each other, attack singly some one of the hostile party, and otherwise do as much damage as possible by plunder and depredation. Everybody began to realize that the resources of the country were thus being wasted, and that, whichever party finally won, there would only be an impoverished land and people to rule over. Bishop Nicholas saw this as well as any one, and consulted the archbishop in Nidaros. The result was a meeting of the chiefs of both parties at Hvitings Island (Hvitingsö), near Stavanger, where the king of the Baglers, Philip, swore allegiance to King Inge, and was, in return, made earl of Viken and the Uplands, and was given Christina, the daughter of Sverre, in marriage.

The war between the Baglers and the Birchlegs was thus ended, and comparative peace was restored. One of the disturbing elements that remained was the jealousy of Earl Haakon Galen and his ambitious wife. As the nephew of King Sverre, he thought he had been as much entitled to the throne as his half-brother, Inge. An open revolt was avoided; but, probably by the intervention of Archbishop Thore, a compact was made between the earl and the king (1212), by which it was decided that illegitimate children were to be excluded from the succession to the throne. This agreement was especially aimed against the young Haakon Haakonson and Inge's own illegitimate child, Guthorm, and gave the succession to Haakon Galen's own offspring. This agreement, however, was not approved by the old warriors among the Birchlegs, who were greatly attached to King Sverre's direct descendant, the young Haakon.

In the evening, after the agreement had been made, the boy came home from school to the court of Earl Haakon, by whom he was being raised, and he hurried to the old veteran, Helge Hvasse, who was especially fond of the boy, and used to give a great deal of attention to him. This time, however, he turned away and would not speak to the child.

"Why are you angry with me?" asked the boy.

"Begone!" said Helge. "I will have nothing to do with you. You were disinherited to-day."

"How did that happen, and who did it?" asked little Haakon.

"It was done at Oere-Thing," said Helge, "and it was done by the two brothers, King Inge and Earl Haakon."

"Be not angry with me, my own Helge," said the boy, "and do not care anything about this; for this decision cannot possibly be valid. My representatives were not present to answer in my behalf."

"And who are your representatives?" asked Helge.

"My representatives are God, the holy Virgin, and Saint Olaf," answered Haakon; "in their hands have I left my case, and they will guard my interests in the best possible way, as you will see, both as to the division of the country and in my other welfare."

Deeply moved, the old Birchleg took the boy in his arms and kissed him, and said:

"That was better said than unsaid, my prince, and I thank you for those words."

What this boy of eight years had said was soon reported among the Birchlegs, who all greatly admired him. The story also soon reached Earl Haakon and his wife Christina. The earl did not say much; but Christina got very angry, and from that day treated the boy more harshly than she had done before.

Earl Haakon was taken sick and died in Bergen in January, 1214, and his wife, Christina, who understood that she had made herself very unpopular, hastened to leave the country with her young son, Knut, and returned to Sweden. Young Haakon Haakonson was transferred to King Inge's court. He and Guthorm, King Inge's son, were sent to school together, and they were in every way treated alike.

In the winter of 1216-17 King Inge was taken sick, and when he could no longer attend to the public affairs he appointed his half-brother, Skule Baardson, as regent with the title of earl. King Inge died April 23, 1217, and Earl Skule had him buried with great ceremony in Christ Church in Nidaros.

CHAPTER XXX

Haakon Haakonson the Old (1217-1263)

AFTER the death of King Inge, the discord which had been fermenting began to show itself. The ambitious Earl Skule, while pretending to favor King Inge's young son, Guthorm, really considered himself the successor to the throne, while a few, who had been special friends of the late Earl Haakon Galen, favored the latter's son Knut, who was with his mother in Sweden. Earl Skule had the aid and sympathy of Archbishop Guthorm and the other dignitaries of the cathedral at Nidaros, and advocated a postponement of the election of a king, until the archbishop, who was absent on a journey, should return. In spite of all intriguing, however, the Birchlegs summoned the Oere-Thing and proclaimed Haakon Haakonson king of Norway, and he swore fidelity to the laws of the country, although he could not, according to usage, do so on the shrine of Saint Olaf, because the canons of the cathedral refused to allow the shrine to be taken out of the church and carried to the Thing. The next day all the court-men and the delegates present took the oath of allegiance to Haakon as king and to Skule as earl. The king and the earl now proceeded to Bergen, where the Gula-Thing was summoned, in order that Haakon might also be proclaimed king there. The day before the Thing a meeting was held by the king and the earl and their advisers. The king's advisers suggested that Earl Skule should swear an oath of allegiance to King Haakon; but this the earl bluntly refused to do, unless he was given in fief one-third of the kingdom and of its dependencies. As it was learned that the earl had been negotiating with the so-called Bagler king, Philip, in Viken, and the king's party was hardly strong enough to fight a combination of that kind, it was thought that there was nothing to do but to acquiesce in the earl's demands. The next day, at the Thing, King Haakon made his oath to uphold the laws, but the wily earl had made use of his position as the king's guardian to insert in the oath a pledge to keep the agreement already made between the king and the earl. Shortly after this, news was received that the Bagler king, Philip, was dead. King Haakon and Earl Skule immediately proceeded to Viken, where, at the suggestion of Bishop Nicholas, negotiations were opened with the Baglers. It was finally decided that the Baglers should retain, during the coming winter, one-half of the fiefs which Philip had held as earl, and that both parties should send men north to the archbishop to request him, next summer, to arrange a permanent peace. The other half of Viken was given up to King Haakon and Earl Skule, who appointed prefects there. Thereupon they summoned the Hauga-Thing, where Haakon was acknowledged as the rightful king.

King Haakon had several enemies to contend with, and the most dangerous among them were by no means those who were in open rebellion. A new band of rebels was organized under the leadership of a chaplain by the name of Benedict, or Bene Skinkniv (Skin knife), as the peasants called him, who claimed to be a son of King Magnus Erlingson. His followers were originally mostly thieves and bandits, who only sought an opportunity for robbery and plunder. On account of their ragged appearance they were called the "Slitungs" (vagabonds or "tramps"). After a short campaign against the Slitungs, the king and the earl returned northward. When they arrived in Nidaros, the earl was received with the utmost courtesy by the archbishop, but the latter refused to show the proper honor to the king; and the reason being given that there was some doubt as to whether Haakon was really the son of Haakon Sverreson, it was agreed that his mother, Inga of Varteig, was to submit to the ordeal of fire. This was done in Bergen in the presence of the king, the earl, the archbishop, and other bishops and chiefs. The result was in every way satisfactory. The church declared that King Haakon had proved his paternity, and Earl Skule was for the time being apparently reconciled with the king.

The strained relations between Earl Skule and the king soon came to the surface again, however, and there were frequent conflicts between the "earl's-men" and the "king's-men." The friends of both finally came to the conclusion that something ought to be done to bind them together by common interests, and as the best means to this end they proposed a marriage between King Haakon and the earl's daughter, Margreta. The plan was accepted by both parties, and the betrothal took place in September, 1219. The actual marriage was preliminarily postponed on account of the tender age of both parties, the king being then about fourteen years and the bride scarcely more than nine years old.

During the next winter a new band of rebels was organized in Viken by Gudolf of Blakkestad, a former prefect, who had been discharged from office on account of his harsh treatment of the peasants. The Slitungs joined the new party, which was commonly called the Ribbungs (robbers). They chose as their leader and candidate for the throne a young man by the name of Sigurd, who claimed to be the son of the former Bagler king, Erling Steinvegg. They seem to have had the secret support of Bishop Nicholas, in spite of the fact that the latter had professed friendship for King Haakon. After having fought this party for about two years and defeated it several times, Earl Skule induced Bishop Nicholas to assist in ending the struggle. In the spring of 1223, Sigurd Ribbung made overtures for peace, but had the audacity to demand as a condition for laying down his arms one third of the kingdom and the earl's daughter in marriage. The earl answered that he would not give his daughter away to live in the woods, and as for the third of the kingdom he would have to apply to King Haakon; but he promised Sigurd and his men amnesty and safe conduct, in case Sigurd wished to apply personally to the king. Although these conditions were more severe than expected, Sigurd Ribbung surrendered. The earl was greatly praised for having gained this victory without a battle, in having induced such a mighty force to lay down their arms, and thus secured peace throughout the country. This peace, however, was not as complete as it was thought; for the earl was at this time cherishing more far-reaching plans than ever before. It appears that he had made a levy of troops and taxes outside of his own fiefs, and had been reprimanded for this in a letter from King Haakon. After having made peace with the Ribbungs, he immediately sailed for Denmark, it being no doubt his intention to renounce his allegiance to King Haakon, and, with the aid of the Danish king, take possession of the country and hold it in fief from him. Upon arriving in Copenhagen he learned that King Valdemar (the Victorious) had been taken prisoner by Count Henry of Schwerin and brought to Mecklenburg. Earl Skule, therefore, was obliged to return and continue to feign friendship for King Haakon. At a state meeting in Bergen in the fall of 1223, where the archbishop, the bishops, and other leading men of the country were present, Haakon's right to the throne was reaffirmed, and Earl Skule agreed to take the northern third of the country in fief instead of the southern part, which he had held before.

By the agreement at the state meeting in Bergen, Norway was divided into two domains, of which that of the king included Viken, the Uplands, and the Gulathingslag, except Söndmöre, while that of the earl included everything north of the king's domain, and this division remained in force for over fifteen years. The earl made his headquarters in Nidaros, while the king took up his residence in Oslo. Sigurd Ribbung remained with the earl, who had promised to watch him, but escaped during the summer of 1224, and again organized a band of rebels who resumed their old guerilla warfare. Whenever they were met by a superior force, they would make their escape across the frontier into the Swedish province of Vermeland, where they had many adherents. At last King Haakon found it necessary to invade Vermeland with an army of 2,400 men, early in 1225, in order to punish the inhabitants. He burned a great number of houses, but did not succeed in meeting the Ribbungs in any decisive battle.

In April, King Haakon proceeded to Bergen, in order to celebrate his marriage with Earl Skule's daughter, Margreta. The earl received him apparently with great cordiality, and grand preparations were made for the wedding, which took place May 25, 1225. This marriage had been dictated by political considerations; but Earl Skule derived no direct benefits from it, for during all the later struggles Margreta stood faithfully by her husband, in spite of the fact that the principal opponent was her own father.

The Ribbungs continued their guerilla warfare, secretly aided by Bishop Nicholas. The latter died in Oslo, November 7, 1225, after having asked and obtained the king's forgiveness for all his treachery. He was between seventy and eighty years old at the time of his death. During the winter Earl Skule and the archbishop at Nidaros attempted to negotiate peace between the Ribbungs and the king, but without any success. In the spring of 1226 Sigurd Ribbung was taken sick and died, and Squire Knut, the son of Haakon Galen and Christina, was induced to become the chief of the Ribbungs. The Ribbungs suffered several reverses, and in the following year Squire Knut disbanded his army and submitted to King Haakon, whose devoted friend he ever remained.

Earl Skule continued his intriguing for the ultimate overthrow of the king, and, while strengthening himself at home, negotiated with the king of Denmark for aid from that quarter. Meanwhile King Haakon did everything to retain the earl's allegiance. In 1233 a meeting was held in Bergen, where a new compact was made, only to be broken shortly afterward by the earl. When the king discovered that the earl had tried to involve him in a conflict with the Church, and had sent damaging reports about him to Rome, he again summoned him to a meeting in Bergen. This time Earl Skule did not see fit to come to the meeting, but proceeded with an army across the mountains to the Uplands, thus entering the reserved territory of the king. Through the mediation of the archbishop peace was patched up for the coming winter, on the condition that the earl was to have one-third of all the prefectures. The following year a new agreement was made, by which Skule was to retain the privileges thus obtained in the southern part of the country, besides which he was raised to the rank of duke, a title which no one so far had held in Norway.

Nothing, however, seemed to satisfy Skule short of the dignity of king. He prepared himself in every way for an open conflict—built and equipped ships, and steadily increased his force of warriors. His followers were called the "Varbelgs," the same name that a rebellious party during the reign of King Sverre had carried. In November, 1239, Duke Skule convened the Oere-Thing, where he had his friends proclaim him king of Norway, whereupon he made the usual oath of fidelity to the laws, with his hand upon Saint Olaf's shrine, which had been forcibly taken from the cathedral and carried to the Thing.

There was now open war between Duke Skule and King Haakon. The duke proceeded south to the Uplands with an army of six hundred men. At Laaka, Raumarike, he met and defeated the king's forces under Squire

Knut, who had been appointed earl in Skule's place. After this victory he proceeded to Oslo, but here he was soon afterward attacked by King Haakon and was badly defeated. A great many of the Varbelgs fell in the battle, while others surrendered to the king and were pardoned. Duke Skule with a few men escaped and fled north to Nidaros. Shortly afterward the town was suddenly attacked by the Birchlegs, who, after the battle of Oslo, had been sent north by King Haakon with a fleet under the command of Aasulf of Austraat, one of Skule's bitter enemies. Duke Skule, awoke by the alarm, armed himself and sent his messengers around in the town to call the Varbelgs together; but they would not obey orders, and his men took refuge in the churches. Skule himself crossed the Nid River and hid himself with a few men in a forest near by. Two days later the monks at Elgeseter Cloister sent them cloaks, and thus disguised they reached the cloister. The Birchlegs, however, discovered the duke's whereabout, and, proceeding to the cloister, demanded that he be delivered up. This being refused they set fire to the building. Skule then came out with his men, and they were all slain, May 24, 1240.

After the fall of Skule the rebellion of the Varbelgs died out completely, the power of King Haakon was undisputed, and the country could at last enjoy peace and order. On Saint Olaf's Day, July 29, 1247, King Haakon was crowned with grand ceremonies in Christ Church in Bergen by Cardinal William of Sabina, whom the Pope had sent north for that purpose. At the grand feast that followed there were so many people present that there was not room enough in the king's mansion, and the king therefore had a huge boat-house temporarily fitted out as a festival hall, the walls being covered with colored cloth, and the hall furnished with costly benches with gold-embroidered silk cushions. This feast lasted for three days, and after that the king gave a party, lasting five days, in the royal home for the cardinal and the most prominent men. When the cardinal departed from Norway, the king sent with him 15,000 marks sterling as a gift to the Pope, and also gave the cardinal personally fine presents.

The reign of King Haakon, after peace had been restored, was very beneficial to the country. He improved the laws, and, among other changes, abolished the ordeal of fire. This was done after consultation with the visiting cardinal, who declared that it was not proper for Christians to challenge God to give his verdict in human affairs. It was decided that at the death of a king the oldest legitimate son was to succeed to the throne, and the kingdom was not to be divided between two or more princes. In architecture great progress was made, and a great deal of money was spent for the erection of monasteries, churches and royal mansions. A wall was built around the royal mansion in Bergen; this wall was the beginning of the fort afterward called Bergenhus. King Haakon also built the grand royal hall in Bergen and a hospital for lepers. In Tunsberg he built a monastery, and the strong wall of the fort is still to be seen. He began to Christianize the Finns and built churches for them. The church which he built at Tromsœ was the northernmost Christian church in the world.

King Haakon gained a high reputation in foreign countries. The Russian grand-duke, Vasilij, asked for the hand of his daughter Christina, and the Spanish king, Alfonso X. of Castile, wooed her for one of his brothers. The latter suit was accepted, and Christina was married to the Spanish prince, Don Philip, in 1257. The pope wanted Haakon for emperor of Germany, and the French king, Louis IX., urged him to take the command of a crusade.

During the reign of King Haakon, in 1261, Greenland was made a dependency of Norway, and the next year Iceland acknowledged the supremacy of Norway. The Icelanders agreed to pay the king of Norway a tribute; but they were to retain their own laws and their own officers.

In the summer of 1263 King Haakon sailed with a strong fleet and a large army westward to make war on Alexander III. of Scotland, who had tried to annex the Norwegian possessions west and north of Scotland. King Haakon proceeded to the Sudr Islands (the Hebrides), where he met with terrible storms, during which his fleet suffered considerable loss. In a battle at Largs, near the entrance to the Firth of Clyde, some of Haakon's best men fell. Scotch and Norwegian accounts differ as to which side was really defeated; but even from Scotch sources it appears that there was for some time afterward a great dread of the reappearance of "the black fleet of Norway." A contemporary Scotch poet and soothsayer, Thomas of Erceldoune, wrote:

It will be seen upon a day
Between the Bass and Bay,
Craigin and Fidderay,
The black fleet of Norroway.
Quhen the black fleet is come and gane,
Then may they bigg thair burgh of lime and stane
Quhilk they biggit of straw and hay—
That will stand till doomes day.

Shortly after the battle at Largs, King Haakon retired to the Orkneys, intending to winter there and to renew the attack in the spring. In the town of Kirkevaag (Orkneys) he was taken seriously ill; dying December 15, 1263. During his illness he had his men read aloud to him portions of the Bible and several books in Latin. Afterward he had Norwegian books read to him, first the stories of holy men (legends) and afterward the sagas of his ancestors, from Halfdan the Black down to his grandfather, King Sverre. During the reading of Sverre's saga he sank rapidly, and toward midnight, when King Sverre's saga was finished, he expired.

King Haakon was fifty-nine years old when he died. He had been king of Norway forty-six years. His body was temporarily entombed in Kirkevaag, and, in the following spring, was brought back to Norway and buried in the Christ Church in Bergen.

CHAPTER XXXI

Snorre Sturlason

DURING the reign of Haakon Haakonson lived the renowned author of sagas, Snorre Sturlason. He was born in the year 1178 at Hvam (or Kvam), in the western province of Iceland. His family traced their lineage from the old Norse kings. In his third year Snorre was sent to the rich and learned Jon Loftson to be fostered. Jon Loftson's grandfather was Saemund Frode, the contemporary of Are, who first committed the historical sagas to writing; Jon's mother, Thora, was an illegitimate daughter of King Magnus Barefoot. In such a family, says Mr. Laing, we may presume the literature of the country would be cultivated, and the sagas of the historical events in Norway, and of the transactions of her race of kings, would be studied with great interest. Jon Loftson died when Snorre was nineteen years of age, but he continued to live with his foster-brothers a couple of years after that. He was quite poor, his mother having wasted his patrimony; but marrying Herdis, the daughter of a wealthy priest, he obtained with her a considerable fortune, which he afterward greatly increased. We are told that he owned six large farms and had so many men under him that he could appear at the Things with an armed body of six hundred or eight hundred men. He fortified his main residence at Reykholt, and also constructed there a bathing-house of cut stone, into which the water was led from a neighboring geyser. This bath-house was called Snorrelaug (Snorre's bath), and ruins of it are still to be seen.

Snorre Sturlason held some important offices in Iceland. On a visit to Norway he won the friendship of Duke Skule and King Haakon, and the latter even appointed him a king's chamberlain. He is said to have promised the king to induce the people of Iceland to submit to the supremacy of the king of Norway; but if this promise was given he seems to have forgotten it. When afterward, during the conflict between Duke Skule and King Haakon, Snorre was said to be a friend or adherent of Duke Skule, the king declared him to be a traitor, and, in a letter, requested Snorre's son-in-law and bitterest enemy, Gissur Torvaldson, to bring Snorre to Norway, dead or alive. On this authority Gissur, and other relatives of Snorre, who were his enemies on account of differences about the division of property, came on the night of September 22, 1241, with seventy armed men to Snorre's residence at Reykholt and murdered him in the sixty-third year of his age. It was the same party which, two years afterward, brought Iceland under subjection to the crown of Norway.

Snorre Sturlason's famous work, the sagas (chronicles) of the kings of Norway, reaches from the earliest times to the fall of Eystein Meyla, in the battle at Ree, in 1177. The book is also called the "Heimskringla"—the world's circle—from the first word of the manuscript. It is written in the old Norse language. Snorre also wrote a book called the "Edda,"[13] which treats of the old Norse mythology and contains rules for the writing of poetry.

Snorre's nephew (his brother's son), Sturla Thordson, afterward wrote the saga of King Haakon Haakonson.

During the reign of King Haakon, another remarkable book was written, "The King's Mirror." In the form of a dialogue between a father and his son, it contains information about the seas and the countries that Norway had communication with, especially Ireland, Iceland and Greenland. It also gives the rules of life and conduct for traders and for men at the royal court.

CHAPTER XXXII

Magnus Law-Mender (1263-1280)

HAAKON'S son Magnus now became king of Norway. He had been crowned six years before his father's death, and there was no one to dispute his right, King Haakon having declared on his death-bed that he left no other son. Magnus was twenty-five years old when he assumed the government in his own name. He was a wise and peaceable ruler, and soon made up his mind that it was not for the benefit of Norway to continue the war with Scotland about the islands which were so distant and had been of so little value to the country. He opened negotiations with Alexander III., and on July 2, 1266, peace was finally concluded. The Norwegian king ceded the Isle of Man and the Hebrides to Scotland, although retaining the rights belonging to the Nidaros archbishopric. On the other hand, the Scotch king agreed to pay the Norwegian king 4,000 marks sterling, besides a permanent annual tribute of one hundred marks.

When King Magnus had succeeded in ending the conflict with Scotland, he turned his whole attention to the improvement of the domestic affairs of the country. He undertook a thorough revision of the laws, and, on account of his efforts in this direction, was given the surname *lagaböter*, *i.e.*, law-mender. He had a common code of laws compiled for the whole country, while formerly there had been four different laws administered respectively at the four Things; viz., the Frosta-Thing for the Throndhjem country, the Gula-Thing for the western coast, the Eidsiva-Thing for the Uplands, and the Borgar-Thing for the country around Viken. The new general law, as codified by King Magnus, remained in force for nearly four hundred years, and some of it is law even yet. Among the new provisions was the one that, in the future, changes in the laws were to be made only by the king and his "good men" at a state meeting or state council. Thus the Things were deprived of the privilege to make laws.

Magnus also compiled a law for the cities and towns, and a new court law (*Hirdskraa*) for his vassals and courtiers. This court law prescribed rules for the proclamation of kings and described the duties and rights of the courtiers, liegemen, etc. Among new offices created were those of ensign (bearer of the colors), the chancellor, who kept the royal seal, and the master of ceremonies.

Toward the bishops King Magnus was very submissive. At a meeting in Tunsberg, in 1277, he made a number of humiliating concessions to the ambitious Archbishop Jon the Red. Thus the king agreed to abstain from all interference in the selection of bishops, and surrendered to the latter the right of filling all clerical offices.

King Magnus granted the city of Lubeck and other North-German cities—the Hanseatic League—a number of commercial privileges in Norway, and from that time a great part of the commerce of Norway gradually came to be controlled by the Hansa towns.

In his legislation, King Magnus showed a disposition to abandon former democratic characteristics of the institutions. He was fond of pomp and ceremony, and adopted foreign, especially English, court customs. In 1277 he ordained that the liegemen were to be called barons, and the court officials, knights and squires. They were given a partial immunity from taxes, but were to render additional services to the king in case of war. The knights and their families soon began to adopt coats-of-arms, and a kind of nobility was gradually formed.

King Magnus died May 9, 1280, at the age of forty-two years.

CHAPTER XXXIII

Erik Priest-Hater (1280-1299)

AT the death of King Magnus only two of his children were alive, Erik, who had already been proclaimed king, and Haakon, who had been made duke at the same time. Erik was twelve, and Haakon ten years old. The royal counsellors, among whom were the barons Hallkell Agmundson, Audun Hugleikson, and Biarne Erlingson of Biarkoe and Giske, thought that King Magnus had made too great concessions to the church and attempted to curtail the power of the bishops. On account of their activity against the clergy they were put in the ban of the church; but they did not seem to pay much attention to this; and, as a result of the struggle, Archbishop Jon the Red and two other bishops were outlawed and compelled to leave the country (1282).

The epithet "Priest-Hater," which, after this, was given King Erik, does not seem to have been well deserved; for he always sought to mediate in the conflicts with the archbishop, and he himself had no ill-feeling toward the bishops, but rather seemed to be too kindly disposed toward them.

King Erik was only a very young man when he commenced a war with Denmark, which lasted for twenty years, and was not terminated until in the time of his successor. His mother, the queen-dowager Ingeborg, was the daughter of the Danish king, Erik Plowpenny, and as her inheritance, consisting of landed estates, had not been turned over to the Norwegian king according to agreement, she induced her son to make war on Denmark. The war was principally a naval war. One who especially distinguished himself was the Norwegian baron, Alf Erlingson of Tornberg (now Tanberg, Ringerike), a great favorite of the queen-dowager. He captured a number of the enemy's ships, and preyed upon the commerce in Danish waters. But the principal sufferers by this warfare were the Hanseatic League, whose members, by the concessions of King Magnus Lawmender, had practically a monopoly of the foreign trade of Norway. Many ditties were composed about Alf Erlingson, and one verse reads thus:

Sailing Germans are northward bound
Carrying malt and meal;
But Alf is lying in Oere Sound
And robs them of all their weal.

The conflict with the Hanseatic towns came to an end, through the arbitration of the Swedish king, by the peace of Kalmar (1285), by which the privileges of the Hansa towns were considerably extended.

The hostilities with Denmark were continued, and the queen-dowager was so well pleased with Alf Erlingson's piratical conduct of the war that she had him created an earl, and induced the king to send him as special ambassador to England. In 1286 a conspiracy was formed in Denmark against King Erik Glipping, and he was murdered during a hunting trip by Marshal Stig, Count Jacob of Halland and others. The murderers, who were outlawed in Denmark, were well received by the Norwegian king, and afterward accompanied him on his campaigns against Denmark.

By the death of Queen Ingeborg (1287), Earl Alf Erlingson lost his special protector, and when he had committed extraordinary outrages in Viken and murdered the commander of Oslo Castle, Baron Hallkell Agmundson, he was sentenced as an outlaw and compelled to flee to Sweden, where, for some time, he took refuge in a cloister. Later he attempted piracy on his own account in Danish waters, but was captured, and, by the command of Queen Agnes, executed on the rack (1290).

King Erik made several successful cruises to Denmark, and that country might have fared badly if his attention had not been drawn in other directions. At an early age he had been married to Margaret of Scotland, a daughter of his grandfather's enemy, King Alexander III. This young queen died a year after the marriage, after having given birth to a daughter, who was christened Margaret. When Alexander III. died in 1286, without leaving any sons, the Scotch leaders acknowledged King Erik's young daughter, Margaret, as the rightful heir to the throne. In 1290 she was proclaimed queen of Scotland, and the young princess—the "Maid from Norway," as she was called—accompanied by the bishops of Bergen and other prominent persons, sailed for Scotland. She was taken sick on the voyage, however, and died at the Orkneys. King Erik afterward claimed the crown of Scotland as the heir of his daughter, but was compelled to abandon the claim upon the armed intervention of King Edward I. of England.

King Erik died July 13, 1299, at the age of thirty-one years.

CHAPTER XXXIV

Haakon V. Magnusson (1299-1319)

AT the death of King Erik the throne of Norway was inherited by his brother Haakon, who had, during his brother's reign, under the title of duke, ruled his part of the country with royal authority. Shortly after his succession to the throne, the knight, Audun Hugleikson Hestakorn of Hegranes, who during the reign of King Erik had been highly esteemed and had conducted negotiations with foreign powers, was imprisoned in Bergen and tried for high treason, and, after three years of imprisonment, was executed. The real nature of this man's crime is not known. By some it was thought that he had insulted the king's bride; but the actual crime was probably some frauds in connection with the negotiation of a treaty with France. Apparently without any reason, rumor has connected his case with another affair, which transpired about the same time. In 1300 a woman arrived from Lubeck and created a great deal of excitement by claiming to be the Princess Margaret—"The Maid from Norway"—who had died at the Orkneys when on her journey to Scotland to assume the Scotch throne. She was proven to be an impostor, and was condemned and burned at the stake in 1301, and her husband, who accompanied her, was beheaded.

During Haakon's reign the war with Denmark, which had lasted for twenty-eight years, was finally ended by the Peace of Copenhagen (1309), by which Haakon obtained the province of Northern Halland in settlement of his maternal inheritance. His rule was also in other respects firm and prudent. He curtailed some of the privileges of the Hansa towns and reduced the power of the bishops. He abolished the positions of earls and liegemen, and adopted stricter regulations for other officers, holding them to a faithful compliance with the laws. He built the fortress of Akershus, near Oslo, where he resided much of the time.

King Haakon had no sons, but only a daughter, Ingeborg. In 1302 he therefore proclaimed a new law of succession extending the right of inheritance to the female line. By the same law a council of twelve men were to conduct the government during the minority of an heir to the throne. The king's daughter, Ingeborg, was afterward married to Duke Erik of Sweden, and, in the year 1316, she bore a son, who was christened Magnus. This caused great joy in Norway, and the king on this occasion conferred knighthood on twenty-five men. But the joy was of short duration. Duke Erik and his brother, Duke Valdemar, had been quarrelling with their brother, King Birger of Sweden. The latter pretended to desire a reconciliation and invited them to a feast at the castle of Nyköping. During the night the sleeping-room of the dukes was entered, and they were thrown into prison, where soon afterward they died. Rumor said that they were starved to death. The tidings of this tragedy so affected King Haakon that it hastened his death. He died at Tunsberg, May 8, 1319, and with him the male line of the royal house of Harald the Fairhaired became extinct.

CHAPTER XXXV

Magnus Erikson "Smek" (1319-1374)—Haakon VI. Magnusson (1355-1380)

MAGNUS, the son of King Haakon V.'s daughter Ingeborg and Duke Erik of Sweden, was only three years old at the death of his mother's father. While he was in his minority the affairs of the government were managed by a regency, the members of which had been selected by King Haakon. In Sweden King Birger, who had become generally hated on account of his treatment of his brothers, was deposed, and Magnus was proclaimed king of Sweden. Thus, for the first time, Norway and Sweden were united under one king. Both countries retained their own government and laws, and the king was to divide his time equally between the two countries. The Norwegians soon became dissatisfied with the government, which was conducted mainly by the king's mother, Duchess Ingeborg, who caused great scandal by her recklessness and wasted much of the revenue on her lover, Knut Porse, duke of Halland, whom she afterward married. At a general Thing, in Oslo, February 20, 1323, the regency was abrogated, and the knight Erling Vidkunson of Biarkoe and Giske was appointed regent.

When King Magnus, who, by the Swedes, was surnamed "Smek" (the fondling), reached his majority, in 1332, he himself assumed the government in both countries. He was a good and kind man, but too weak to govern two countries. Sweden took up most of his time, and he did not come to Norway as often as he was expected to, and made no proper arrangement for the government during his absence. This caused general discontent, and a virtual separation of the countries was finally arranged. At a great meeting in Varberg, August 15, 1343, King Magnus's oldest son, Erik, was declared heir-apparent and co-regent in Sweden, and his other son, Haakon, in Norway. On the same day the Norwegian state counsellors acknowledged Haakon, who had been educated in Norway, as their king, with the understanding that King Magnus was to conduct the government until his son became of age. The separation of the countries was further confirmed in 1350 in Bergen, where King Magnus placed Haakon in the royal seat and arranged a separate court for him. According to public documents, however, Haakon's reign dates only from 1355, when probably he had reached his majority.

The Swedes were no more satisfied with King Magnus than the Norwegians were. He succeeded in annexing the provinces of Scania, Halland and Blekinge, which he bought for 34,000 marks silver from Duke

John of Holstein, who held them as a pledge; but the taxes he had to levy, in order to raise this sum, caused great dissatisfaction.

The king's recklessness and the great influence wielded by his vain and malicious queen, Blanca of Namur, and his favorite, the young Swedish knight, Bengt Algotson, increased the dissatisfaction to such a degree that Prince Erik took up arms and declared Bengt to be a public enemy. Erik died shortly afterward, but quiet was not restored. King Magnus's ambiguous and pusillanimous action in allowing the wily King Valdemar Atterdag of Denmark to seize the dearly-bought provinces of Scania, Halland and Blekinge, created great discontent, which was increased when his son, Haakon, married King Valdemar's eleven year old daughter Margaret, although the Swedes, who expected Haakon to become their future king, had decided upon another bride for him. When, after an uprising, King Magnus banished forty of the most turbulent magnates, the latter offered the crown to Albrecht of Mecklenburg, a nephew of King Magnus, and returned with him to Sweden, where Magnus was deposed and Albrecht elected king of Sweden (1363). Haakon, who shortly before that had been elected king of Sweden, did not intend to give up the kingdom without a fight, especially as he had several fortresses and provinces in his possession. Both sides armed themselves, and a battle was fought at Enköping, March 3, 1365. Magnus was taken prisoner and brought to Stockholm, and Haakon, severely wounded, had to flee to Norway. The war was continued with varying success until the Hanseatic League interfered in the struggle, because Haakon had attempted to expel the Germans from the country. The German merchants had obtained great power in the country and shamefully abused it; they refused to receive the king's coin, monopolized all trade, and defied the laws. Haakon finally made peace with them, but only after granting them some new privileges. After that he collected a great army and invaded Sweden; even marching against Stockholm. An agreement was reached in 1371 with King Albrecht, by which Haakon was to pay 12,000 marks and surrender the Swedish fortresses for the liberation of his father. The latter had to give up all claim to the Swedish throne, but was to have for his support Skara Stift, West Gautland and Vermeland. Haakon afterward inherited these provinces. Magnus was drowned three years later in the Hardanger Fjord at the age of fifty-eight years. His son survived him only six years. He died at Oslo in June, 1380, about forty-two years old, after having had the pleasure to see his only son Olaf chosen king of Denmark.

Great calamities befell the country during the reigns of Magnus and Haakon. On April 4, 1328, the great cathedral in Throndhjem, the Christ Church, was destroyed by fire. In 1344 the Gaula River suddenly changed its course, owing to a mountain slide, flooded the Gaula Valley, and caused great destruction. Forty-eight farms and some churches were destroyed, and two hundred and fifty people and a great number of cattle were drowned. Iceland suffered from earthquakes, and in 1341 the sixth eruption of the volcano Hekla spread alarm and desolation. In 1323 and 1346 the winters were so severe that a great number of people froze to death. But the greatest calamity occurred in 1349, when the Black Death, a terrible pestilence, after having ravaged Southern Europe, was brought to Bergen by a merchant vessel from England. Before the cargo of the vessel had been discharged, the whole crew died, and immediately the pestilence spread with great rapidity over the whole country. In a single day ninety persons were buried from a church in Bergen, including fourteen priests and six deacons. In Throndhjem, Archbishop Arne and the whole chapter, with the exception of a single canon, died. Only one bishop in Norway, Salemon in Oslo, survived the plague. In many districts the entire population was swept away. The cattle died from hunger. For want of horses and laborers the farmers were unable to cultivate their farms, and famine and distress resulted. Many districts which had been fertile and populous were laid waste, and were in time covered by a new growth of forests. Industries, trade and commerce stagnated, and Norway sank into a state of debility from which it took her centuries to recover.

CHAPTER XXXVI

Olaf Haakonson the Young (1381-1387)

OLAF, the only son of King Haakon Magnusson and the Danish Margaret, was, at the death of his maternal grandfather, Valdemar Atterdag (1376), proclaimed king of Denmark under the guardianship of his parents, and at the death of his father four years later, when he was ten years old, he inherited the throne of Norway. His mother proceeded to Oslo, where a meeting of the Norwegian chiefs was held early in January, 1381. Here it was arranged that Queen Margaret was to be the guardian of her son and conduct the government in his name, when she was in the country, but in her absence the administration should be conducted by the chieftain Ogmund Finnson, as leader of the state council. Olaf was crowned in Nidaros on Saint Olaf's Day, July 29, 1381. Thus commenced the union between Norway and Denmark, which lasted for over four hundred years and proved so unfortunate for Norway. To the great sorrow of the Norwegians, King Olaf, when scarcely seventeen years old, was taken suddenly sick at Falsterbro Castle, Scania, and died August 3, 1387.

Fifteen years after Olaf's death an adventurer appeared who claimed to be King Olaf, and the rumor soon spread that Olaf had escaped from his mother shortly before the time of his alleged death. It was proven, however, that the pretender was a German, and that some merchants, who had noticed the great likeness he bore to Olaf, had induced him to make the claim. The impostor was condemned to death and burned.

CHAPTER XXXVII

Margaret (1387-1389)—Erik of Pomerania (1389-1442)—The Kalmar Union (1397)

AS young Olaf left no offspring, it was quite generally supposed in Norway that the kingdom would be given to his nearest relative, Haakon Jonson, a grandson of King Haakon V.'s illegitimate daughter Agneta; but the wily Queen Margaret (who had already been acknowledged as reigning queen of Denmark), induced Archbishop Vinald and the majority of the clergy to take her part, and, at the state council in Oslo, February 2, 1388, she was, as Haakon's widow and Olaf's mother, declared to be the rightful ruler of Norway and its dependencies. According to law, however, the Norwegians were to be ruled by a king, and could not long be satisfied with having the government conducted in the name of a woman. She therefore induced the council to choose her grandnephew, Erik of Pomerania, as king of Norway (1389), she to continue the regency during his minority.

King Albrecht of Mecklenburg, who was at this time reigning in Sweden, had caused a great deal of discontent among the Swedish nobility, because he had surrounded himself with Germans, whom he had given places of influence and honor. The ambitious Queen Margaret, who hated Albrecht deeply, because he had laid claim to the Danish throne, made overtures to the Swedish magnates, with the result that they chose her as "the mistress and rightful ruler of Sweden," and transferred several fortified places to her, while she promised to reunite West Gautland and Vermeland with Sweden. Albrecht proceeded to Germany to collect an army, and swore that he would not put his hood on before he had conquered Norway and Denmark. He sent Margaret several insulting messages, called her "Queen Breechless," and sent her a whetstone on which to sharpen her scissors and needles, saying that the good woman ought to remain quietly at her spinning wheel. The queen's chiefs, Ivar Lykke and Henrik Parow, invaded Sweden with an army, and won a battle at Falköping in West Gautland. Albrecht was taken prisoner and was brought before the queen, who reminded him of his insults. She gave him a long fool's-cap to wear instead of the crown of Denmark, and sent him to prison in the castle of Lindholm in Scania, where he remained six years.

Queen Margaret soon won the whole of Sweden except Stockholm, where the German merchants and the hood-brothers made a determined resistance. They received aid from the North German cities Rostock and Wismar, whose rulers proclaimed that any one who would harry the coasts of the Scandinavian countries could find refuge in their harbors; and the result was a number of pirates, the so-called Victualia-Brethren, made the northern waters unsafe for several years, and plundered many of the coast towns. Thus they twice attacked and plundered Bergen. In order to gain his liberty, Albrecht, in 1395, made an agreement that within three years he would either pay 60,000 marks silver or release Stockholm. He could not pay the money, and Stockholm's gates were opened to Queen Margaret.

In 1397 Queen Margaret's sixteen-year-old grandnephew, Erik of Pomerania, was crowned in Kalmar as king of Sweden, Denmark and Norway, in the presence of prominent men from the three countries. A document was drafted containing the provisions regarding the triple union, and it was signed on Margaret's Day, July 20, 1397. It could scarcely be considered binding upon the three countries, as it was signed by only seventeen of the gentlemen present, and they had not been given power to act for their countrymen. The main stipulations of the agreement were the following:

1. The three countries were always hereafter to have the same king.

2. One king was to be elected by authorized delegates from the three countries.

3. The countries were to help each other against foreign foes.

4. Each country was to be governed by its own laws.

Queen Margaret died at Flensborg, October 27, 1412, aged fifty-nine years, leaving the government in the weak hands of King Erik.

In the union Denmark soon assumed the position of the chief country. In Sweden and Norway the people complained that the revenues of the countries went to pay the expenses of the war with the Counts of Holstein about Schleswig, although this war, which lasted for twenty-six years, concerned only Denmark. The counts received aid from the Hansa towns, which hated King Erik, because he encouraged the Dutch trade with the northern countries. In 1427 he defeated the Hanseatic fleet in Oere Sound, and in 1428, when they tried to attack Copenhagen, the city was saved by his brave queen, Philippa of England. She armed the citizens and the peasants, and the Germans were obliged to withdraw. The final outcome of the war was, however, that King Erik had to cede Schleswig to Count Adolph of Holstein by the peace at Vordingborg (1435).

Norway had occasion to feel the effects of King Erik's weakness. The inhabitants of Finmark and Halogaland were attacked by Russians and other enemies from the northeast, who did great damage and abducted men and women, and the town of Bergen was left defenceless against the attacks of the daring Victualia-Brethren. Thus in 1428 the pirate from Wismar,

Bartholomew Vot, came to Bergen with six hundred men, just as the English traders were waiting there for the vessels from Northern Norway to bring herring, stock-fish and other goods. The Englishmen, believing that the whole fighting force of the Hansa towns was coming, hastened aboard their ships and took flight. The bishop of Bergen, who was seized with a similar fear, left everything behind for the enemy and fled with the Englishmen. The robbers then went ashore and plundered the town. At the bishopric they forced the iron doors to the book-room and took away all the books, besides many other valuables. As the traders from the north arrived with their full cargoes, the booty of the pirates became so much larger, as they took possession of their fish, furs and other goods. This success encouraged the robbers to renew their attack on Bergen next year, when they again plundered the bishopric, and then laid a great part of the town in ashes.

In all three countries the people were dissatisfied with King Erik; he coined bad money, levied new taxes, and appointed foreigners, especially Germans, to the chief offices. In Sweden the first uprising started. The peasants in Dalarne twice sent the gallant Engelbrekt Engelbrektsson to Denmark to complain of the cruel prefects, but he could obtain no redress. On his return he placed himself at the head of a rebellion, which spread itself to the whole country. Engelbrekt was murdered (1435); but in his place Carl Knutsson Bonde became the leader of the rebellion and regent.

In Norway the people followed the example of the Swedes. The peasants in Viken revolted under Amund Sigurdson Bolt, captured Oslo, and drove some of the Danish and other foreign officers out of the country. In a proclamation issued, after this uprising, by the Norwegian Council of State, calling upon the people to be loyal to King Erik (1436), the council promised to request the king in the future not to appoint foreigners to the high offices unless they had married into Norwegian families.

In Denmark also the people complained of the heavy taxes and the many Germans who were imported and given high positions. Wearied of all these complaints, and taking with him his mistress, Cecilia, the money left in the treasury, and a number of important documents, King Erik left the country and took up his residence on the island of Gotland, where he had a fortified castle (1438). Shortly after this he was formally deposed in Denmark and in Sweden, while in Norway they still, for a time, remained loyal to him. As regent in Norway, during his absence, the king appointed the influential Norwegian, Sigurd Jonson. The latter descended from a powerful old family; he had inherited Biarkoe, Giske and other estates, and was the richest man in the country. For ten years King Erik lived in his castle in Gottland, supporting himself by piracy, but was finally driven away by the Swedes. He returned to his native country, Pomerania, where he ended his long but inglorious life in 1459.

CHAPTER XXXVIII

Christopher of Bavaria (1442-1448)

ACCORDING to the provisions of the Kalmar Union, a new king was to be elected by the authorized delegates of the three countries; but, instead of that, the Danish Council of State summoned Erik's nephew (sister's son), Christopher of Bavaria, who was first elected regent and shortly afterward (1440) proclaimed king. In Sweden, Carl Knutsson Bonde endeavored to prevent a renewal of the Union; but, with the aid of the clergy, the rights of Christopher were acknowledged, and he was proclaimed king of Sweden at Morasten, September 14, 1441. In Norway, King Erik had many adherents, and his favorite, Bishop Thorleif, did all in his power to retain Erik, or his cousin, Bugislav, as king; but when it appeared that neither of them was coming to assert his claim, the Norwegians finally also acknowledged Christopher, and he was hailed as king of Norway, in Oslo, in 1442. He had thus succeeded in reuniting the three countries, although he was crowned separately in each of them.

Christopher was a good-natured and jolly man, who wished everybody well. In Sweden, there was naturally objection to the piracy committed by his uncle from the island of Gottland; but when the Swedes complained of this to the king, he answered merrily: "Our uncle is sitting on a rock, and he, too, must have something to live off."

In Norway, the administration of public affairs was fairly good. There were no complaints against the king, and the country's own people had their share in the government. The king made an effort to restrict the Hanseatic League, which, together with the "Victualia-Brethren," caused so much damage to Norway. For this purpose he tried to give them commercial rivals by giving the citizens of Amsterdam trading privileges in Norway. In 1444 he gave the town of Bergen new privileges and announced several restrictions of the privileges of the Hansa towns. The power and influence of the latter was shown by the fact that this ordinance was repealed the next year, and the king was obliged to confirm their old and "just" privileges. King Christopher, however, did not abandon his purpose; but, just as he was about to bring new plans into execution, death overtook him, January 6, 1448, when he was about thirty-two years old.

CHAPTER XXXIX

The Union with Denmark—Christian I. (1450-1481)

AFTER the death of King Christopher, the Swedes elected Carl Knutsson Bonde king of Sweden, while the Danes elected Count Christian of Oldenborg, at the age of twenty-two, because he was heir to Schleswig and Holstein, and it was generally desired to have Schleswig reunited with Denmark. In the Norwegian Council of State there was dissension. The regent, Sigurd Jonson, the commander at Bergen, Olaf Nilsson, and the commander at Akershus, Hartvig Krumedike, who was from the duchy of Holstein, wanted to elect the Danish king, Christian, who was remotely related to the old Norse kings, while another more popular party, led by the Archbishop, Aslak Bolt, preferred the Swedish king, Carl Knutsson. The council finally elected Christian, at Oslo, in the spring of 1449; but, after his return to Nidaros, the archbishop declared the election void, not having been voluntary, and joined the people of the Throndhjem country and the Uplands in inviting King Carl to come to Norway. With a mounted force of five hundred men, King Carl proceeded through Vermeland and Solver to Hamar, where he was proclaimed king of Norway, October 25, 1449, and a month later he was crowned in Throndhjem by the archbishop. Early in 1450, however, when King Carl attempted to capture Oslo, he was defeated, and an armistice was arranged. The archbishop died shortly afterward, and, at a meeting in Halmstad, in May, 1450, between Swedish and Danish magnates, the Swedish delegates, in the name of King Carl, relinquished all claims to Norway. Thus, when Christian came to Norway in the summer, he was acknowledged by everybody, and was crowned in Throndhjem on Saint Olaf's day, July 29, 1450. He then went to Bergen, where, on the 29th of August, 1450, a closer union between Norway and Denmark was concluded. The main provisions of the agreement were: 1. That both countries were hereafter to be united in brotherly love, neither country being the superior of the other; 2. That each country should be governed by native-born officials, and enjoy their own laws, liberties and privileges; 3. That both countries should henceforth remain under one lord and king forever; 4. When the king died the councils of both kingdoms were to meet at Halmstad and elect a new king from among the late king's legitimate heirs.

Thus the house of Oldenborg acquired the throne of Norway and continued to rule the country for three hundred and sixty-four years.

For several years there was war between Kings Carl and Christian, and in this war Norway was also involved. In 1452 King Carl invaded Norway with an army and captured Throndhjem; but he was afterward driven back across the frontier by the commander in Bergen, Sir Olaf Nilsson.

The German merchants (Hansa, Hanseatic League), who, after the war under King Erik, had returned to Bergen, had become more powerful and insolent than ever before. They drove the citizens of the town away from the wharves and continually increased their own number by importations. The commander, Olaf Nilsson, was very severe with the Germans, and made them pay heavy taxes. They complained to the king, and, as he feared that the Hansa might aid his enemy, King Carl, he removed Olaf. The latter now set out as a pirate against the Hansa towns, and captured several of their ships at sea. He also succeeded in capturing the Swedish fort, Elfsborg, at the mouth of the Gaut River, and offered it to the king if he were reinstated as commander at Bergen. This offer was accepted, and Olaf returned to Bergen. Enraged at this, the Germans armed themselves to the number of over 2,000, intent upon killing the commander. Olaf sought refuge in the cloister of Munkeliv, where his friend, Bishop Thorleif, tried in vain to appease the Germans. They burned the cloister, killed the bishop—who came out carrying the Sacrament—and three other priests, besides Olaf Nilsson and his brother, with families and children; in all, sixty people. This was the 1st of September, 1455. The king, who needed the help of the Hansa towns, neither would nor could punish this great crime. But the Pope placed the murderers in the ban of the church, and compelled them to pay heavy fines for the murder of the bishop and to rebuild the cloister.

Internal dissensions in Sweden, involving a struggle between the king, the bishops and the nobility, resulted in the expulsion of Carl and the acceptance of Christian as the king of Sweden. Thus the three countries again became united under one king (1457), and the next year the state councils promised that, after the death of Christian, his son Hans was to be king of all three countries. But King Christian made himself hated by his oppression, and when he caused the imprisonment of the powerful archbishop, Jens Bengtson Oxenstierna, the latter's nephew, Ketil Carlsson Wasa, bishop of Linköping, swore that he would not put on his bishop's robes until his country had been rid of its oppressor, and he kept his word. Carl was recalled, and died, as king of Sweden, in 1470, after several unsuccessful attempts by Christian to regain the Swedish crown. In 1471 Christian was defeated in battle at Brunkeberg (now a part of Stockholm) by King Carl's nephew, Sten Sture, whom the Swedes had elected regent. After that King Christian made no further attempts to recover Sweden.

King Christian was a reckless spendthrift, and was always financially embarrassed. The annual tribute for the Hebrides, which Scotland was to pay to the king of Norway according to the peace made with King Magnus the Law-Mender, had not been paid for some time, and King Christian in vain demanded payment. In order to settle the matter peaceably it was arranged that Christian's daughter Margaret was to marry the Scotch king, James III., and her dowry was fixed at 60,000 gulden. As Christian could not raise this amount, he obtained the consent of the Norwegian Council of State to pawn the Orkneys for 50,000 gulden, besides remitting the tribute for the Hebrides. Not being able to pay the balance, he also, without consent, pawned the Shetland Isles. Thus these ancient dependencies were lost to Norway, for they were never redeemed, although each new king solemnly promised to do so.

King Christian died May 21, 1481, at the age of fifty-five years, and lies buried at the Cathedral of Roskilde.

CHAPTER XL
Hans (1483-1513)

CHRISTIAN'S eldest son, Hans, or Johannes, had already as a child been proclaimed as his father's successor in all three countries, but after the death of Christian neither the Norwegians nor the Swedes showed any great disposition to renew the union. The Norwegian Council of State entered into a league with the Swedish regent, Sten Sture, at Oslo, February 1, 1482, where it was agreed that hereafter Norway and Sweden were to act together and mutually support each other for the maintenance of their liberties, rights and welfare. But as Sten Sture hesitated in openly declaring himself against Denmark, the Norwegians again turned to that country and agreed to a joint election of a king at Halmstad (January 13, 1483), where King Hans succeeded in inducing Archbishop Gaute and the other delegates to acknowledge him as king of Norway, after having promised to redress all wrongs and otherwise comply with the wishes of the people. He was crowned in Throndhjem, July 20, 1483.

The king's chief efforts were now directed toward effecting the submission of Sweden. The authorized delegates of the three countries assembled at Kalmar, where the union was renewed, and the Kalmar Recess was published (November, 1483); but through the influence of Sten Sture the acknowledgment of King Hans was postponed from year to year. Finally, in 1497, Hans invaded Sweden with a strong army, defeated Sten Sture, and was proclaimed king of Sweden. Thus Hans had become ruler of the three countries, and his son Christian was proclaimed his successor. This power, however, was not of long duration. In the western part of Holland there lived a people called the Ditmarshers, whom the emperor had transferred to King Christian, although they had always formerly been a free people. King Hans wished to subdue them, and, in the year 1500, he and his younger brother, Duke Frederick of Schleswig-Holstein, invaded the country with a large army. They suffered a terrible defeat, however, as the inhabitants opened the dikes and called in the ocean as their ally. The king and his brother escaped with a loss of 4,000 slain or drowned, while enormous treasures were lost. No sooner did the news of this disaster reach Sweden than the Swedes took up arms. Sten Sture was again made regent, and King Hans's own queen was made a prisoner in Stockholm.

At the same time the Norwegians also revolted. The most powerful man in Norway at that time was Sir Knut Alfson, owner of Giske and many other estates. He had long been commander at Akershus; but had had a quarrel with Henrik Krummedike, the commander at Bahus, and the king, suspecting him of being friendly to the Swedes, had removed him. Now that the Swedes had revolted, Sir Knut joined them and defeated the Danes, after which he invaded Norway and captured the fortresses Akershus and Tunsberghus. Henrik Krummedike proceeded with a strong army to Oslo, in order to besiege Akershus. Negotiations were opened for peace, and Henrik invited Sir Knut to a conference on board his ship under safe conduct, but, on his arrival, foully murdered him and threw his body into the water. The struggle of the discontented Norwegians was continued under the leadership of Knut Alfson's widow, the brave Lady Mette Dyre; but when the Danes received reinforcements from Denmark the rebellion was soon suppressed, and Lady Mette was obliged to flee to Sweden. Knut Alfson's large estates were confiscated to the crown.

The attempt to subdue the Swedes was not so successful, although some strong attacks were made. The able regent, Sten Sture, died in 1503, but his successor, Svante Nilsson Sture, who married Knut Alfson's widow, defended his country's independence with courage and ability. He died in 1512, and was succeeded by Sten Sture the Younger.

In the year 1506 King Hans sent his son Christian to Norway to rule the country in his name. Christian tried to rule as an autocratic king, and to place Norway entirely under Danish rule. He installed Danes as commanders of the fortresses, and also had Danes elected bishops. His faithful servant and chancellor, Erik Valkendorf, was made archbishop in Throndhjem. He understood that it was detrimental to the country that the Hansa towns had a monopoly of the trade, and therefore tried to restrict their privileges and to encourage the competition by the merchants from Holland, and took many steps to help the Norwegian towns. But in dealing with revolts he was very severe. An uprising by the peasants of Hedemarken, under the leadership of Herlog Hudfat, was promptly crushed, and the leaders were beheaded outside of Akershus. Some of the captured peasants were tortured until they confessed that Bishop Carl of Hamar was the real instigator of the rebellion. The bishop was captured and held in prison until his death, and Christian took possession of his estate.

The Hansa towns were greatly enraged against Christian; but they hated King Hans even more, because he interfered with their trade with Sweden and encouraged the Dutch traders. It finally came to open war, and the traders of Lubeck attacked and plundered the Danish islands. King Hans, however, returned the attack with a strong fleet, defeated the Lubeckers, and compelled them to make peace and to pay 30,000 gulden in war indemnity. This was the first time that a Scandinavian king had dared to go to war with the powerful Hansa towns.

King Hans died at Aalborg, February 20, 1513, fifty-eight years old.

CHAPTER XLI

Christian II. (1513-1523)

AFTER the death of King Hans, his only son, the cruel Christian, mounted the throne; but the Council of State and the nobility, well knowing that he would be a less compliant monarch than his father, sought to secure their alleged rights by a new charter, which he was compelled to sign before he was crowned.

During his stay in Norway as viceroy, Christian had become acquainted with a Dutch girl in Bergen, the beautiful Dyveke. They first met at a ball, which he gave for the most prominent citizens in Bergen, and where they fell in love with each other. He afterward brought the girl and her wily mother, Sigbrit Willums, with him to Oslo and later to Copenhagen, where Sigbrit continued to wield a great influence during the whole of Christian's reign. Two years after his accession to the throne, Christian married the wealthiest princess of Europe, Isabella, a sister of Charles V., who afterward became emperor of Germany and king of Spain. The wedding was celebrated with great pomp at Copenhagen. The young queen brought him a dower of 250,000 gulden, and she was as good and lovely as she was rich. Archbishop Erik Valkendorf had brought the bride to the country, and had promised Charles V. to see that Dyveke was kept out of the way. Sigbrit Willums heard of this, and henceforth was the archbishop's bitter enemy. Neither did the king listen to the archbishop's advice. Dyveke retained the favor of the king until, a year and a half later, she suddenly died, and the king's passionate love for her now led him to a cruel and unjust act. The governor of the castle in Copenhagen, Torben Ox, had also fallen in love with Dyveke, and, as she died shortly after having eaten some cherries, it was rumored that the cherries had been poisoned, and that Torben Ox had caused her death. The king summoned Torben before the Council of State, which acquitted him. The king became enraged when he heard the decision, and said: "If we had had as many friends in the council as Torben had, the judgment would have been different; but even if this ox has a neck as thick as that of a bull, he shall yet lose it." Although, according to law, a nobleman could only be tried by the Council of State, the king summoned twelve peasants to retry the case. They found him guilty, and although the counsellors and the nobility, the queen and the court ladies, all begged for mercy, the king was unmoved, and Torben Ox was executed.

The crown of Sweden was the great object of King Christian's ambition; but it took years before he reached this goal. The Swedish regent,

Sten Sture the Younger, was very popular and had undisputed power, until he was antagonized by the newly-elected archbishop at Upsala, Gustaf Trolle, who, with many members of the old nobility, became jealous of the power enjoyed by the Sture family and preferred to support King Christian. Sten Sture defeated Gustaf Trolle, who was deprived of his see and compelled to flee from his castle. Afterward Sten Sture was placed in the ban of the church, and the archbishop received aid from Denmark. King Christian made several expeditions to Sweden, and finally his general, Otto Krumpen, defeated Sten Sture's army in a battle on the ice at Bogesund, where Sten Sture was mortally wounded (February, 1520). Sture's widow, the courageous Christina Gyldenstierna, tried to hold the party together, and, for a few months, defended Stockholm; but finally had to surrender the city. The Swedes now acknowledged Christian as hereditary king, and, on the 4th of November, 1520, he was crowned by Gustaf Trolle in the Grand Church in Stockholm. After the coronation great festivities were held for three days. On the fourth day a number of the Swedish nobles were summoned to meet at the palace. While the king was surrounded by his court, the representatives of Gustaf Trolle stepped forward and demanded reparation for the wrongs committed against the archbishop. Christian, who wished to subdue the Swedish nobles, availed himself of the opportunity and followed the bad advice given him. The document by which Gustaf Trolle had been deposed was produced, and all who had signed it were arrested on the spot. The following day, November 8, 1520, the accused were brought before a court consisting of eleven Swedish priests and one Danish bishop. The only question asked was whether men who had raised their hands against the Pope and the Holy Church were heretics. The members of the court answering in the affirmative, the accused were declared to be heretics, and the king fixed the punishment at death. The condemned were at once conveyed to the great market-place, where two bishops, thirteen Counsellors of State and knights, and many other prominent men, in all about fifty, were beheaded. This was the notorious Carnage of Stockholm.

After having left the conduct of the fight in Sweden in the hands of his able admiral, Soefren Norby, King Christian now returned to Denmark, where, during the next two years, he introduced several excellent laws for the improvement of commerce, industry and culture. But he also tried to establish himself as an autocratic king. He abolished several of the privileges of the nobility and the bishops, and planned the gradual extinction of the Council of State, by not appointing any successors to members who died.

The Swedes did not long endure the rule of King Christian and the insolence of his officers. The people of the province of Dalarne (Dalecarlia) rose under the leadership of Gustavus Eriksson Wasa, a young nobleman whose father was among those beheaded in the Carnage of Stockholm. They successfully fought the Danes and captured one town after another, and elected Gustavus Wasa regent of Sweden. King Christian prohibited all trade by the Hansa towns with Sweden, and let his men capture their ships; thus he incensed the people of Lubeck, who declared war against him and helped the Swedes. King Christian then levied a new tax to cover the war expenses and summoned a meeting of nobles. But now the nobles of Jutland rose against him and offered to proclaim his uncle, Duke Frederick, king. Frederick accepted the offer, and the nobles sent Christian a letter revoking their allegiance to him. An inexplicable faint-heartedness now seized Christian, and, instead of summoning his many faithful adherents to his support, he commenced to negotiate with his enemies, and when that proved of no avail, he embarked, April 20, 1523, with his queen, his children, Lady Sigbrit and others, and sailed to Holland in order to seek the aid of his powerful brother-in-law, Emperor Charles V. Duke Frederick was now proclaimed king, but he had to divide the power with the Council of State and sign a charter which gave the nobility many improper privileges. Shortly afterward the Swedes elected Gustavus Wasa king, and thus ended the union of the three countries. Both kings were obliged to restore to the Hansa towns all trading privileges, in order to be assured that they would not help King Christian to return.

CHAPTER XLII

Frederick I. (1524-1533)

NORWAY had taken no part in the expulsion of King Christian, and for a time remained loyal to him. The newly-elected archbishop, Olaf Engelbrektson, proceeded to Rome in order to obtain the recognition of the Pope. During his absence Norway was to be governed by the Council of State, which consisted of the bishops and a few noblemen. The mightiest among the latter was Nils Henrikson of Oestraat, whose wife, Inger Ottesdatter, was related to the old Norwegian royal house. This ambitious woman, commonly called Lady Inger of Oestraat, took quite a prominent part in public affairs, three of her daughters being married to prominent Danes.

King Frederick soon gained a number of influential adherents in Norway. He sent to Bergen the Danish nobleman, Vincentz Lunge, who married one of the daughters of Nils Henrikson and Inger of Oestraat. After the death of Nils, Vincentz became a member of the Council of State and commander at the fortress of Bergenhus. He used his influence in favor of King Frederick; but he wanted the Council of State to be as powerful in Norway as the Danish council was in Denmark. He was supported by Archbishop Olaf, and the Council of State finally elected Frederick king of Norway; but the king had to grant the council, and especially Vincentz Lunge, great authority. The king issued a "Recess," by which he pledged himself: 1. In the future not to sign himself heir to Norway, as the country was a free elective kingdom; 2. To redeem the Orkneys and the Shetland Isles, which his father had illegally pawned; 3. That the coronation was hereafter to take place in Throndhjem. The king did not care so much about keeping these promises as about filling the most important offices with Danish noblemen, who conducted public affairs to suit themselves. Among those who were specially favored were: Mogens Gyldenstierne, who became commandant at Akershus; Eske Bilde, who was placed in command at Bergenhus, relinquished by Vincentz Lunge in consideration of having the nunnery at Bergen (afterward called Lungegaarden) deeded to him; Vincentz's brother-in-law, Nils Lykke, and Henrik Krummedike, notorious from the slaying of Knut Alfson.

King Frederick was an adherent of the doctrines of Luther, which had now been commonly accepted in Northern Germany, and from thence were introduced into Denmark. He compelled the Danish bishops to acknowledge him as the head of the Church instead of the Pope, and took possession of a number of cloisters, which he either kept for himself or gave to the nobles. In Norway, too, he gave away some of the cloisters, which, of course, caused great dissatisfaction among the clergy. The discontent in Norway took a very definite form, when, contrary to the Recess, the king sent his son Christian to Norway to be proclaimed heir to the throne. Archbishop Olaf Engelbrektson and a majority of the Council of State then declared that this could not be done, inasmuch as Norway was an elective kingdom; and here the king was obliged to let the matter rest. Meanwhile, the exiled King Christian, encouraged by messages from Norway and Sweden, thought he saw a chance to regain his lost throne. With the aid of Charles V., and some private parties, he gathered an army and a fleet in Holland, and sailed for Norway in October, 1531, with twenty-five ships and 7,000 men. On the way he suffered by great storms and lost ten of his ships, but landed in Norway with the remnants of his fleet. He gained a large number of adherents, and, proceeding to Oslo, laid siege to the fortress of Akershus. Mogens Gyldenstierne, however, defended it well, and when, in the spring (1532), reinforcements arrived, in the form of a strong army of Danes and Lubeckers, Christian made an agreement with Mogens, by which he was to proceed, under a safe conduct, to Copenhagen, in order to personally conduct peace negotiations with his uncle. Upon his arrival in Denmark, however, the agreement was shamefully broken, and the unfortunate king was thrown into prison at Sonderborg. He was placed in a cell having a small barred window high up; the entrance was closed with masonry, and the food was sent in through a hole in the wall. Here he remained for eighteen years. In 1550 he was transferred, by Frederick's successor, to a milder prison in Kallundborg Castle, where he remained until he died, in the beginning of 1559, seventy-eight years old.

The Norwegians were severely punished for their alliance with Christian. The chieftains of the Danish party, Bishop Olaf in Bergen and the Danish noblemen, Eske Bilde, Vincentz Lunge and Nils Lykke, held a meeting in Bergen shortly after Christian's defeat and levied a heavy tax on the whole country. The archbishop was fined 15,000 Danish marks. The Norwegians were compelled to relinquish any right, through the Council of State, to elect any other king than the one elected for Denmark.

Shortly after Frederick had been again recognized by the Norwegians as their king, he died, without being missed, at the age of sixty-two years, April 10, 1533. During his reign the Lutheran faith was preached throughout Denmark, but only in a few towns in Norway; for instance, in Bergen.

CHAPTER XLIII

Interregnum (1533-1537)

AT the death of Frederick I. an interregnum occurred, as the Danish estates were unable to agree upon the election of a new king. The nobles favored the late king's oldest son, Duke Christian, but he being devoted to Protestantism, the clergy wanted his younger brother, Hans, who was only a child, and whom they hoped to win for the Catholic faith. The bourgeoisie and the peasants desired to have the imprisoned Christian II. reinstated. Under the pretext that a new king could not be elected without the presence of the Norwegian Council of State, the clergy succeeded in having the election postponed to a joint meeting of the councils of both countries, to be held the following year. In the meantime, the so-called "Count's Feud" broke out. The Lubeckers, who were dissatisfied on account of the trading privileges granted to the Dutch, sent an army to Denmark, under command of Christopher of Oldenborg, who desired to recover the Danish throne for his cousin, the captive king, Christian II. The count discovered the lower estates to be such bitter enemies of the nobility, and ardent adherents of the captive king, that he found no great difficulty in taking possession of the Danish Isles and Scania. The Council of State, or a part of it, now hastened to elect Frederick's son, Duke Christian, king (July 4, 1534). An alliance was formed with the Swedish king, Gustavus Wasa, against the Lubeckers, and the fortunes of war soon turned in favor of the new king. His brave general, Johan Rantzau, defeated the enemy at Aalborg, crossed over to Fyn, and won a complete victory over the count at Oexneberg, while Gustavus Wasa helped the king's party to retake Scania. After the capture of Copenhagen, July 29, 1536, King Christian III. was recognized by the whole of Denmark.

While the Count's Feud was going on in Denmark, there was also strife and disorder in Norway. Both parties had tried to win the support of the powerful archbishop in Throndhjem, Olaf Engelbrektson, and through him the control of Norway; but, while for several reasons he could not recognize Christian III., he was for a time uncertain whom to support. It was decided to hold a meeting in Throndhjem at Christmas, 1535, for the purpose of electing a king; but the followers of Vincentz Lunge and Eske Bilde in the southern and western parts of the country held a meeting at Oslo, shortly before Whitsuntide, 1535, where they proclaimed Christian III. king of Norway. A special embassy from the queen-regent of Holland visited Archbishop Olaf, and, in the name of Emperor Charles V., promised him powerful support if he would persevere in his old loyalty to the captive king, Christian II.; and when the agents of Christian III. arrived in Throndhjem, about Christmas time, there was an uprising of the people, said to be instigated by the archbishop, and many of the Danish magnates were imprisoned and otherwise maltreated. Two of them, the counsellors Vincentz Lunge and Nils Lykke—who were not only public opponents, but personal enemies, of the archbishop—were murdered.

The archbishop now adopted a vigorous policy, and tried to get possession of the fortresses of Bergenhus and Akershus, but his armies were defeated. When the adversity of Christian II.'s party in Denmark further convinced the archbishop that the cause was hopeless, he released the imprisoned agents and requested them to mediate with the king, offering allegiance to Christian III. on condition that he be allowed to retain his rank and property. The king, however, did not accept the offer, but, in the spring of 1537, sent a fleet of fourteen ships and 1,500 men, under the command of Truit Ulfstand and Christopher Hvitfeld, to Throndhjem. Foreseeing the destruction of his party, Archbishop Olaf Engelbrektson gathered the treasures of the cathedral and fled to Holland, where this last champion of Norwegian independence died the following year.

CHAPTER XLIV

Christian III. (1537-1559)—The Reformation Introduced

AT the great Diet, held in Copenhagen, in 1536, it was decided that the Catholic faith should be abolished, the property of the bishops and the cloisters was confiscated to the crown, and the Lutheran faith was introduced into Denmark. A new ecclesiastical law was adopted, called the Ordinance. The king also promised the rapacious nobility of Denmark that henceforth Norway was to be, and remain, under the crown of Denmark as any other part of the country, and not to be called a separate kingdom, but a province of the Danish crown. The Norwegian Council of State was abolished, the Catholic bishops were removed, and Danish noblemen were installed at the fortresses to rule the country in the king's name. From this time the Danish Council of State exerted great influence in the government of Norway; but, in spite of all this, Norway remained a separate state; it retained its old laws, and the chancellor was still to be the supreme judge.

After the flight of the archbishop, and the submission of Norway, the Danish Church Ordinance was also made to apply to Norway; but the new faith was little known there, and the Norwegians long clung to the old faith. When the bishops had been removed, Danish magnates were sent around in the country to take possession of "the silver, treasures and goods of the old idolatry." In performing this function the Danish magnates showed especial reformatory zeal. Thus, in Bergen, the church robber, Eske Bilde, spared neither churches nor the graves of the departed kings, while in Throndhjem Otto Stigson burned the library and archives of the cathedral chapter, and Thord Roed committed havoc in the same manner in Stavanger. Saint Olaf's costly shrine—which stood on the high altar in the cathedral of Throndhjem, and was ornamented with precious stones—as well as many other treasures of the church, were sent to Copenhagen. Lutheran superintendents or bishops were installed in place of the Catholic bishops; but the government could not at once remove all the Catholic priests, because there were not Lutheran ministers enough to put in their places, and, when Lutheran ministers were appointed, they were generally treated with ill-will, and sometimes even driven away or killed. The majority of the Lutheran ministers were Danes, and Danish became the language of the Church. The ablest of the new Lutheran bishops was Geble Pederson in Bergen, who showed great zeal in educating Lutheran ministers. Theological seminaries were established at each of the episcopal sees of Throndhjem, Bergen, Stavanger and Oslo. The bishopric of Hamar was consolidated with that of Oslo.

The Hansa towns, in making peace with Christian III. after the Count's Feud, had succeeded in retaining their trading privileges in Norway, and, during the greater part of this reign, acted in their old insolent and oppressive manner. In Bergen they made themselves especially obnoxious, so that the people complained bitterly to the king. He finally appointed, as commander in Bergen, the able Danish nobleman, Christopher Walkendorf, who commenced to put limits to the arbitrary and violent conduct of the Germans, and subdued them in such a way that they never regained their old power. After this the Norwegian citizens of Bergen gradually asserted themselves, and soon had the control of the whole fishery trade with the northern districts.

Christian III. died on the 1st of January, 1559, at the age of fifty-five years. Although he reigned for twenty-three years, he never visited Norway as king.

CHAPTER XLV

Frederick II. (1559-1588)

CHRISTIAN III. was succeeded by his oldest son, Frederick II., who was then twenty-five years old. This vain and worthless monarch commenced his reign with a successful war on the liberty-loving Ditmarshers. Later he waged war on the Swedish king, Erik XIV. The causes of this disastrous war, the so-called Northern Seven Years' War (1563-1570), were apparently trivial. Both kings wanted to carry the three crowns in their coats-of-arms, and some Swedish messengers, who were on their way to Germany, had been arrested in Denmark; but the real reasons were the jealousy between the two kings and the desire of the Danes to again unite the three countries under a Danish king. At sea the Danes were unsuccessful, although they had very able admirals in Herluf Trolle and Otto Rud. On land they fared no better in the beginning; but, in 1565, the hero, Daniel Rantzau, won a great victory over a much larger army than his own in the battle of Svarteraa in Halland.

Norway, whose defences had been sadly neglected, suffered greatly, during this war, from Swedish incursions. A Swedish army of 4,000 men, under the command of the Frenchman, Claude Collart, conquered Jemteland and Herjedalen and crossed the mountains to Throndhjem. The fortress Stenviksholm was forced to surrender, and the people of Throndhjem and the surrounding districts submitted without resistance and paid homage to the Swedish king. Later, however, Claude Collart was defeated by a fleet sent against him by the governor at Bergenhus, the rich and highly-esteemed Erik Rosenkrands. Claude Collart took refuge in the fortress Stenviksholm; but here he was besieged, and was finally obliged to surrender. He was sent in irons to Copenhagen. Especially hard for the Norwegians was the year 1567, when the Swedes harried Hedemarken, Romerike and Soloer, and captured Hamar. The cathedral of Hamar was burned, and the Swedes marched against Akershus, which was bravely defended by the commander, Kristen Munk. The citizens of Oslo burned their town in order to prevent the Swedes from obtaining a foothold there. On this occasion the Swedes lay encamped on the mountain side above the town, on a plain afterward called the "Swedish plain." The Norwegians were hard pressed; but Erik Rosenkrands again sent assistance from Bergen, and the Swedes were obliged to leave the country with considerable loss. The incursions of the Swedes were, however, repeated from time to time, and, during one of them, the town of Sarpsborg was burned, January, 1570. Finally, in December, 1570, peace was concluded at Stettin, and the terms were, on the whole, favorable to Denmark. In return for relinquishing her claims to Sweden, which could never have been established, she secured an acknowledgment of her rights to Norway, Scania, Halland and Blekinge, while Sweden returned the Norwegian provinces of Herjedalen and Jemteland, and paid 150,000 Rigsdalers for war expenses. Both countries retained the right to carry the "three crowns" in their coats-of-arms.

The Seven Years' War was not the only cause of suffering in Norway during the reign of Frederick II. From 1572 Norway was given its own *Statholder* or viceroy, always a Danish nobleman, who was to reside at Akershus, the fortress near Oslo. But the viceroy did not not have the power, if indeed he desired it, to prevent the prefects and other officers from subjecting the people to cruelties and extortions. They arbitrarily levied taxes, conducted illegal trading, and treated the peasants in a shameful manner. For ten years Erik Munk continued his violent rule in Nedenes. At last, on complaint of the people, he was sentenced to return illegal taxes and indemnify a peasant, whose property he had taken. Later he was deprived of his office and placed in a prison, where he committed suicide. Ludvig Munk, prefect in Throndhjem, even became viceroy, although his conduct as prefect had been such as to cause a conspiracy, which cost the instigators their lives.

The city of Fredericksstad, which was built to replace the ancient Sarpsborg, was named after King Frederick.

During his reign of twenty-nine years, Frederick II. was only once in Norway on a short visit, and knew little of the distress of the country. He amused himself at the palace of Copenhagen, where he led a dissolute life, shortened by drink. He died, April 4, 1588, at the age of fifty-four years.

CHAPTER XLVI

Christian IV. (1588-1648)

FREDERICK II. was succeeded by his son, Christian IV., a king who became very popular with the Norwegians. Christian was only eleven years of age at his father's death. According to the desire of the late king, his widow, Sophia of Mecklenburg, was to act as regent during Christian's minority, but the powerful Council of State refused to confirm such regency, and appointed four members of their own body, Chancellor Niels Kaas, Admiral Peder Munk, and the Counsellors Jorgen Rosenkrands and Christopher Walkendorf, as regents and guardians of the prince. Christian was given an excellent education by competent teachers. He early showed great love for the sea, and Admiral Munk caused a little frigate to be built expressly for him, and had it launched in a lake in Jutland, where he was taught by expert sailors how to navigate his ship.

When he was nineteen years old, Christian assumed the government in his own name, and was crowned, with great ceremony, in Copenhagen, 1596. None of the other Danish kings have been so zealous for the welfare of Norway. He frequently visited the country, and once even (1599) sailed along the northernmost coast into the White Sea, as he wished to acquaint himself with the circumstances of the northern boundary conflict with Sweden. On his return voyage he came to Bergen, where he witnessed a trial in court, visited the German wharf and watched the games of the Germans. He attended a jolly party at the apothecary's, where the guests smashed the windows; the king's crowned monogram was painted on the new panes. He also visited the peasants and drank toasts with them, according to their custom. King Christian listened to the complaints from Norway of the extortions of the Danish prefects, who, one after another, were deposed from office or compelled to pay heavy fines. He made the Norwegian-born nobleman, Hans Pederson Basse (or Little), Chancellor of Norway.

The old Norwegian laws, which were written in the old Norse language, and therefore now hard to understand, were abolished, and, in their stead, the king directed the learned chancellor, Hans Pederson Basse, with the assistance of other experienced men, to elaborate a new code of laws. Hans Pederson died (November, 1602) before this work was completed, but his assistant and successor as Chancellor of Norway, Anders Green, continued it, and the new laws were published in 1604. A Norwegian ecclesiastical law (Ordinance) was also given, because the Danish one was not suited for Norway.

Christian IV. had three wars during his long reign, two with Sweden and one with the Catholics in Germany.

The first Swedish war (1611-1613) was fought principally for Norway's sake. The Swedish king, Charles IX., called himself, at his coronation, King of the Lapps, and laid claim to the Norwegian province of Finmark. There was also a renewal of a conflict about "the three crowns" in the coats-of-arms. Christian made a successful attack, destroyed the newly-founded town of Gothenburg, and captured Elfsborg and the town and fortress of Kalmar; hence this war is called the Kalmar War. During the war, the old king, Charles IX., died, and was succeeded by his son, the great Gustavus Adolphus. The war was largely conducted with foreign mercenaries, as it was not yet usual to have standing armies. Gustavus Adolphus had secured two such hired armies, which were to try to proceed across Norway in order to reach Sweden, as the Kattegat was closed with Danish ships. Colonel Munchaven landed with eight hundred men from Holland in Söndmöre, where he plundered the country, then tried in vain to attack Throndhjem, and afterward proceeded through Stjördalen, where the people had become so frightened, on account of his depredations, that they did not dare to offer any resistance. Ravaging and plundering he made his way across the mountain ridge Kjölen into the province of Jemteland, which he conquered before joining the army in Sweden. The second foreign army was given a different reception. It consisted of nine hundred men, who came from Scotland under the command of Colonel George Sinclair. They landed at Veblungsnes in Romsdal and proceeded up to Gudbrandsdal. Under the leadership of Bailiff Lauritz Gram, the brave peasants of the Gudbrandsdal armed themselves as best they could. The peasants from the parishes of Lesje, Vaage, Fron, and Ringebu, gathered at the narrow mountain pass, Kringen, near the river Laugen, to await the arrival of the enemy. The advance guard was allowed to pass; but on the arrival of the main body, with Colonel Sinclair himself, the Norwegians suddenly attacked the Scotchmen, who were all shot down or driven into the river. The advance guard was then overtaken and killed. Of the whole force of nine hundred men, not one man, it is said, escaped. At Kvam's Church a grave is still pointed out as being that of Colonel Sinclair, and at Kringen there is a plain stone monument bearing this inscription: "Here Colonel George Sinclair was shot, August 26, 1612." After the Scotchmen the Norwegians call this war the "Scotch War."

Peace was finally concluded at Knaeröd, January 26, 1613. Gustavus Adolphus abandoned his claim to the Norwegian Finmark, and Christian relinquished the captured fortresses upon being paid a million Rigsdalers. Both countries were again allowed to use the three crowns in their coats-of-arms.

In his second war Christian IV. was not successful. This was his participation in the Thirty Years' War as the ally of the German Protestants against Emperor Ferdinand II. and the Catholics (1625-1629). After his defeat in the battle of Lutter am Barenberge, the imperial armies, under Tilly and Wallenstein, overran Holstein, Schleswig, and Jutland, and, at the Peace of Lubeck, Christian was obliged to pledge himself not to take any further part in the war.

King Christian's third war was with Sweden. The Swedish king, Gustavus Adolphus, had been fighting for the cause of the Protestants in Germany, and, after his fall in 1632, the Swedes continued the war under his able generals with much success. King Christian viewed with alarm the growing power of the Swedes, and secretly allied himself with the enemies of Sweden. The Swedes, however, anticipated his designs, and, in December, 1643, the Swedish general, Torstensson, left the scene of war in Bohemia and suddenly invaded Holstein, while another Swedish army attacked the province of Scania; a Swedish and a Dutch fleet were to convey these armies over to the Danish isles. The duchies and Jutland were in a very short time conquered by the Swedes, and it was only by Christian's wise and prompt proceedings that Funen and the other islands were saved from falling into the hands of the enemy. Although King Christian was then an old man of sixty-seven years, he took command of his fleet, won a battle at Listerdyk, and fought valiantly in the terrible naval battle of Kolbergheide, Femern, July 1, 1644, where he himself was badly wounded. On account of a lack of vigilance on the part of the old Danish admiral Galt, the Swedish fleet succeeded in escaping and uniting with the Dutch, and this combined fleet, of sixty-four ships, thereupon attacked the Danish one of seventeen ships, between Lolland and Falster. Unfortunately, a number of the sailors were ashore, and some of the commanders took to hasty flight. The remainder gathered around their admiral, the Norwegian, Pros Nilson Mund, who would neither flee nor surrender, but fought to the last man against the overwhelming force of the enemy. This defeat placed Denmark in such a dangerous position that an immediate peace became an absolute necessity. The peace was concluded at Bromsebro, August 13, 1645, and King Christian was compelled to cede the Norwegian provinces of Herjedalen and Jemteland, and the island of Gottland to Sweden.

In Norway, where the king had lately established a standing army, this war had been conducted with some success. It was named the Hannibal's Feud, after the viceroy, Hannibal Sehested, who, with the assistance of the brave warrior, the clergyman in Ullensaker, Kield Stub, not only kept the enemy out of Norway, but also collected heavy tributes from the nearest Swedish provinces. After peace had been concluded, Kield Stub returned to his pastorate, which he managed to his death, in 1663.

Christian IV. did a great deal to promote the industries and commerce of Norway. The Hanseatic office in Bergen was held in check, and Norwegian trading enterprises were encouraged. The mining industry, which had heretofore been neglected, became quite active. When silver had been discovered in Sandsvaer, in 1623, he founded the mining-town of Kongsberg. He also established the copper-works at Röros, where copper was accidentally discovered by the peasant, Hans Aasen, in 1640. Oslo having been destroyed by fire, King Christian requested the inhabitants to move across the bay, closer to the fortress of Akershus, where he laid out the new town, the present capital of Christiania (1624). At the mouth of the Otter River he founded the town of Christianssand (1643), which afterward became the seat of the bishop instead of Stavanger.

King Christian was very often in Norway. The last time was during the year following the Peace of Bromsebro. After a pleasant sojourn of seven weeks he returned to Denmark, where, shortly afterward, he died (February 28, 1648), in the seventy-first year of his life.

Christian IV. was first married to Anna Katherina of Brandenburg, who died in 1612. In 1615 he entered into a morganatic marriage with Kristine Munk, a lady of noble family, to whom he gave the title of Countess of Schleswig-Holstein, and with whom he lived happily many years. They had several children, among whom was the highly gifted Eleonora Kristine, who was married to the Danish nobleman, Corfitz Ulfeld, and who, with her ambitious husband, exerted a great influence over the king during the latter years of his life.

CHAPTER XLVII

Frederick III. (1648-1670)—Absolutism Introduced (1660)

AFTER the death of Christian IV. some months elapsed before the Council of State would agree to elect his son, Frederick III., to the throne. He was finally elected toward the end of the year 1648, after having given the nobility still greater power, by signing a more humiliating charter than any king had yet granted; but it also became the last one. The conditions were such that he could not exercise any of the powers of a king without the consent of the council.

During the first nine years of Frederick's reign the country had peace; but the war which then broke out was most fatal in its result. The Swedish king, Charles X. Gustavus, was at war with Poland, and rumor had it that he had suffered serious defeats. Although the country highly needed peace, the army and navy, as well as the finances, being in a miserable condition, King Frederick believed there was an opportunity to recover the lost provinces, and war against Sweden was declared, 1657. But King Charles hastily left Poland and invaded Denmark, and, before the year was closed, he had conquered Holstein, Schleswig and Jutland. The winter being unusually severe, he could march across the ice to the islands of Langeland, Lolland, and Falster, and, in February, he stood with his whole army in Zealand (Sjælland) and threatened Copenhagen. King Frederick was obliged to sign the peace at Roskilde (February 26, 1658), by which he ceded to Sweden the Norwegian provinces of Bahus-Len and Throndhjem Stift and the Danish provinces of Scania, Halland, Blekinge, and the island of Bornholm. Thus Norway was again deprived of some territory, although the Norwegians, under Iver Krabbe (after whom the war was called the Krabbe War), had repulsed the attacks of the Swedes, while General Jorgen Bjelke had conquered Jemteland, which, however, had to be evacuated when peace was concluded.

Having discovered the great weakness of Denmark, King Charles thought he saw a chance to place the three crowns on his head, and five months later he broke the peace, under some pretext, and again landed with a well-equipped army, with which he besieged Copenhagen. He captured the castle of Kronborg and other points of defence, and arrogantly declared, to the Danish messengers sent to him, that "it could matter little whether the king of the Danes was called Charles or Frederick, and that he would explain the causes of the war after Denmark had been taken." At Copenhagen, however, King Charles met a stronger resistance than he had expected. A Dutch fleet, under Admiral Opdam, succeeded in forcing its way past Kronborg and the Swedish fleet, and brought provisions and help to the starving citizens. When Charles, during the night of February 10, 1659, tried to take the city by assault, he was repulsed after a desperate conflict, leaving 2,000 dead and wounded in the hands of the Danes. Later in the year King Frederick succeeded in securing the assistance of France, England and Holland. After a conference held at the Hague, a Dutch fleet, under Admiral de Ruyter, was sent to aid the Danes, and in November, 1659, the Swedish army was defeated at Nyborg.

King Charles, after this defeat, turned his principal attention to Norway, where his forces needed reinforcements. The able Major-General Reichwein had proceeded to Throndhjem, shortly after the renewal of the war, with a force of soldiers from the southern part of Norway, and, with the aid of the inhabitants, had driven the Swedes out of Throndhjem Stift. In the south, the citizens of Halden (now Frederickshald) had especially distinguished themselves under the brave Colonel Tonne Hvitfeld, the commandant at the fortress, and the merchant, Peter Olafson Normand. Halden was twice visited by the Swedes, and both attacks were heroically repelled by the citizens. In the beginning of 1660 King Charles sent an army of 5,000 men, under Field-Marshal Kagg, against Halden, and a vigorous siege was commenced. For six weeks one assault after another was repulsed. About half of the able-bodied citizens had fallen, the town was partly destroyed, and the fortifications were badly damaged. But the Swedish army had also suffered great losses, and on February 23d the siege was discontinued and the army returned home, upon learning of the death of Charles X. at Gothenburg (February 13). The Swedes now desired peace, and King Frederick had no reason to wish to continue the war. He readily concluded a peace with the queen-regent of Sweden, which was signed at Copenhagen, May 27, 1660. The Swedes relinquished Throndhjem Stift and the island of Gottland; but otherwise the terms of the Peace of Roskilde were confirmed.

Denmark was in a miserable condition at the end of the war, without fleet, without money, and hopelessly in debt. In his great need the king summoned the nobles, the clergy, and the burgher class to a diet at Copenhagen. The nobles, as usual, asserted their special privilege of exemption from taxation; but the other estates joined in an appeal to the king for the curtailment of the privileges of the nobles, and proposed a disposal of the crown fiefs to the highest bidders without regard to rank. While these propositions were made, the gates of the city were closed by order of the burgomaster, Hans Nansen, and a strong guard was placed at the doors of the hall where the meeting was held. The nobles, being taken by surprise, were obliged to agree to the payment of the taxes demanded of them. Later, by similar means, the nobles were compelled to assent to an important change in the government. The charter signed by the king at the time of his election was declared void, the Council of State was abolished, and Denmark was declared henceforth to be a hereditary kingdom. Thus, by a bloodless and sudden revolution, King Frederick had become perfect master of the situation. He was authorized to draft a new constitution, which might be for the benefit of all classes; but this constitution never appeared. He prepared a charter setting forth the absolute power of the king, and this document was signed by all classes throughout Denmark. Later he published the so-called Royal Law, which confirmed the absolute power of the king. The only unconditional demands upon him were, that he must belong to the Lutheran Church, that he must reside within the country, and that he must not divide his countries.

The effect of the establishment of absolutism in Norway was at first only that the country was placed under one master, the king, instead of the many who had composed the Danish Council of State. Having, since 1537, been ruled principally by Danish nobles, the country gained by having absolutism introduced, as it was placed on an equal footing with Denmark. The king now ruled with the same absolute power in both countries, and the power of the Danish nobles was abolished or greatly reduced. They were obliged to take their share of the burden of taxation, and they suffered a great loss by the abolition of the fiefs. The fiefs were changed into *Amts*, or counties, to be administered by officers appointed and paid regular salaries by the king. The revenues of the state were increased almost fivefold. In the new government "colleges," which superseded the Council of State, citizens without rank of nobility might become members. Thus able citizens, who were not noblemen, obtained a chance to rise to power and dignity. Among those who thus rose to high positions were Peter Schumacher and Kort Adeler.

Kort Syvertson Adeler was born in Brevig, Norway, December 26, 1622, learned seamanship in Holland under the famous Admiral Tromp, and distinguished himself as a brave fighter, first in Dutch, and afterward in Venetian service, against the Turks, where he performed great heroic deeds. Once he forced his way, with a single ship, through a line of seventy-seven Turkish galleys, and another time he boarded the Turkish admiral's ship, fought single-handed with Admiral Ibrahim, and beheaded the admiral with his own sword. Several powers desired to get the experienced naval hero in their service; but Frederick III. called him home and made him admiral in the Danish navy. For twelve years he labored with great zeal in establishing an efficient navy for Denmark and Norway, but died in 1675 without having had a chance to make use of it.

Frederick III., who had not inherited his great father's affection for Norway, visited this country only once in great haste. He died February 9,

1670, about sixty years old. During his last years he busied himself a great deal with alchemy, and an itinerant Italian, who claimed to know the mystic art, helped him to squander a couple of millions of Danish dollars on this foolishness.

The fortress of Fredericksteen and the city of Frederickshald (formerly Halden) were named after Frederick III.

Frederick III. was married to the proud and ambitious Sophie Amalie of Hesse-Cassel, who, on account of her jealousy and hatred, caused the king's half-sister, Eleonore Kristine Ulfeld, to be tried on some false and absurd charges, and imprisoned in Blaataarn (the Blue Tower) in Copenhagen, where she remained for twenty-two years. She was liberated on the death of her enemy in 1685. King Frederick's and Sophie Amalie's children were, besides Crown Prince Christian, George, who was married to Queen Anna of England; Anne Sophie, who was married to John George III. of Saxony, and became the mother of Augustus II.; Ulrike Eleonore, who was married to the Swedish king Charles XI., and became the mother of the famous Charles XII.; Frederikke Amalie, married to Duke Christian Albrecht of Gottorp, and Wilhelmina, married to Prince Charles of the Palatinate.

CHAPTER XLVIII

Christian V. (1670-1699)

CHRISTIAN V., who succeeded his father, Frederick III., in 1670, was the first Danish-Norwegian king who mounted the throne by hereditary right, and was not obliged to sign a charter, dictated by the nobles, in order to be elected. He was a brave and vigorous young man; but he early disappointed those who had placed great hopes in him, as he wasted his time and strength on hunting and other amusements, and left the government to the care of his favorites, who were often incapable and selfish men. He loved pomp and splendor, and sought to imitate the extravagant Louis XIV. of France, spending much more money than the treasury could afford. He especially fancied everything that was German, and surrounded himself with indigent German noblemen, whom he helped to make their fortunes in Denmark. At court the language spoken was the German, the ministers preached in German, actors played in German, and the highest officers were Germans. As many of the old noble families had withdrawn from the capital, where they no longer exercised their old influence, and had retired to their estates, where they were still powerful on account of their wealth, King Christian, determined to secure other support for the throne, created a new and higher nobility, and established the titles and ranks recognized in Germany. Thus he filled his court with counts and barons, and adopted the strict etiquette and ceremonies of the French court. He also established two orders of knighthood, the order of Dannebrog and the order of the Elephant. In Norway, the earldom (county) of Laurvik was established (1671) for the benefit of the king's friend and half-brother, Ulrik Frederick Gyldenlöve, whose descendants, the Counts of Danneskiold-Laurvik, and later Ahlefeldt-Laurvik, for a long time owned this beautiful county. The old royal estate Sem, together with the deanery of Tunsberg, was made into another earldom (1673) for the then very powerful Minister of State Griffenfeld, who called himself Count of Griffenfeld and Tunsberg; after he had fallen from grace, this county was transferred to his rival, Gyldenlöve, who, with the permission of the king, sold a part of it—afterward called Jarlsberg—to the German-born field-marshal of Norway, Gustav Wilhelm Wedel, the progenitor of the family of Wedel-Jarlsberg. Rosendal, the only barony in Norway, was founded, in 1678, by Ludvig-Rosenkrands, a Danish nobleman, who, by marriage, had come into possession of large estates in Bergen Stift.

King Christian's adviser was, for some years, the eminent Danish statesman, Peter Griffenfeld. His original name was Peter Schumacher, and he was the son of a wine-seller in Copenhagen. His father died in poverty, after which Bishop Brochmann took him into his home. Here King Frederick saw him and had him sent abroad for six years at his expense. After his return he became librarian to the king, and occasionally assisted the king in state affairs. On his death-bed the king asked his son to take care of Peter Schumacher, saying: "Make a great man of him, but not too rapidly." Christian did not exactly follow this advice: in the following year he made him Count of Tunsberg, with the name of Griffenfeld, and appointed him great chancellor of the realm. Griffenfeld became greatly renowned. The emperor made him an imperial count, and Louis XIV. called him one of the greatest statesmen in the world. But, on account of this, he soon had many jealous rivals at the court, who aroused the king's suspicions as to his loyalty; he was deposed and accused of several great crimes, although some of the acts construed as crimes were acts of statesmanship for which he had deserved the greatest praise. He was condemned to death and brought to the scaffold; but, at the last moment, a message arrived from the king, that the sentence had been commuted to imprisonment for life. "This mercy is more cruel than death," exclaimed Griffenfeld. He was first imprisoned in the castle of Copenhagen, and remained there for four years; but as the king missed his able services, and his enemies feared that he might again be put in power, they caused him to be removed to the fortress of Munkholmen at Throndhjem, where he remained for eighteen years. At first he whiled away the time by reading and writing; but later they cruelly took away pen and ink. He wrote numerous apothegms in the margins of his books with little bits of lead, which he tore from the window-panes, or with coals on the wall. He was given his liberty in 1698, but died the following year (March 11, 1699), in Throndhjem, at the age of sixty-four years.

As the ally of the Elector of Brandenburg, but principally in the hope of recovering the lost provinces, King Christian, against the advice of Griffenfeld, commenced war against the Swedish king, Charles XI. This war, which lasted from 1675 to 1679, was called the Scania War, because that province was the principal scene of action. The Danes captured Wismar and some places in Scania, but lost the battles of Halmstad, Lund, and Landskrona. At sea, however, the Danes were generally successful. Admiral Kort Adeler had put the navy in good condition and had a worthy successor in the naval hero, Niels Juel, who won victories at Oeland and Kolbergerheide, and especially in the great naval battle of Kjögebugt (October 4, 1677). As Griffenfeld had foreseen, however, the Danes could accomplish little against the allies of France, and Christian was obliged to accede to peace proposed by Louis XIV. The peace was concluded at Lund (1679), and all that Christian V. obtained, for his efforts during an expensive four years' war, was permission to take with him ten cannons from each of the conquered fortresses.

During this war, which the Norwegians called the Gyldenlöve Feud, after their leader, the brave Ulrik Frederick Gyldenlöve, the Norwegians several times defeated the Swedes. In February, 1676, Gyldenlöve marched into Bahus Len with 11,000 men, conquering Udevalla and Wenersborg. The following year he took the fortified town of Marstrand by storm and compelled the fortress of Carlsten to surrender. In order to prevent the Norwegians from making further progress, the Swedish chancellor, Magnus de la Gardie, hastened into Bahus Len with 8,000 men, but was defeated by a much smaller Norwegian army, under Major-General Hans Lövenhjelm, at Udevalla, August 28, 1677. About 1,500 Swedes were slain and two hundred were captured, together with fourteen pieces of artillery and all the supplies. The following year the ever-active Gyldenlöve attacked Bahus Castle, which, however, he was unable to capture, as it was defended with great heroism and perseverance. The war ended, on the part of Norway, with an incursion by Gyldenlöve into Sweden in 1679, in order to avenge a similar expedition which the Swedish General Sparre had made into the region of Throndhjem the previous year, on which occasion the copper works at Röros had been burned.

The Norwegian code of laws, which is yet partly in force, was elaborated by direction of Christian V., dated April 15, 1687, and published April 14, 1688. He abolished Latin singing in the churches, introduced a new church ritual and a Danish hymn-book.

Christian V. visited Norway only once (1685). On Dovre Mountain he laid the foundation for a monument, with an inscription in the German language. He died August 25, 1699, leaving a debt of 1,110,000 Danish dollars, although he had tried to replenish his treasury by hiring out Norwegian and Danish soldiers as mercenaries to other countries. He was married to the gentle Charlotte Amalie of Hesse-Cassel.

CHAPTER XLIX

Frederick IV. (1699-1730)

AT the death of Christian V., his oldest son ascended the throne under the title of Frederick IV. His education had been sadly neglected; but, by untiring industry and energy after his accession to the throne, he gained considerable practical knowledge of the affairs of the government. He gave especial attention to the finances of the country, and, by a careful reduction of all unnecessary expenses, he succeeded in almost obliterating the great public debt. To his discredit, however, it must be admitted that this result was obtained partly with the blood of his subjects, as he secured large sums for the treasury by hiring out to the emperor 8,000, and to England and Holland 12,000, of the soldiers of Denmark and Norway, for service in the Spanish war about the order of succession. These soldiers distinguished themselves and fought with honor in many battles.

From his father, King Frederick had inherited certain disputes with Duke Frederick of Holstein, which led to a war; but the duke received aid from his brother-in-law, the Swedish king, Charles XII., who invaded Zealand (Sjælland) and marched against Copenhagen, and King Frederick was obliged to accept a hasty peace at Traventhal, Holstein, August 18, 1700, on unfavorable terms.

After the peace at Traventhal Charles XII. turned his forces against Russia and Poland, where he won victory after victory, until finally, on the 27th of June, 1709, he lost the battle of Pultowa. On account of the dangerous position in which this defeat placed the Swedish king, King Frederick thought the opportunity had come to recover the lost provinces. He renewed his old allegiance with Russia and Poland, and began the Great Northern War (1709-1720). With 16,000 men he invaded Scania and captured several towns; but the Swedish field-marshal, Magnus Stenbock, hastily gathered an army of undisciplined peasants and defeated the Danes at the battle of Helsingborg (1710). In this war also the Danish-Norwegian fleet rendered great service, fighting the Swedish fleet with success in the Baltic and especially in the North Sea. On October 4, 1710, it was attacked by the Swedish fleet in Kjögebugt. The Norwegian, Ivar Hvitfeld (a son of Tonne Hvitfeld, who had distinguished himself at Frederickshald), commanded the ship "Dannebrog," which took fire early in the fight. He might have saved himself by beaching the ship, but there was danger of thus spreading the fire to the rest of the Danish fleet and to the town. He therefore stayed where he was, drew closer to the enemy and fired volley after volley from the forward guns, until the fire reached the powder magazine. The ship was blown up, and he and his five hundred men perished.

In the latter part of 1715, Charles XII. returned to Sweden, after an absence of fifteen years, and succeeded in giving new courage to the Swedes, who were exhausted from the hardships of the long war. The winter was very severe, so that the Sound was frozen over, and, in January, 1716, Charles intended to lead his army of 20,000 men across the ice and invade the Danish islands; but, just as he was ready for this exploit, a thaw suddenly set in, so that he could not effect the crossing, and, not having sufficient transports, Charles decided to direct his attacks against Norway.

The defences of Norway were in a miserable condition. The trained regiments had been sent south to Denmark, so that the army consisted almost wholly of the National Guards, which were without training, poorly clothed, and without the necessary supplies. The fortresses were short of provisions, arms, and ammunition, and there was no money in the treasury. The commanding general, the old and feeble Barthold von Lützow, had to confine his operations to garrisoning the silver works at Kongsberg and the principal passes. The natural advantages of the country and the patriotism and perseverance of the inhabitants constituted the principal defence.

By three different routes the Swedes invaded Norway. Charles himself entered Höland in March, 1716. At the Riser farm the Swedish advance guard was attacked by two hundred Norwegian dragoons under the brave Colonel Ulrich Christian Kruse, and, during the fight, the colonel himself killed fifteen men and wounded Charles's brother-in-law, the prince of Hesse. After a desperate fight, and the fall of the brave Captain Michelet, Colonel Kruse, who was so severely wounded that he could not hold his sword, surrendered to King Charles with twenty men; sixty lay dead or wounded, and the remainder had escaped. The Swedes had one hundred and seventy killed and wounded. Charles highly praised his brave opponent, had his own surgeon attend to his wounds, gave him a sword, and asked him if his brother, King Frederick, had many such officers. Kruse answered: "Of them he has many, and I am far from being among the ablest."

Charles thereupon occupied Christiania and commenced to besiege the fortress of Akershus, but could not accomplish much for lack of heavy artillery. While he lay in camp there he sent out expeditions in different directions. The Swedish colonel, Axel Löwen, was sent out with six hundred dragoons to destroy Kongsberg silver works. He was to proceed by way of Ringerike, because the road from Drammen was blocked by the Norwegians; and, on the evening of March 28, 1716, he arrived with his force at the Norderhov parsonage, Ringerike. The parson, the learned Jonas

Ramus, was confined to his bed by sickness, but his wife, the intrepid Anna Kolbjörnsdatter, received the soldiers well in order to avoid plundering. Having learned, by paying close attention to her guests, that it was their intention early the next morning to surprise a number of Norwegian dragoons, who lay encamped at the Steen farm and knew nothing of the arrival of the Swedes, she asked and obtained the permission of the colonel to send her servant-girl out to a neighboring farm for something that was needed for the table. Thus she was enabled to send warning to the Norwegians about the plans of the enemy. Under the leadership of Captain Sehested and Sergeant Thor Hovland the Norwegians set out at midnight, and, guided by the fires which Anna had started under pretext of warming the chilly soldiers, they surprised and overpowered the Swedish force. Colonel Löwen was captured, together with one hundred and sixty men; thirty were killed, and the remainder escaped.

In April a Swedish force, under Colonel Falkenberg, was attacked and defeated at Moss by the Norwegians, under the command of Major-General Vincents Budde and Colonel Hvitfeld, who took four hundred prisoners and captured a large quantity of supplies. At the parsonage of Skieberg the Swedish general, Ascheberg, lay with 2,000 men and could hear the shooting at Moss; but the parson, Peter Rumohr, who had intercepted the correspondence between the Swedes at the parsonage and those at Moss, gave such exaggerated accounts of the defeat of the Swedes and of large reinforcements to the Norwegians, that General Ascheberg hastily broke camp and returned to Sweden. When King Charles, some time afterward, heard of this, he became so enraged at the minister that he caused him to be captured and brought to Sweden, where he died in prison.

As the roads were becoming very bad, and Charles feared that the Norwegians contemplated cutting off his retreat, he suddenly withdrew from Christiania and shortly afterward attacked the city of Frederickshald. Here the citizens had armed themselves under the brave brothers Peter and Hans Kolbjörnson, nephews of Kield Stub, and half-brothers of Anna Kolbjörnsdatter, and the Swedes had to buy every step with blood. Charles captured the city on the night between the 3d and 4th of July, 1716, and the Norwegians had to retire to the fortress, Fredericksteen. That the enemy might not find shelter behind the houses against the shots from the fortress, the citizens put fire to the town. Peter Kolbjörnson commenced with his own house, and soon the whole city was in flames. Charles had to withdraw from Fredericksteen, with a loss of 1,500 men and three generals, to his headquarters at Torpum, intending to renew the siege as soon as he could get his heavy artillery from his transport ships at Dynekilen, near Svinesund. But in this hope he was disappointed, as the Norwegian naval hero, Peter Tordenskiold, by a daring attack shortly afterward, succeeded in capturing or destroying the whole transport fleet at Dynekilen.

Peter Wessel, afterward ennobled under the name of Tordenskiold, was born November 7, 1691, in Throndhjem, where his father, Jan Wessel, was a merchant. As he showed no disposition for college studies, he was placed with a tailor as apprentice; but he ran away from his master, came to Copenhagen, where he hired out as a sailor, and made journeys to the West Indies and to India. Afterward he became a naval cadet, made another trip to India, and on his return came to Bergen just as the Great Northern War had broken out. He immediately proceeded overland to Christiania, where the commanding general, Waldemar Lövendahl, took a fancy to him and gave him the command of a ship of four guns, "Ormen" (the Serpent), with which he made cruises along the Swedish coast. He soon became renowned for his courage, and was given a better ship called "Lövendahl's galley," a frigate of twenty guns. By his heroic deeds and brilliant bravery he rose, in the comparatively short time of ten years, from cadet to vice-admiral, and was ennobled by King Frederick IV. "For your rare courage and loyalty," the king said to him, "we have raised you to our nobility. Your name shall hereafter be Tordenskiold (Thunder-shield)." "Well, then," answered the young man, "I will so thunder in the ears of the Swedes that they will say you have not given me the name without reason."

The entrance to the harbor of Dynekilen is at most places only four hundred to four hundred and fifty feet wide. On a little peninsula in the inlet the Swedes had erected a battery of six twelve-pounders, and on each side of the narrow inlet 4,000 infantry were stationed. On the evening of July 7th, when Tordenskiold lay with two frigates, three galleys and two other vessels outside of Stromstad, he learned from some Swedish fishermen, who were brought aboard as prisoners, where the Swedish fleet lay, and also that a number of the officers had been invited to a wedding, while the admiral was to have a banquet on board for the others. He concluded that the officers, therefore, would be in poor condition for fighting, and at daybreak he weighed anchor, and cried over to the brave Lieutenant Peter Grib, who was commanding the other frigate: "I am informed that the Swedish admiral is going to have a carousal on his fleet to-day. Would it not be advisable if we went in with our ships and became his unbidden guests? The pilot says we have favorable wind." Peter Grib was ready, and Tordenskiold at once steered into the harbor. Without firing a shot he ran his ship in through a heavy fire from all sides. It was not till he came so near that his six-pounders could be of effect, and when he had reached the widest part of the inlet where he could arrange his ships with the broadsides toward the enemy, that he commenced to fire. After three hours of uninterrupted cannonading the Swedish fire began to slacken, and at one o'clock (July 8, 1716) the Swedish flag was lowered. The Swedes had then beached as many of their ships as possible, and soldiers and sailors were trying to save themselves by flight. Tordenskiold's victory was complete; forty-four ships, carrying sixty guns, were either burned or sunk. Not a single ship was saved, and the next day King Charles was on his retreat to Sweden.

In September, 1718, King Charles again attacked Norway. He sent General Armfeldt with 14,000 men into Throndhjem Stift, where the commanding general, W. Budde, had to confine himself to the defence of the city of Throndhjem. King Charles himself moved against Fredericksteen with 20,000 men and began a vigorous siege. The outer redoubt was stormed and taken after a brave resistance, and the Swedish trenches were only two hundred and fifty paces from the fortress when King Charles was killed in one of the trenches by a bullet from the fortress, December 11, 1718. A few days later the Swedish army withdrew and returned to Sweden. General Armfeldt, on receiving this intelligence, retreated from Throndhjem and started to return to the frontier across the Tydal Mountains. On the mountain his army was overtaken by a fearful snowstorm; many hundreds froze to death, and many of those who escaped became cripples for life.

Frederick IV. now proceeded to Norway himself, and invaded Sweden with 15,000 men and occupied Stromstad, while Tordenskiold, by daring strategy, took possession of Marstrand and captured the fortress Carlsten. The war, which had lasted eleven years, was ended by a peace, which Charles's sister, Ulrika Eleonora, concluded at Fredericksborg Castle, 1720. By this peace Sweden was compelled to agree never to help the Duke of Holstein to recover Schleswig, to pay 600,000 Rigsdalers, and to relinquish its right to exemption from tolls in the Oere Sound, a right which Sweden had had since 1645.

Peter Tordenskiold lived only a few months after peace had been concluded. He was allowed to make a journey abroad, and at Hanover he thrashed a gambler, Colonel Stahl, who had cheated one of his friends. For this he was challenged to a duel with the colonel, and in their encounter he was killed, November 12, 1720, being then a little over twenty-nine years of age.

The interests of Norway were often neglected during the reign of Frederick IV. In order to raise money the government sold all the Norwegian churches, and the lands belonging to them, to private parties, because the people, who from time immemorial had owned the churches, could not produce deeds or other documents showing title. The northern districts of Norway were especially neglected. The trade with Finmarken had, to the great detriment of that part of the country, for a long time been leased to the citizens of Bergen; in 1720 it was sold to three citizens of Copenhagen, and the result was greatly increased distress among the people.

During the reign of Frederick IV., two Norwegians distinguished themselves by missionary work. One of them was Thomas von Westen from Throndhjem, who worked with great zeal for the cause of Christianity in Finmarken. The other was Hans Egede, a clergyman from Vaagen in Nordland, who proceeded to Greenland, where, for years, he indefatigably devoted himself to the work of promoting the spiritual and material welfare of the inhabitants.

Frederick IV. died in 1730, fifty-nine years old.

CHAPTER L

Christian VI. (1730-1746)

CHRISTIAN VI., who succeeded his father, Frederick IV., in 1730, commenced his reign by discharging the most of his father's experienced advisers and friends. The very able Bartholomew Deichmann, bishop at Akershus, who was most highly esteemed during the former reign, was deposed and indicted, but died shortly after his degradation, April, 1731. The king allowed himself to be controlled by his German queen, the proud and extravagant Sophie Magdalena. The language and customs of the country were banished from the court, and a proud and haughty tone introduced. The king rarely spoke with any of his subjects unless they belonged to the higher nobility or were Germans. The queen had a mania for building, and large sums were expended on costly palaces in and about Copenhagen.

The Danish-Norwegian Church had also been affected by the pietistic revivalism brought about in the German Protestant Church by Spener and Francke. Christian himself was a pious man, but his religion was mournful and morbid. He was, to a great extent, controlled by his pietistic court-chaplain, Bluhme. A Sabbath ordinance was enacted (1735), by which several preposterous rules about church-going were introduced and some antiquated laws were again put in force. Neglect of attendance at church was punished in the cities by money fines, and in the country by being placed in the stocks, which, for that purpose, were erected outside of every church door. Public amusements hitherto considered harmless—dancing, games and festivities—were forbidden; weddings and social parties were not to be held on a holiday or the evening before. A general Church Inspection College was established in 1737, a kind of Court of Inquisition, whose duty it was to watch over the proper performance of church services. The result of this unwise zeal for religion was a general state of hypocrisy and intolerance. Unscrupulous people, who feigned holiness and imitated the pietists at court, were given offices, while those who were sincere and independent were left out.

One of the beneficial results of the pietism which ruled during the reign of Christian VI. was the introduction of the Confirmation in the Lutheran faith. This was introduced upon the advice of court chaplain Bluhme, by the ordinance of January 13, 1736; the same year in which the second centennial of the introduction of the Reformation was celebrated. The Confirmation led to an improved Christian education of the people, and indirectly compelled all classes of the people to read. Great zeal was also shown in the printing of Bibles and other religious books, and some improvement was made in the Norwegian Church organization by an ordinance of August 13, 1734. The Latin schools were reorganized in 1739, the teachers being given better salaries, while more suitable text-books were introduced.

Some efforts were also made to improve the trade, manufactures and navigation of Norway, but these efforts were not always well directed. The trade with Finmarken, Iceland and Greenland was leased to companies, whose aim seemed to be the greatest possible extortion. Very unwise and harmful to the country was the king's decree forbidding the people of southern Norway to buy grain from any other country than Denmark. The navy was greatly improved under the supervision of Count Frederick Danneskiold-Samsoe, Admiral Suhm and Constructor Benstrup; but their work took large sums of money.

Toward the close of this reign Norway suffered a great deal from hard times and famine, in common with the greater part of Northern Europe. During the years 1720 and 1741 there died in Norway 31,346 more persons than were born. Many died of starvation, and, in many districts, the people had to make meal from bark, bones and straw. A collection amounting to about 14,000 Rigsdalers (Danish dollars) was made in Denmark in order to help some of the most needy.

During the reign of Christian VI. lived "the father of the Danish-Norwegian literature," the witty and very productive author, Ludvig Holberg (born in Bergen, 1684, died 1754); also the active and eloquent Peter Hersleb (born in Throndhjem, 1689), who from 1730 to 1737 was bishop at Akershus, and from 1737, until his death in 1757, bishop of Zealand, and who may be considered the father of the public school system. Two Danish bishops of this time who are held in respectful memory by the Norwegians are Erik Pontoppidan, who was bishop in Bergen from 1747 to 1755,—author of "Explanation of Luther's Catechism," which is still extensively used in the Norwegian schools—and Hans Brorson (bishop in Ribe, 1694-1764), the author of many church hymns.

Christian VI., during his reign of sixteen years, only visited Norway once, in the summer of 1733. He died August 6, 1746, in his forty-seventh year. In spite of the long peace, a flourishing trade, and large subsidies from foreign powers for mercenaries, which he had furnished from Norway and Denmark, he left a debt of over two million Rigsdalers.

CHAPTER LI

Frederick V. (1746-1766)

WHEN Christian VI. died, his eldest son, Frederick V., ascended the throne. He was a man of limited intelligence, but of a kindly disposition. By his affability and his taste for the language of the country he stood in sharp contrast with his late father, and he and his lovely young queen, Louisa, daughter of George II. of England, soon won the hearts of the people. He abolished all the harsh ordinances against amusements, the national theatre was opened again, and Ludvig Holberg had the pleasure, in his old age, to again see his comedies played and received with great applause. The change was at first beneficial, especially as long as Queen Louisa lived; but, after her death, in 1751, when her place had been taken by Juliana Marie of Brunswick, the liberal tone at court often degenerated into giddiness and license, and, in an attempt to imitate the French manners, a luxury was introduced which was too expensive for the ordinary resources of the crown.

The reign of Frederick V. was, like that of his father, peaceful, although a war with Russia seemed very imminent, when one of the Holstein-Gottorp princes, Charles Peter Ulrik, had ascended the throne of Russia, under the title of Peter III., and laid claim to a part of the duchy of Schleswig. A Russian army was sent into Mecklenburg with orders to advance on Holstein, where an army of 70,000 Danish and Norwegian soldiers had been drawn together. The armies lay within a few miles of each other, when the conflict was suddenly averted by the news that Peter III. had been deposed, and, shortly afterward, murdered by his wife (July, 1762). The empress, Catherine II., who succeeded her husband, had always been averse to the war, and a treaty of peace was concluded with her, principally as the result of the able diplomacy of the king's adviser, Count Johan Hartvig Bernstorf.

The great preparations for this threatened conflict had, however, necessitated an increase of taxation. The so-called "extra-tax" was felt as a great burden; every person above twelve years of age had to pay a tax of one Rigsdaler (about fifty-five cents) per year. This was especially felt as a burden by the common people in the districts around Bergen, where the fisheries had been a failure, and a revolt was the result. About 4,000 peasants armed themselves and made an assault upon the city, maltreated the magistrates, and plundered about 8,000 Rigsdalers of the public means. Quiet was soon restored, and the participants in the revolt were punished. A few years afterward the "extra-tax" was abolished.

A great deal was done during this reign for the promotion of science and art, trade, manufactures and agriculture. At Kongsberg a mineral school was established and two hundred German experts employed as teachers. The bishop at Throndhjem, Johan Gunnerus, Rector Gerhard Schöning, and the Danish scholar, Peter Suhm (who had married the daughter of a merchant at Throndhjem), established the Royal Academy of Sciences in Throndhjem. A free school of mathematics, afterward reorganized as the Norwegian Military Academy, was founded in Christiania.

Frederick V., who shortened his life by all kinds of excesses, died in his forty-third year, January 14, 1766. He left a public debt of about twenty millions. By his first wife he had one son, Christian, and three daughters; his second wife became the mother of Prince Frederick.

CHAPTER LII
Christian VII. (1766-1808)

AT the death of Frederick V., his son Christian, who was hardly seventeen years of age, ascended the throne; and, shortly afterward, married the fifteen year old Caroline Mathilde, a sister of the English king, George III. Christian led a most dissipated life, eventually resulting in insanity. In 1768 the king made a journey abroad, during which his body physician, the German free-thinker, Johan Frederick Struensee, became his dearest favorite, and got him completely under his influence. Upon their return the king's old counsellors, including the experienced and deserving Bernstorf, were discharged and replaced by a privy council, in which the strong and ambitious Struensee soon became the real master. By the influence which he had gained over the debilitated, and at times insane, king, and the queen, he succeeded in reaching the highest positions. He was made a count and prime minister and became an almost absolute ruler, the cabinet orders being given the force of royal commands simply by being signed by Struensee. His power lasted only sixteen months; but during this time he introduced many reforms, which were in themselves commendable, but, in many cases, came too abruptly and without preparation. On account of the violent changes, and his contempt for the Danish language and customs, he soon had many enemies, chief among whom was the queen-dowager, Juliana Maria, who wished to get her son, the king's half-brother, Prince Frederick, into power. With the aid of the prince's teacher, the learned Ove Hoeg Guldberg, she formed a conspiracy against Struensee and obtained the signature of the insane king to an order for his arrest, together with that of others. On the night of January 17, 1772, after a ball at the palace, Queen Caroline Mathilde, Struensee, Count Brandt, and others, were arrested. The queen was imprisoned at Kronborg, and afterward at Celle, Hanover, where she died in her twenty-fourth year (1775). The others were accused of high treason and condemned to death. Struensee was cruelly executed, April 28, 1772.

During the following twelve years (1772-1784) Prince Frederick's teacher, Ove Guldberg, virtually conducted the government, and this period has therefore been called the Guldberg period. A great many of Struensee's reforms were revoked, and former rules were re-established. The liberty of the press, which Struensee had granted, was curtailed and a censorship again introduced. The plan of establishing a university in Norway, which had been promised, was given up. Everything was now to be "Danish," even Norway. Guldberg even wished to abolish the very name of Norwegian, and wrote: "No Norwegian exists; all are citizens of the Danish state."

Many of the strong men, whom Struensee had made use of, were removed, and mediocrity was again raised to dignity. In spite of the large revenues which flowed into the treasury during the flourishing commercial period, the public debt, which had been reduced to sixteen millions, rose to twenty-nine millions. Still, there are some things to the credit of the Guldberg ministry. Thus the foreign minister, Andreas Bernstorf, by his negotiations, succeeded in removing any cause for conflict with the powerful Russia, when the Russian grand-duke, Paul, relinquished his part of Holstein to the king of Denmark, in return for Oldenborg and Delmenhorst. On February 15, 1776, the so-called *native right* was published, an ordinance providing that hereafter only native citizens could be appointed to office under the government. Finally, it was ordained that the Danish language should be used both in the army and as a business language.

During the long period of peace (since 1720) Norway had made great progress in commerce, shipping and population. The population, which, in 1660, was only 450,000, had reached about 723,000 in 1767, and the merchant marine had grown from fifty to 1,150 ships, many of them large and engaged in trade with distant countries. The peasant class had advanced considerably, as a consequence of the sale of the estates of the crown in order to raise revenue; the number of freeholders was now nearly double that of the tenant farmers. The officials sent their sons to be educated at the University of Copenhagen, so that the country was gradually furnished with a native class of officials, who could replace the Danish and advocate the cause of their countrymen.

In 1784 Crown Prince Frederick was confirmed, and immediately took charge of the government as regent for his insane father. He had the sense to surround himself with able counsellors, and the foremost among them was Andreas Bernstorf, a nephew of the elder Bernstorf. While he was at the head of the government (1784-1797), the united countries had happy and prosperous days. He succeeded in maintaining an honorable neutrality, while the French Revolution, which commenced in 1789, shook Europe and involved nearly all the countries of Europe in war. Much was done for Norway during this period. The trade of Finmarken was made free, and the cities of Tromsœ, Hammerfest and Vardœ were founded. In order to expedite judicial matters four superior courts were established, and, in order to avoid litigation as much as possible, courts of conciliation were introduced in all parts of the country.

During Bernstorf's administration, Norway was involved in a short war with Sweden, the Swedish king, Gustavus III., having attacked Russia, whereupon the Russian empress, Catherine II., demanded, according to agreement, an attack upon Sweden by Denmark. A Norwegian army of 10,000 men, under Prince Charles of Hesse, invaded Sweden in the fall of 1788, and, after some successful encounters, marched against Gothenburg; but an armistice was concluded, which was changed into a convention, November 5th, the Norwegians agreeing to retire from Sweden.

England continued the war with France with great vigor, and, in order to weaken the enemy as much as possible, raised the point with neutral powers that meat, flour and grain must be considered as contraband of war, and should not, therefore, be shipped to France or any other enemy of England. In order to protect their commerce, Denmark-Norway then, in 1800, together with Russia and Sweden, renewed the so-called "Armed Neutrality," which, through the untiring efforts of Andreas Bernstorf, had been agreed upon in 1780, based upon the principle that "free ship carries free cargo." After an unsuccessful attempt, through negotiations, to persuade Denmark to withdraw from this alliance, England declared war against her, and sent a fleet, under the command of Admirals Parker and Nelson, to Oere Sound. On April 2, 1801, a battle was fought in the roadstead of Copenhagen. Although the Danish and Norwegian sailors defended themselves with great bravery, they finally had to yield to superior force. An armistice was concluded, which, at the death of the Russian emperor, Paul, ended with a peace, by which Denmark consented to withdraw from the Armed Neutrality.

The country now enjoyed peace until 1807, when a new war with England broke out. At the peace of Tilsit, July 7, 1807, Emperor Napoleon and Alexander I. of Russia made certain arrangements of European affairs with a view to helping Napoleon in his conflict with England. Russia was to be allowed to conquer Finland from Sweden, and Napoleon was to take possession of the Danish fleet, by means of which he might dispute the dominion of England at sea. Although this agreement was to be kept strictly secret, the English government, in some way, heard of it, and decided to anticipate the action of Napoleon. A strong fleet was sent to Copenhagen, where the British commanders demanded that Denmark should surrender its fleet to England, where it was to remain until peace was concluded between England and France. The demand was answered by the Danish minister, who protested that there was no cause for it, since Denmark had no idea of letting Napoleon have the fleet. The British, however, would not listen to any assurances of Denmark's peaceful attitude. An army of about 38,000 men was landed and defeated the Danish force outside of Copenhagen, which, all told, hardly amounted to 10,000 men. Thereafter preparations were made for bombarding the city. The bombardment commenced on September 2d and lasted for three days. During this bombardment the cathedral and three hundred and five other buildings were burned, and 1,200 buildings were, more or less, damaged. Valuable libraries, and collections of art and other valuable property, were destroyed by fire, 1,100 soldiers and citizens were killed and eight hundred wounded. The Danes had to surrender their whole fleet, which was then brought to England. The English government now gave Denmark the choice between three conditions: neutrality, an alliance, or war. In case of war Denmark was threatened with destruction of the Danish and Norwegian merchant marine, the occupation of Copenhagen by the Swedes, and, possibly, the forcible transfer of Norway to England's ally, Sweden. Crown Prince Frederick answered that, after what had taken place, peace was impossible, and so the war was continued, Denmark entering into a close alliance with France.

When it became difficult to maintain communication between Norway and Denmark, the Danish government, in August, 1807, established a "Government Commission" for Norway, consisting of Prince Christian August of Augustenborg as chairman, "Stiftamtmand" Gerhard Moltke, Justice Enevold Falsen, and Chamberlain Marcus Rosenkrantz. Prince Christian August was commander of the troops in the southern part of Norway, having been appointed as such in 1805. He was greatly beloved by the Norwegians. After having performed its arduous duties for three months, the commission lost its ablest member, Enevold Falsen, whose body was found in the bay, November 17, 1807. His health had been greatly impaired, and he had probably been driven to suicide by his sufferings. While performing his duties on the Government Commission, he also edited the journal "Budstikken," in which he did much to arouse and maintain the courage and perseverance of the people. He was succeeded, in January, 1808, by Count Herman Wedel Jarlsberg, who had gained the high respect of his countrymen by the zeal and vigor which he had shown in his efforts to provide the famine-threatened country with the necessary grain by importation from Denmark, which numerous British cruisers tried to prevent.

CHAPTER LIII

Frederick VI. (1808-1814)

WHEN, on the death of his insane father, Frederick VI. changed his title of regent to that of king of Denmark, his domains were in a sad condition. They were at war with England, but had no fleet. The finances were in great disorder, which became still worse when the Danish government tried to improve the situation by issuing a large amount of paper currency. The English men-of-war blocked the navigation, and hundreds of Danish and Norwegian trading-ships, together with their cargoes, were seized by the enemy. In Norway, all industries were paralyzed, there had been failures of crops, and there was a great deal of want and suffering. When the Danish government, as the ally of France and Russia, also declared war on Sweden, the situation was most desperate. The Government Commission was daily begged, by petition, to open the public grain magazines to relieve the distress of the people, and it taxed their judgment and firmness to the utmost to control the situation and distribute aid where the need was most pressing. In this condition Norway was attacked, in April, 1808, by a large Swedish army under the command of General Armfeldt, and threatened by a British army and fleet, which lay at Gothenburg. In the hour of distress and danger, however, the Norwegians had awakened to a consciousness of the fact that they had only themselves to rely upon, and, during their struggles, they showed a patriotism which shunned no sacrifice. Men like Marcus Rosenkrantz, Peter Anker, Herman Wedel, Jacob Aall, Severin Lövenskiold, Thygesen, John Collett, Ludvig Maribo, and many other patriots, offered their time, energy, and fortunes to the service of the country, and the popular commander, Prince Christian August, was strengthened and aided by a strong national spirit among all classes, when he made his preparations to meet the enemy.

General Armfeldt, on April 17, 1808, advanced toward the fortress of Kongsvinger, and a battle was fought at Lier, near that place. The Swedes were at first repulsed, but later received reinforcements and compelled the Norwegians to retreat across the Glommen River. It is said that some of the Norwegian troops had to cease firing, during the battle, for want of ammunition. About the same time a Swedish force captured the Blaker Redoubt, about twenty-five miles to the southwest of Kongsvinger, but this position they soon afterward abandoned, upon hearing of the approach of a Norwegian force which had been hurriedly despatched against them by Christian August. The Norwegians proceeded beyond Blaker, and at Toverud (in Urskog Parish, Romerike) surrounded, and, after a sharp fight, captured a Swedish force under Count Axel Mörner. On April 24th a Swedish force, under Colonel Gahn, crossed the frontier and marched along the left bank of the Flisen River, a tributary of the Glommen. Near Trangen, in Aasnes Parish, Soloer, they were attacked by the Norwegians, and, after a fight of three hours and a half, the Swedes surrendered, having suffered a loss of two hundred killed and wounded. About three hundred and thirty men, including Colonel Gahn, were taken prisoners. The Norwegians were also successful in a battle fought on June 10th at Prestebakke in Enningdal, in the southern part of Smaalenene, near Svinesund. The attack was made early in the morning, and, after a desperate fight, the Swedes were forced to surrender; four hundred and forty-five men, including twenty-seven officers, being taken prisoners. A large amount of arms and ammunition was also taken. A few days later the Swedish force which was commanded by General Armfeldt's aide-de-camp, George Adlersparre, received large reinforcements and recaptured the lost positions in Enningdal; but, shortly afterward, the Swedish troops again retreated, the Swedish government desiring to give more attention to the war in Finland. Negotiations were now opened for an armistice. King Frederick VI. several times requested Christian August to invade Sweden with his army; but the prince, as well as his tried advisers, considered an invasion very unwise, the army being destitute of all necessary supplies. An armistice was finally entered into on December 7, 1808. A definite peace was not concluded till a year later.

Great changes took place in Sweden during the following year. King Gustavus IV. Adolphus had shown great incompetence in the management of the affairs of Sweden, and after the reverses in Finland, resulting in the loss of this province, the feeling against the king became very strong. Early in 1809 rumors began to circulate of the renewal of an old project, by which Napoleon and Alexander I. had agreed to divide Sweden between Denmark and Russia, and great excitement was created among the leading men in Sweden. A conspiracy was formed by a number of influential men, including George Adlersparre, who marched with his army toward Stockholm. On March 13, 1809, the king was arrested and brought to the castle of Drotningholm, and a few days later to Gripsholm Castle, where finally he was induced to write and sign an unconditional abdication. He was later transported to Pomerania, and from there proceeded to Switzerland. When King Gustavus had abdicated, his aged uncle, Charles, duke of Södermanland, was prevailed upon to take charge of the government as regent. The Swedish Diet, which met in May, 1809, confirmed the deposition of King Gustavus and elected Charles king under the title of Charles XIII. The newly-elected king being old and childless, a successor to the throne also had to be chosen, and the choice fell upon the general-in-chief of the Norwegian army, Prince Christian August, whom the Swedes also had learned to respect during the war, and whose election, it was supposed by many, would eventually result in uniting Norway with Sweden. After peace had been concluded between Denmark and Sweden, at Jönköping, December 10, 1809, Prince Christian August accepted the election as Crown Prince of Sweden, his name being changed to Charles (or Carl) August. No royal or princely person had ever, to such a degree, won the affection of the Norwegians. He left Norway for Sweden January 4, 1810, accompanied by the blessings and well-wishes of the whole people. Only a few months later, May 28, 1810, he suddenly died during a military review.

Shortly before the prince's departure from Norway, and at the suggestion of Count Wedel and other patriotic men, a society was founded in Christiania under the name of the Society for Norway's Welfare, which did much to encourage the feeling of independence and the national spirit in the country and to advocate the wishes of the people. Thus the long-felt want of a national university was strongly set forth by Count Wedel. The government having pointed to the lack of money, such an amount was collected by voluntary subscriptions from the whole country, especially the cities, that King Frederick at last yielded, and, by royal decree, the Norwegian University was established September 2, 1811, and given the name of the king. This event was celebrated with great joy by the Norwegian people by a national festival, December 11, 1811.

The condition of the country, however, became very serious during the next year. Failure of the crops caused a famine, and the use of bark-bread became quite general throughout the country. The paper currency became more and more depreciated, and the government was finally obliged to partially default payment. The British continued to prevent all importation, and the distress was increased by the breaking out of a new war between Denmark and Sweden.

During the distressing years of war, when a foreign fleet intercepted the communication with Denmark, many Norwegians had become convinced that the union with Denmark was a very unnatural one. Many able and patriotic men believed that a union or a strong defensive alliance with Sweden would be much more advantageous to the country, and no doubt many considered such a union among the future probabilities, when the beloved Prince Christian August was elected Crown Prince of Sweden. The sorrow that was felt in Norway at the sudden death of Christian August was universal. A rumor, probably unfounded, that he had been poisoned by some of his opponents in Sweden, was, for a time at least, generally believed in Norway, and extinguished, for the time being, any desire that may have existed in Norway for a union of the two countries. In Sweden, however, the plan grew in strength, especially after the election of the new Crown Prince.

CHAPTER LIV

Marshal Bernadotte

THE election of a new successor to the Swedish throne was no easy problem. Under the conditions prevailing in Europe it was thought necessary to make a choice that would be approved by Napoleon, and it had even been suggested that it might be necessary to elect one of Napoleon's marshals. Among the different candidates considered, the most popular one was the Duke of Augustenborg, an elder brother of Prince Christian August. His election was opposed by King Frederick VI. of Denmark, who hoped to be chosen himself, and held out as inducement a promise to give each of the three countries a constitution. King Frederick at first had the support of quite a party in the Swedish Diet; but his opponents strongly argued that to make the Danish king successor to the Swedish throne would eventually result in Sweden becoming a province of Denmark, and the Duke of Augustenborg, who was supported by King Charles XIII., was the choice of a majority in the Swedish Diet. A messenger, Baron Mörner, was sent to Paris to ascertain whether such an election would have the approval of Napoleon; but upon arriving in Paris he was told that, according to the latest reports, the election of the Danish king was being seriously considered, and believing that this would be a great misfortune, the baron took upon himself to open negotiations with one of Napoleon's marshals, Jean Baptiste Bernadotte, Prince of Pontecorvo, and requested him to become a candidate for the Swedish succession. After a conference with Napoleon and a consultation with the Swedish minister in Paris, Bernadotte declared himself willing to accept the election, if it were offered to him.

When Baron Mörner returned to Sweden and reported the result of his unauthorized step, he caused great surprise, and the king ordered his arrest; but, on second thought, the plan to elect Bernadotte was generally favorably considered by leading men in Sweden. Count Platen had a consultation with his Norwegian friend, Count Wedel, and the latter, who had made the personal acquaintance of Bernadotte, advised the Swedes to elect him in preference to the Duke of Augustenborg. The result was that in August, 1810, the Swedish Diet, with practical unanimity, elected Bernadotte Crown Prince of Sweden, and King Charles XIII. adopted him as his son, under the name of Charles John (Carl Johan). When, in September, 1810, Bernadotte was about to leave Paris for Sweden, and Napoleon asked him to promise never to wage war on France, he declined to bind himself by such a promise, but assured the emperor of his sincere friendship. "Go, then," said Napoleon, "and let us fulfil our several destinies."

Crown Prince Charles John, on his arrival in Sweden, immediately assumed the chief control of the government, and set about the very difficult task of raising the country from the wretched and defenceless condition into which it had fallen. Sweden was at the time practically at the mercy of the great Powers. Napoleon forced Sweden to declare war on England, and when, a year later, he found that this war was not carried on with satisfactory vigor, he sent an army into Swedish Pomerania, which he occupied, while two Swedish regiments were sent as prisoners to France (January, 1812). This caused Charles John to look around for other alliances, which would be of greater benefit to his adopted country. He once more offered Napoleon the faithful services of Sweden, on condition that Sweden was to receive Norway in compensation; but Napoleon would not listen to any proposition to take anything from his faithful ally, Denmark.

Charles John immediately opened negotiations with Russia, and the result was a secret treaty, concluded at St. Petersburg, April 18, 1812, by which Russia promised to help Sweden, by negotiations or force of arms, to acquire Norway, and Russia was guaranteed the possession of Finland, while Charles John was to take an active part in the military operations in Germany against Napoleon. This agreement was confirmed at a personal meeting between the Russian emperor Alexander and Crown Prince Charles John at Åbo, Finland, August 27, 1812. The stipulation that Norway was to be united with Sweden was afterward also agreed to by the other Powers at war with France. Charles John took an active part in the great campaign against Napoleon in Germany. After the complete defeat of Napoleon's army at Leipsic, October 16-19, 1813, Charles John marched with an army of 40,000 men into Holstein in order to compel Denmark to cede Norway. The Danish-Norwegian army in Holstein and Schleswig made a brave defence; but the resistance against the overwhelming force of the enemy could not last long, and Frederick VI. was compelled to conclude peace at Kiel, January 14, 1814, where Norway was ceded to Sweden. The Norwegian dependencies, Iceland, the Faroe Islands, and Greenland, were not included in the cession. Four days later King Frederick VI., for himself and his successors, relinquished all his rights to the kingdom of Norway to the Swedish king, Charles XIII., and his successors. In his proclamation to the Norwegians, King Frederick released them from their oath of allegiance, and requested them to peaceably and quietly transfer their allegiance to the Swedish king.

Thus ended the union between Denmark and Norway, which had lasted for more than four hundred years.

CHAPTER LV
Norway Declares Her Independence

PRINCE CHRISTIAN FREDERICK, a cousin of King Frederick VI. and heir presumptive to the Danish-Norwegian throne, had, in May, 1813, been sent up to Norway as viceroy (*Statholder*), and had become very popular with the Norwegians. When, on January 24, 1814, he received the message from the king, informing him of the treaty of Kiel and commanding him to transfer the forts and the public offices to the Swedes and return to Denmark, Christian Frederick became highly indignant and resolved not to obey the commands. In his diary the prince wrote:

"That the king could believe that the Norwegian people will voluntarily surrender, and that he could believe me base enough to desert them now—indeed, I do not understand it. People would be justified in throwing stones after me, if ever I were able to deceive a nation which loves me and places its trust in me. I should leave it now without so much as trying to defend it—never in the world, while I live!"

On a journey, which the prince made north to Throndhjem, he found that the people all wished to defend the independence of Norway, and on the 16th and 17th of February he held a conference with notables at Eidsvold in order to discuss the needs of the hour. It was at first the idea of the prince that, since the king had relinquished the throne, he, as the legal heir, might ascend the throne of Norway as absolute monarch; but the members of the meeting at Eidsvold, especially Professor George Sverdrup, convinced him that, as King Frederick, contrary to law, had relinquished Norway, the sovereignty had now reverted to the Norwegian people, who thus recovered their natural right to adopt their own constitution and choose their executive. According to his diary the prince said at the meeting: "I have heard with great pleasure a speech made to me at a private audience by Professor Sverdrup, in which he conjured me not to place the crown on my head in a manner which was contrary to the views of the most enlightened men of the nation. The rights which Frederick VI. has relinquished revert to the people, and it is from their hands that you must receive a crown which will be far more glorious when you owe it to the love of the people." The result was that Christian Frederick took temporary charge of the government as regent, and issued a call for a constitutional convention or diet, consisting of representatives of the people from all parts of the country.

In all his efforts, by the aid of the great Powers and by force of arms against Denmark, to secure Norway for the king of Sweden, Charles John had never taken the will or desire of the Norwegians themselves into consideration. While Count Wedel, who considered a union with Sweden desirable or necessary, had emphatically declared that Norway would never consent to a union attempted by force, Crown Prince Charles John said that a people which for centuries had tolerated the supremacy of a foreign power without a murmur would not seriously resist a change of masters. The Swedish king issued a proclamation to the Norwegians, in which he promised to give them a constitution, and he appointed a viceroy for Norway; but his offers were rejected. The Swedish army being occupied in Germany, with the war against Napoleon, there was no force available with which to enforce the Swedish demands, and this gave the Norwegians time to arrange their own affairs; but there was considerable suffering in the country, because the British, upon learning that the Norwegians would not accept the treaty of Kiel, sent their fleet to prevent the importation of grain to Norway.

The diet, which met at Eidsvold, April 10, 1814, consisted of one hundred and twelve representatives. There were thirty-three army officers, fourteen clergymen, twenty-six other officials, twenty-three farmers, twelve merchants, and four mine-owners and landed proprietors. There were two parties in the convention. The most numerous one was the so-called "party of independence," whose principal leaders were Judge Christian Magnus Falsen, Professor George Sverdrup, Judge Christie, and Captain Motzfeldt. The other party, which numbered about thirty members, favored a union with Sweden, and was called the Swedish party, although hardly any of them advocated their policy from any love for the Swedes, but rather from what they considered a necessity, believing that Norway would not, under the circumstances, be able single-handed to maintain her independence. The prominent men of this party were Count Wedel-Jarlsberg, Chamberlain Peter Anker, Mine-owner Jacob Aall, *Amtmand* (prefect) Lövenskiold, and the Reverend Nicolai Wergeland. But all members agreed in the demand that Norway must henceforth have a liberal constitution. The following were agreed upon as the fundamental principles of the constitution:

1. Norway shall be a limited, hereditary monarchy; it shall be a free, independent and indivisible kingdom, and the ruler shall have the title of king.

2. The people shall exercise the legislative power through their representatives.

3. The people shall alone have the right to levy taxes through their representatives.

4. The right to declare war and to make peace rests with the king.

5. The king shall have the right of pardon.

6. The judicial power shall be separate from the legislative and executive power.

7. There shall be liberty of the press.

8. The evangelical Lutheran religion shall remain the religion of the state and of the king.

9. Personal or mixed hereditary privileges shall not be granted to anybody in the future.

10. All citizens, irrespective of station, birth, or property, shall be required to render military service for a certain length of time.

Upon the basis of these principles the constitution was drawn and finally adopted on the 17th day of May, 1814. On the same day Christian Frederick was elected king of Norway. He accepted the election and solemnly made oath to the constitution, May 19, whereupon the members of the diet swore allegiance to the constitution and to the new king. They held their last meeting on May 20, in order to sign the record of the proceedings. That done, they formed a circular chain, each person giving his right hand to his neighbor on the left, and his left hand to his neighbor on the right, and standing thus, hand in hand, they all exclaimed in chorus: "United and true, until Dovre (mountain) falls!"

CHAPTER LVI

War With Sweden—Union of November 4, 1814

AFTER the final defeat of Napoleon, the allied powers, Russia, Prussia, Austria, and England, granted the request of Charles John and promised to urge Norway to accept the supremacy of Sweden. The special envoys of the powers arrived in Christiania, June 30, 1814, bringing with them, besides their instructions from their respective governments, a letter from the Danish king to Christian Frederick, in which the latter was again commanded, under pain of being disinherited and otherwise punished, to abdicate and return to Denmark. The day after their arrival the commissioners had an audience with King Christian Frederick and acquainted him with the intention of the powers to demand the acceptance of the provisions in the treaty of Kiel. The king declared himself willing to convene the Storthing (Parliament) in extra session, in order to open negotiations for a peaceable union, if, in the meantime, the powers would guarantee an armistice and allow the free importation of breadstuffs; but when the commissioners demanded that the Norwegians should surrender to the mercy of the Swedish king, and allow the forts to be occupied by Swedish soldiers, the king declined to accept their propositions, and war commenced. The Norwegian army, which stood along the frontier, was poorly equipped and ill-provided with clothing and provisions. The king himself was no great soldier, and the information that all the foreign powers were against Norway had considerably lessened his courage. The Swedish fleet, under the personal command of Charles XIII., took up a position outside of Fredericksstad, which was insufficiently defended and was compelled to surrender, August 4. About the same time, the main Swedish army, under Charles John, crossed the frontier south of Frederickshald. One division of it laid siege to the fortress of Fredericksteen, which was bravely defended by General Ohme. The Norwegian army was eager for a general action; but the king, who thought this would be unwise, ordered a retreat across the Glommen River. North in Soloer, where Lieutenant-Colonel Krebs had the command, the Norwegian forces were much more successful. A Swedish force, under General Gahn, crossed the frontier and marched in the direction of Kongsvinger, but was defeated by the Norwegians at Lier, August 2. The Norwegians, under Col. Krebs, afterward attacked the Swedes at Matrand and drove them back across the frontier, August 5. The battle at Matrand was the most bloody encounter during this war. General Gahn's loss, in killed, wounded, or captured, was sixteen officers, seven non-commissioned officers and three hundred and twelve men. The Norwegian loss, in killed, wounded or captured, was five officers, four non-commissioned officers and one hundred and thirty men. The number of dead was about equal on both sides, about fifty men; of the wounded there was sixty-four on the Norwegian, and one hundred and twenty-six on the Swedish side.

On August 5, Charles John took steps to communicate with the Norwegians with a view to the arrangement of an armistice, offering to recognize the Norwegian Constitution of May 17, if Norway would agree to a union with Sweden. The result at these negotiations was the Convention signed at Moss, August 14, by which Christian Frederick promised to call an extra session at the Storthing to negotiate with the Swedish king through commissioners appointed by him; he also solemnly agreed to surrender the executive power intrusted to him into the hands of the nation; in the meantime the country east of the river Glommen and the fortress of Frederickssteen were to be occupied by Swedish troops. According to a secret agreement Christian Frederick was, under some pretext, to immediately transfer the executive power to the ministers, who were to conduct the necessary functions of the government until the Storthing had definitely decided upon the future form of government. This ended the war, which had not been a very bloody one. The loss, in killed, wounded, and captured, was about equal on both sides; namely, about four hundred dead and wounded and three hundred prisoners.

On the 16th day of August Christian Frederick issued a proclamation ordering elections to an extraordinary Storthing to be opened at Christiania, October 7, and on August 19 he ordered the cabinet to take charge of the executive power, signing all executive acts "by high command." The Storthing met at the time designated, the number of representatives being eighty, of whom about twenty had been members of the diet at Eidsvold. The Storthing was solemnly opened by the oldest minister in the name of King Christian Frederick. Two days later a committee of the Storthing, at the request of the king, had an audience with him at his residence on Bygdö, when he surrendered the Norwegian crown into the hands of the people, and for himself and his descendants relinquished all rights to the country. On the same day he went on board a ship and sailed from Norway.[14] The Storthing now, under the presidency of Judge Christie, began negotiations with the commissioners of the Swedish king, and on the 20th day of October it was decided, by seventy-two votes in the affirmative to five in the negative, that Norway as an independent state, upon certain conditions, was to be united with Sweden under the same king. The changes in the Constitution made necessary by reason of the union with Sweden were then made and finally ratified, November 4, 1814, and, on the same day, Charles XIII. was unanimously elected king of Norway.

A committee of the Storthing, headed by Count Wedel-Jarlsberg, was sent to Crown Prince Charles John at Frederickshald, to inform him of the action of the Storthing; whereupon Charles John and his son, Prince Oscar, proceeded to Christiania and delivered to the Storthing the king's written oath to the Constitution. As soon as the report of the action of the Norwegian Storthing had reached Stockholm, the Swedish Minister of Foreign Affairs, Lars von Engeström, despatched a circular to each of the Swedish representatives at the foreign courts, informing them of the union of Norway and Sweden. In this circular the minister said:

"The Norwegian Storthing having, of its own accord and by a free election, chosen his Swedish majesty as king of Norway, it is plain that it is not to the provisions of the treaty of Kiel, but to the confidence of the Norwegian people, that we owe the Union of Norway with Sweden."

CHAPTER LVII

The Union With Sweden

THE first Storthing (Parliament), after the union had been accomplished, remained in session a year, and together with the Swedish Diet adopted the "Act of Union," or Rigsakt (1815), based upon the Norwegian Constitution and defining the terms of the union. At the same time the Supreme Court of Norway was established in Christiania. The Bank of Norway was established at Throndhjem in 1816. At the death of Charles XIII., in 1818, Charles John ascended the throne of both countries as Charles XIV. John.

On several occasions there was friction between the king and the Norwegian Storthing. At the treaty of Kiel, Charles John had promised that Norway would assume a part of the Norwegian-Danish public debt; but as the Norwegians had never acknowledged this treaty, they held that it was not their duty to pay any part of the debt, and declared besides that Norway was not able to do so. But as the powers had agreed to help Denmark to enforce her claims, a compromise was effected in 1821, by which the Storthing agreed to pay three million dollars, the king relinquishing his civil list for a certain number of years. The same Storthing adopted the law abolishing the nobility in Norway. This step was also strongly opposed by Charles John, but as it had been adopted by three successive Storthings, the act under the Constitution became a law in spite of any veto. It was believed by many that the manœuvres of Norwegian and Swedish troops and the Swedish fleet, which was collected at Christiania at the time that these matters were under consideration, had been called together by the king in order to intimidate the Storthing.

For a number of years there existed a want of confidence between the king and the Norwegian people. The king did not like the democratic spirit of the Norwegians, and the reactionary tendencies of his European allies had quite an influence upon his actions. In 1821 he proposed ten amendments to the Constitution, looking to an increase of the royal power, among which was one giving the king an absolute instead of a suspensive veto; another giving him the right to appoint the presidents of the Storthing, and a third authorizing him to dissolve the Storthing at any time. But these amendments met the most ardent opposition in the Storthing, especially from the former cabinet-minister, Christian Krogh, and were unanimously rejected by the Storthing in 1824. The king renewed these propositions before several successive Storthings, but they were each time rejected.

When the Norwegians commenced to celebrate the anniversary of the adoption of the Constitution (May 17), the king thought he saw in this a sign of a disloyal spirit, because they did not rather celebrate the union with Sweden, and he forbade the public celebration of the day. The result of this was that "Independence Day" was celebrated with so much greater eagerness. The students at the university especially took an active part under the leadership of that champion of liberty, the poet Henrik Wergeland (born 1808, died 1845). The unwise prohibition was the cause of the "market-place battle" in Christiania, May 17, 1829, when the troops were called out, and General Wedel dispersed the crowds that had assembled in the market-place. There was also dissatisfaction in Norway, because a Swedish viceroy (Statholder) was placed at the head of the government, and because their ships had to sail under the Swedish flag.

The French July Revolution of 1830, which started the liberal movement throughout Europe, also had its influence in Norway. Liberal newspapers were established at the capital, and the democratic character of the Storthing became more pronounced, especially after 1833, when the farmers commenced to take an active part in the elections. Prominent among them was Ole Gabriel Ueland. The king was so displeased with the majority in the Storthing of 1836 that he suddenly dissolved it; but the Storthing answered this action by impeaching the Minister of State, Lövenskiold, for not having dissuaded the king from taking such a step. Lövenskiold was sentenced to pay a fine. The king then yielded and reconvened the Storthing. He also took a step toward conciliating the Norwegians by appointing their countryman, Count Wedel-Jarlsberg, as viceroy. This action was much appreciated in Norway. During the last years of this reign there existed the best of understanding between the king and the people. Charles John's great benevolence tended to increase the affection of the people, and he was sincerely mourned at his death, March 8, 1844, Charles XIV. John being then eighty years old.

Charles John was succeeded by his son, Oscar I., who very soon won the love of the Norwegians. One of his first acts was to give Norway her own commercial flag and other outward signs of her equality with Sweden. His father had always signed himself "King of Sweden and Norway"; but King Oscar adopted the rule to sign all documents pertaining to the government of Norway as "King of Norway and Sweden." During the war between Germany and Denmark, King Oscar gathered a Swedish-Norwegian army in Scania, and he succeeded in arranging the armistice of Malmœ in 1848. The war broke out anew, however, the following year, and he then occupied northern Schleswig with Norwegian and Swedish troops, pending the negotiations for peace between Germany and Denmark. During the Crimean War, King Oscar made a treaty with England and

France (1855), by which the latter powers promised to help Sweden and Norway in case of any attack from Russia. General contentment prevailed during the happy reign of King Oscar, and the prosperity, commerce and population of the country increased steadily. These satisfactory conditions did not, however, result in any weakening of the national feeling, and the Storthing, in 1857, declined to promote a plan, prepared by a joint Swedish and Norwegian commission, looking to a strengthening of the union. After a sickness of two years, during which his eldest son, Crown Prince Charles, had charge of the government as prince-regent, King Oscar I. died in July, 1859, at the age of sixty years. He was married to Josephine of Leuchtenberg, daughter of Napoleon's stepson, Engene Beauharnais.

Charles XV. was thirty-three years old when he ascended the throne. The progress in the material welfare of the country was continued during his reign, and, like his father, he was very popular. Numerous roads and railways were started, all parts of the country were connected by telegraph, and the merchant marine grew to be one of the largest in the world. In 1869 a law was passed providing for annual sessions of the Storthing instead of triennial as heretofore.

The first Storthing under Charles XV., with only two negative votes, resolved to abolish the right of the king to appoint a viceroy (Statholder) for Norway. This action of the Storthing enraged the ruling party in the Swedish Diet, who claimed a right to be consulted in this matter, in which they considered that Sweden had an interest, and they demanded a revision of the terms of the union. A serious conflict was avoided for the time being, the king vetoing the resolution of the Storthing. Not till 1865 were negotiations opened for a revision. A joint committee was appointed to prepare a plan; but the question was not solved, for the Storthing, in 1870, rejected the plan proposed by the committee.

Charles XV. died September 18, 1872, and, having no sons, was succeeded by his younger brother, Oscar II. The king and the Storthing at first showed themselves mutually accommodating. The Storthing appropriated the necessary funds for the expense of the coronation at Throndhjem (July 18, 1873), while the king sanctioned the bill abolishing the office of Statholder. But in 1880 the difference between the Storthing and the ministry had brought on a sharp conflict. The liberal majority of the Storthing, in order to introduce parliamentarism, had three times adopted an amendment to the Constitution admitting the cabinet ministers to participation in the debates of the Storthing, and each time the measure had been vetoed by the king. The king, supported by the conservative party and by the opinion of the faculty of law of the university, claimed that the Constitution was a contract between the people and the royal house, and could not, therefore, be changed without the sanction of the king, who thus had an absolute veto in the matter of amendments to the Constitution. The liberal party claimed that in constitutional amendments, as well as in the matter of ordinary laws, the king had only a suspensive veto; and on the 9th of June, 1880, the Storthing adopted a resolution declaring that the amendment providing for the attendance of the cabinet ministers at the meetings of the Storthing was law in spite of the veto. The conflict steadily grew sharper, and in 1883 the members of the ministry (headed by Minister of State Selmer) were impeached for failure to promulgate the resolution of June 9, 1880. The ministers were found guilty and removed from office in the spring of 1884. The king once more tried a ministry which was not in accord with the majority of the Storthing, the so-called April Ministry, headed by Schweigaard; but the latter soon resigned, and in June, 1884, the king finally called upon Johan Sverdrup, the acknowledged leader of the liberal majority (the Left), to form a ministry.

The king now signed the constitutional amendment, and Sverdrup and his colleagues took their seats in the Storthing. For a time the legislative and the executive power worked in harmony, and several liberal reforms were introduced. A reorganization of the army in accordance with the views of the majority was brought about, the suffrage was extended, and trial by jury was introduced. In 1887, however, when the government introduced a bill for a new church-law, a division in the party of the left had taken place, and Sverdrup found himself without a majority in the Storthing. He retained office until after the elections of 1888, which resulted in three legislative parties, the "Left," the "Moderate," and the Conservative, or "Right." Neither of them had a majority in the Storthing. Sverdrup resigned (July, 1889), and the Conservative leader, Emil Stang, formed a new ministry. At the elections in 1891, the "pure left," having made a separate consular service independent of Sweden the main issue of the campaign, again obtained a majority, and their leader, Rector Steen, became the chief of the new ministry. The principal occasion of this movement was the rapid increase in Norwegian commercial interests, which, as was claimed, were imperfectly protected by a joint consular service.

The Steen Ministry resigned in May, 1893, and a ministry from the minority was formed by Stang. On June 7, 1895, the Storthing adopted a resolution declaring that, with a ministry possessing the confidence of the Storthing, it would be willing to negotiate with Sweden for a peaceable settlement of the matters in dispute. A coalition ministry, consisting of members from each of the three political groups and headed by Hagerup, was appointed in October, 1895, and a joint Swedish and Norwegian Union Committee was chosen to adjust disputed points. This committee, having failed to reach any agreement, was discharged in 1897.

At the elections of 1897 the left obtained an increased majority in the Storthing, and, in February, 1898, the Hagerup Ministry resigned, and Steen was again placed at the head of a ministry. The Storthing of 1898-99 adopted a constitutional amendment extending the suffrage to all male citizens who have attained the age of twenty-five years. A bill was also passed, for the third time, removing from the Norwegian merchant flag the "union jack," the symbol of the union with Sweden. This bill was twice vetoed by the king; but, after its third passage, was promulgated, having been passed, according to the Constitution, over the royal veto.

The secession movement was largely in abeyance during the years 1900-1902, owing to the popular fear of a Russian invasion. However, in 1903, the anti-union sentiment again came strongly to the front, reaching an acute stage in March, 1905, when a new cabinet, headed by Peter Christian Michelson, was formed. A bill demanding separate consular service was again passed by the Storthing, only to be vetoed by the Swedish crown. Compromise measures were proposed and rejected. In June the cabinet offered its resignation, which was refused by the King on the ground that a new ministry could not be formed in the existing state of feeling in Norway. The cabinet, thereupon, delegated its powers to the Storthing, which immediately passed a resolution declaring the dissolution of union between Sweden and Norway on the ground of the King's inability to conduct the government and his constructive relinquishment of authority. At the same time a letter was addressed to the King of Sweden expressing Norway's desire for the continuation of peaceful relations, and asking that a prince of the royal house of Sweden be designated as King of Norway. The latter request was refused, but other matters were adjusted by a joint commission.

The crown was finally offered to Charles, Crown Prince of Denmark, and son-in-law of King Edward of England, who was elected by a popular majority of 259,563 against 69,264, and assumed the throne November 20th under the name Haakon VII.

CHAPTER LVIII

Norwegian Literature

THE people who emigrated from Norway and settled in Iceland, after Harald the Fairhaired had subdued the many independent chiefs and established the monarchy (872), for the most part belonged to the flower of the nation, and Iceland naturally became the home of the old Norse literature. Among the oldest poetical works of this literature is the so-called "Elder Edda," also called Sæmund's Edda, because for a long time it was believed to be the work of the Icelander Sæmund. "The Younger Edda," also called Snorre's Edda, because it is supposed to have been written by Snorre Sturlason (born 1178, died 1241), contains a synopsis of the old Norse religion and a treatise on the art of poetry. Fully as important as the numerous poetical works of that period was the old Norse Saga-literature.[15] The most prominent work in this field is Snorre Sturlason's "Heimskringla," which gives the sagas of the kings of Norway from the beginning down to 1177. A continuation of the "Heimskringla," to which several authors have contributed, among them Snorre Sturlason's relative, Sturla Thordson, contains the history of the later kings down to Magnus Law-Mender.

The literary development above referred to ceased almost entirely toward the end of the fourteenth century, and later, during the union with Denmark, the Danish language gradually took the place of the old Norse as a book-language, and the literature became essentially Danish. Copenhagen, with its court and its university, was the literary and educational centre, where the young men of Norway went to study, and authors born in Norway became, to all intents and purposes, Danish writers. But Norway furnished some valuable contributors to this common literature. One of the very first names on the records of the Danish literature, Peder Claussön (1545-1614), is that of a Norwegian, and the list further includes such illustrious names as Holberg, Tullin, Wessel, Steffens, etc.

One of the most original writers whom Norway produced and kept at home during the period of the union with Denmark was the preacher and poet, Peder Dass (1647-1708). The best known among his secular songs is "Nordlands Trompet," a beautiful and patriotic description of the northern part of Norway.

Ludvig Holberg was born in Bergen, Norway, December 3, 1684. His father, Colonel Holberg, had risen from the ranks and distinguished himself, in 1660, at Halden. Shortly after his death the property of the family was destroyed by fire, and at the age of ten years Ludvig lost his mother. It was now decided to have him educated for the military service; but he showed a great dislike for military life, and, at his earnest request, was sent to the Bergen Latin School. In 1702 he entered the University of Copenhagen. Being destitute of means, he took a position as private tutor. As soon as he had saved a small sum he went abroad. He was first in Holland, and afterward studied for a couple of years at Oxford, where he supported himself by giving instruction in languages and music. Upon his return to Copenhagen he again took a position as private tutor and had an opportunity to travel as teacher for a young nobleman. In 1714 he received a stipend from the king, which enabled him to go abroad for several years, which he spent principally in France and Italy. In 1718 he became a regular professor at the Copenhagen University. Among Holberg's many works the following are the most prominent: "Peder Paars," a great comical heroic poem, containing sharp attacks on many of the follies of his time; about thirty comedies in Molière's style, and a large number of historical works. Holberg, who was ennobled in 1747, died in January 29, 1754, and was buried in Sorö Church. His influence on the literature and on the whole intellectual life of Denmark was very great. He is often called the creator of the Danish literature.

Christian Baumann Tullin (1728-1765), a genuine poetical genius, who has been called the Father of Danish lyrical verse, was born in Christiania, and his poetry, which was mainly written in his native city, breathes a national spirit. From his day, for about thirty years, Denmark obtained the majority of her poets from Norway. The manager of the Danish national theatre, in 1771, was a Norwegian, Niels Krog-Bredal (1733-1778), who was the first to write lyrical dramas in Danish. A Norwegian, Johan Nordal Brun (1745-1816), a gifted poet, wrote tragedy in the conventional French taste of the day. It was a Norwegian, Johan Herman Wessel (1742-1785), who, by his great parody, "Kjærlighed uden Strömper" (Love without Stockings), laughed this taste out of fashion. Among the writers of this period are also Claus Frimann (1746-1829), Peter Harboe Frimann (1752-1839), Claus Fasting (1746-1791), Johan Wibe (1748-1782), Edward Storm (1749-1794), C. H. Pram (1756-1821), Jonas Rein (1760-1821), and Jens Zetlitz (1761-1821), all of them Norwegians by birth.

Two notable events led to the foundation of an independent Norwegian literature: the one was the establishment of a Norwegian university at Christiania in 1811, and the other was the separation of Norway from Denmark in 1814. At first the independent Norwegian literature appeared as immature as the conditions surrounding it. The majority of the writers had received their education in Copenhagen, and were inclined to follow in the beaten track of the old literature, although trying to introduce a more national spirit. All were greatly influenced by the political feeling of the hour. There was a period when all poetry had for its subject the beauties and strength of Norway and its people, and "The Rocks of Norway," "The Lion of Norway," etc., sounded everywhere. Three poets, called the Trefoil, were the prominent writers of this period. Of these, Conrad Nicolai Schwach (1793-1860) was the least remarkable. Henrik A. Bjerregaard (1792-1842) was the author of "The Crowned National Song," and of a lyric drama, "Fjeldeventyret" (The Adventure in the Mountains). The third member of the Trefoil, Mauritz Chr. Hansen (1794-1842), wrote a large number of novels and national stories, which were quite popular in their time. His poems were among the earliest publications of independent Norway.

The time about the year 1830 is reckoned as the beginning of the new Norwegian literature, and Henrik Wergeland is called its creator. Henrik Arnold Wergeland was born in 1808. His father, Nicolai Wergeland, a clergyman, was a member of the Constitutional Convention at Eidsvold. Henrik studied theology, but did not care to become a clergyman. In 1827, and the following years, he wrote a number of satirical farces under the signature "Siful Sifadda." In 1830 appeared his lyric dramatic poem, "Skabelsen, Mennesket og Messias" (The Creation, Man and Messiah), a voluminous piece of work, in which he attempted to explain the historical life of the human race. As a political writer he was editorial assistant on the "Folkebladet" (1831-1833), and edited the opposition paper "Statsborgeren" (1835-1837). He worked with great zeal for the education of the laboring class, and from 1839 until his death edited a paper in the interest of the laborer. The prominent features of his earliest efforts in literature are an unbounded enthusiasm and a complete disregard of the laws of poetry. At an early age he had become a power in literature, and a political power as well. From 1831 to 1835 he was subjected to severe satirical attacks by the author Welhaven and others, and later his style became improved in every respect. His popularity however decreased as his poetry improved, and in 1840 he had become a great poet but had no political influence. Among his works may be named "Hasselnödder," "Jöden" (The Jew), "Jödinden" (The Jewess), "Jan van Huysums Blomsterstykke" (Jan van Huysum's Flower-piece), "Den engelske Lods" (The English Pilot), and a great number of lyric poems. The poems of his last five years are as popular to-day as ever. Wergeland died in 1845.

The enthusiastic nationalism of Henrik Wergeland and his young following brought on a conflict with the conservative element, which was not ready to accept everything as good simply because it was Norwegian. This conservative element maintained that art and culture must be developed on the basis of the old association with Denmark, which had connected Norway with the great movement of civilization throughout Europe. As the poetical leader of this "Intelligence" party, as it was called, appeared J. S. Welhaven.

Johan Sebastian Cammermeyer Welhaven was born in Bergen in 1807, entered the university in 1825, became a "Lector" in 1840, and afterward Professor of Philosophy. "His refined æsthetic nature," says Fr. Winkel Horn, "had been early developed, and when the war broke out between him and Wergeland he had reached a high point of intellectual culture, and thus was in every way a match for his opponent. The fight was inaugurated by a preliminary literary skirmish, which was, at the outset, limited to the university students; but it gradually assumed an increasingly bitter character, both parties growing more and more exasperated. Welhaven published a pamphlet, 'Om Henrik Wergelands Digtekunst og Poesie,' in which he mercilessly exposed the weak sides of his adversary's poetry. Thereby the minds became still more excited. The 'Intelligence' party withdrew from the students' union, founded a paper of their own, and thus the movement began to assume wider dimensions. In 1834 appeared Welhaven's celebrated poem 'Norges Dæmring,' a series of sonnets, distinguished for their beauty of style. In them the poet scourges, without mercy, the one-sided, narrow-minded patriotism of his time, and exposes, in striking and unmistakable words, the hollowness and shortcomings of the Wergeland party. Welhaven points out, with emphasis, that he is not only going to espouse the cause of good taste, which his adversary has outraged, but that he is also about to discuss problems of general interest. He urges that a Norwegian culture and literature cannot be created out of nothing; that to promote their development it is absolutely necessary to continue the associations which have hitherto been common to both Norway and Denmark, and thus to keep in *rapport* with the general literature of Europe. When a solid foundation has in this manner been laid, the necessary materials for a literature would surely not be wanting, for they are found in abundance, both in the antiquities and in the popular life of Norway." Welhaven continued his effective work as a poet and a critic. Through a series of lyrical and romantic poems, rich in contents and highly finished in style, he developed a poetical life, which had an important influence in the young Norwegian literary circles. He died in 1873.

Andreas Munch (1811-1884), an able and industrious poetical writer, took no part in the controversy between Wergeland and Welhaven, but followed his Danish models independently of either. His "Poems, Old and New," published in 1848, were quite popular. His best work is probably "Kongedatterens Brudefart" (The Bridal Tour of the King's Daughter), 1861.

In the period of about a dozen years following the death of Wergeland, the life, manners and characteristics of the Norwegian people were given the especial attention of the literary writers. Prominent in this period was Peter Christian Asbjörnsen (1812-1885), who, partly alone and partly in conjunction with Bishop Jörgen Moe (1813-1882), published some valuable collections of Norwegian folk tales and fairy tales. Moe also published three little volumes of graceful and attractive poems. Among other writers of this period may be named Hans H. Schultze ("Fra Lofoten og Solör"), N. Östgaard ("En Fjeldbygd"), Harald Meltser ("Smaabilleder af Folkelivet"), M. B. Landstad (hymns), and the linguist Sophus Bugge.

The efforts to bring out the national life and characteristics of the people in the literature also led to an attempt to nationalize the language in which the literature was written. The movement was the so-called "Maalstræv," and had in view the introduction of a "pure Norwegian" book-language, based upon the peasant dialects. The most prominent supporter of this movement was Ivar Aasen (1813-1898), the author of an excellent dictionary of the Norwegian language. A prominent poetical representative of this school was Aasmund Olafson Vinje (1818-1870), while Kristofer Janson (born 1841) has also written a number of stories and poems in the *Landsmaal* (country tongue).

A new and grand period in the Norwegian literature commenced about 1857, and the two most conspicuous names in this period—and in the whole Norwegian literature—are those of Henrik Ibsen and Björnstjerne Björnson.

Henrik Ibsen was born in Skien in 1828. He has written many beautiful poems; but his special field is the drama, where he is a master. His first works were nearly all historical romantic dramas. His first work, "Catilina," printed in 1850, was scarcely noticed until years afterward, when he had become famous. In 1856 appeared the romantic drama, "Gildet paa Solhaug" (The Feast at Solhaug), followed by "Fru Inger til Oestraat," 1857, and "Hærmændene paa Helgeland" (The Warriors on Helgeland), 1858. In 1863 he wrote the historical tragedy "Kongsemnerne" (The Pretenders), in which the author showed his great literary power. Before this play was published, he had been drawn into a new channel. In 1862 he began a series of satirical and philosophical dramas with "Kjærlighedens Komedie" (Love's Comedy), which was succeeded by two masterpieces of a similar kind, "Brand," in 1866, and "Peer Gynt," in 1867. These works were written in verse; but in "De Unges Forbund" (The Young Men's League), 1869, a political satire, he abandoned verse, and all his subsequent dramas have been written in prose. In 1873 came "Keiser og Galilæer" (Emperor and Galilean). Since then he has published a number of social dramas which have attracted world-wide attention. We mention:

"Samfundets Stötter" (The Pillars of Society), "Et Dukkehjem" (A Doll's House), "Gengangere" (Ghosts), "En Folkefiende" (An Enemy of the People), "Rosmerholm," "Fruen fra Havet" (The Lady from the Sea), "Little Eyolf," "Bymester Solnes" (Masterbuilder Solnes), "John Gabriel Borkman."

Björnstjerne Björnson (born in Österdalen in 1832) is the more popular of the two giants in the Norwegian literature of to-day. His works are more national in tone. It has been said that to mention his name is to raise the Norwegian flag. His first successes were made in the field of the novel, and the first two, "Synnöve Solbakken" (1857), and "Arne" (1858), made his name famous. These, and his other peasant stories, will always retain their popularity. He soon, however, entered the dramatic field, and has since published a great number of dramas and novels. "Halte Hulda," 1858; "Mellem Slagene," 1859; "Kong Sverre," 1861; "Sigurd Slembe," 1862; "Maria Stuart," 1863; "De Nygifte" (The Newly-married Couple), 1865; "Kongen," 1877; "Leonarda," 1879; "Det ny System," 1879; "Over Ærne," 1883; "En Fallit," "Det flager," etc., and many others.

In the field of belles-lettres there is, at the present time, a number of other talented authors. Jonas Lie (born 1833) has produced a number of excellent novels. Then there are Alexander Kielland (born 1849), Magdalene Thoresen (born 1819), Arne Garborg, Gunnar Heiberg, and a number of young authors.

In the field of science, also, modern Norway has a rich literature with many prominent names, such as the historians Peter Andreas Munch (1810-1863), Rudolph Keyser (1803-1864), Johan Ernst Sars (born 1835), and O. A. Överland.

CHAPTER LIX

The Constitution of Norway

THE following is the Constitution adopted at the Convention at Eidsvold on the 17th day of May, 1814, and amended and ratified by the Storthing on the 4th day of November, 1814, with all the subsequent amendments incorporated:

A. RELIGION AND FORM OF GOVERNMENT:

Article 1. The Kingdom of Norway is a free, independent, indivisible and inalienable state, united with Sweden under one king. Its form of government is a limited, hereditary monarchy.

Article 2. The Evangelical Lutheran religion shall continue the established religion of the state. Such inhabitants as profess the same shall educate their children therein. Jesuits shall be excluded.

B. THE EXECUTIVE POWER, THE KING, AND THE ROYAL FAMILY:

Article 3. The executive power shall be vested in the King.

Article 4. The King shall constantly profess, maintain and defend the Evangelical Lutheran religion.

Article 5. The King's person is sacred; he shall neither be censured nor impeached. His Ministry shall, however, be accountable.

Article 6. The succession shall be lineal and agnatic as prescribed in the ordinance of succession of September 26, 1810, adopted by the Legislative Assembly of Sweden and accepted by the King, a translation of which is attached to this Constitution. A posthumous child shall be deemed in the line of succession, and shall take his appropriate place therein as soon as born. When a prince, who is heir to the United Crowns of Norway and Sweden, is born, his name and time of birth shall be reported to the next Storthing in session and entered in its journal.

Article 7. If no Prince, heir to the Crowns, be living, the King may propose a successor to the Storthing of Norway, at the same time as to the Legislative Assembly of Sweden; and, as soon as the King has made his nomination, the legislative bodies of both nations shall appoint a committee from their midst, with power to choose a successor, in case the nominee of the King is not confirmed by a majority in each legislative body. The number of members of this Committee, which must be equal from each kingdom, and the manner in which the choice shall be made, shall be determined by a law, simultaneously proposed by the King to the next Storthing and to the Legislative Assembly of Sweden. One member shall withdraw, by lot, from the assembled committee.

Article 8. The age of majority of the King shall be prescribed by a law, to be enacted pursuant to an agreement between the Storthing of Norway and the Legislative Assembly of Sweden, or, in case they cannot agree concerning the same, by a committee appointed by the legislative bodies of both kingdoms, conformable to the provisions of the preceding Article 7. The King shall publicly proclaim himself of age as soon as he has attained his majority.

Article 9. As soon as the King, on coming of age, assumes the government, he shall take the following oath before the Storthing: "I promise and depose that I will govern the Kingdom of Norway conformable to its Constitution and laws, so help me God and His Holy Writ." If no Storthing is then in session, the oath shall be deposited in writing with the Ministry, and shall solemnly be renewed by the King at the next Storthing, either orally or in writing through his representative.

Article 10. The King shall be crowned and anointed, when he is of age, in Throndhjem's Cathedral, at such time and with such ceremonies as he himself may prescribe.

Article 11. The King shall reside in Norway a part of each year, if not prevented by serious obstacles.

Article 12. The King shall appoint a Ministry of Norwegian citizens, who shall not be less than thirty years of age. The Ministry shall consist of two Ministers of State, and not less than seven Secretaries of State. The King shall apportion the public business among the members of the Ministry in such manner as he deems best. The King, or, in his absence, the Minister of State, in conjunction with the Secretaries of State, may, on extraordinary occasions, in addition to the regular members of the Ministry, summon other Norwegian citizens, not members of the Storthing, to a seat in the Ministry. Father and son, or two brothers, shall not have a seat in the Ministry at the same time.

Article 13. The King shall commit, during his absence, the administration of the domestic affairs of the realm, in such cases as he may prescribe, to one of the Ministers of State, and not less than five of the Secretaries of State, who shall carry on the government in the name, and on behalf, of the King. They shall sacredly conform as well to the provisions of this Constitution as to the several instructions in harmony therewith, prescribed to them by the King. They shall present to the King a respectful application concerning the affairs they resolve upon. Their transactions shall be determined by vote, and in case of an equal division the Minister of State, or, in his absence, the senior Secretary of State, shall have two votes.

Article 14. (Repealed.)

Article 15. One of the Ministers of State, and two of the Secretaries of State, the latter to be changed yearly, shall constantly remain with the King while he resides in Sweden. They shall be subject to the same obligations and to the same constitutional accountability as the governing Ministry, named in Article 13, existing in Norway, and only in their presence shall Norwegian affairs be disposed of by the King. All applications from Norwegian citizens to the King shall first be presented to the governing Ministry in Norway, and supplemented with their opinion, before passed upon. As a rule, except where serious obstacles prevent, no Norwegian affairs shall be disposed of without obtaining the advice of the governing Ministry in Norway. The Minister of State shall move the consideration of public business, and shall be responsible for the due expedition of all resolutions taken.

Article 16. The King shall prescribe rules for all public religious and church service, and for all meetings and conventions relating to religious affairs, and he shall take care that the public instructors of religion adhere to the standards prescribed them.

Article 17. The King may enact and repeal ordinances relating to commerce, customs, industrial pursuits and public order, not, however, in conflict with the Constitution or the laws of the Storthing, passed pursuant to the provisions of Article 77, 78 and 79 of this Constitution. Such acts of the King shall remain provisionally in force until the next Storthing.

Article 18. The King shall, ordinarily, cause the taxes and imposts, levied by the Storthing, to be collected. The Norwegian Treasury shall remain in Norway, and its revenue shall be devoted to the requirements of Norway alone.

Article 19. The King shall take care that the estates and regalia of the State be used and managed in the manner prescribed by the Storthing, and for the greatest advantage of the public.

Article 20. The King shall have power, in council, to pardon offenders after conviction. The offender shall, however, have the option to accept the pardon of the King or to suffer the punishment adjudged. No pardon or reprieve, except the remission of the death penalty, shall be granted in cases prosecuted by the Odelsthing in the Court of Impeachment.

Article 21. The King, after hearing his Ministry in Norway, shall appoint and induct all civil, ecclesiastical and military officials, who shall take an oath of obedience and fealty to the Constitution and the King, or who, if relieved by law from such an oath, shall solemnly declare their fealty to the same. Royal Princes shall hold no civil office.

Article 22. The King may, after taking the advice of the Ministry, without the warrant of judicial decree, remove from office the Ministers and Secretaries of State, together with officials in the bureaus of the Ministry, Ambassadors and Consuls, the chief civil and ecclesiastical officials, and the chiefs of fortifications and ships of war. Whether pensions shall be granted to officials thus removed shall be determined by the next Storthing, but, in the meantime, they shall continue to receive two-thirds of their former salary. Other officials are only liable to suspension by the King, and, when suspended, shall at once be proceeded against in the courts, and shall not, without judgment, be removed, nor transferred without their consent.

Article 23. The King, at his pleasure, may confer orders of merit, in recognition of distinguished services, to be publicly announced, but no other rank or title than that conferred by an office occupied. Such orders shall relieve no one from the duties and burdens common to all citizens, nor shall they confer any preference in securing admission to the public service. Officials, honorably discharged, shall retain the title and rank of the office they occupied. No personal or mixed hereditary prerogatives shall hereafter be conferred on any one.

Article 24. The King may, at pleasure, select and dismiss the employees and officers of his royal household.

Article 25. The King shall be Commander-in-Chief of the land and naval forces of the realm. These forces shall neither be increased nor diminished without the consent of the Storthing. They shall not be placed in the service of foreign powers, nor shall the military forces of any foreign powers, except auxiliary troops to repel hostile attack, be brought within the realm without the consent of the Storthing. In times of peace, none but Norwegian troops shall be stationed in Norway, and no Norwegian troops shall be stationed in Sweden. The King, however, may retain in Sweden a Norwegian guard of volunteers, and he may, for a short time not exceeding six weeks in any year, assemble for manœuvres, within the limits of either country, the nearest troops of the armies of both realms; but in no case, in times of peace, shall more than three thousand soldiers, of all arms combined, of the military force of one country, be brought within the limits of the other country. Norway's troops and coast flotilla shall not be employed in offensive war without the consent of the Storthing. The Norwegian fleet shall have its dock yards, and in times of peace its stations or havens in Norway. The ships of war of one country shall not be manned with sailors of the other country, except by voluntary enlistment. The home guard and the other Norwegian troops, not classed as troops of the line, shall never be employed outside of the boundaries of Norway.

Article 26. The King shall have power to call out the troops, to commence war and make peace, to enter into treaties, and to abrogate the same, and to send and receive diplomatic representatives. When the King intends to commence war, he shall communicate his purpose to the governing Ministry in Norway, and obtain their judgment concerning the same, together with a full report upon the condition of the country in respect to its finances, means of defence, and other matters. When these steps have been taken, the King shall convene the Norwegian Minister of State and the Norwegian Secretaries of State stationed in Sweden, together with the members of the Swedish Ministry, in an extraordinary cabinet council, and shall present to them the grounds and circumstances which should in such cases be taken into consideration, and shall also place before them the report of the Norwegian Ministry concerning the condition of that country, and a like report concerning the condition of Sweden. The King shall thereupon demand their judgment in the premises, which each of them for himself shall give and have entered in the journal of the proceedings, to be accountable for as provided in the Constitution. When this has been done, the King shall have the power to take and execute such resolution as he deems for the best interest of the country.

Article 27. All members of the Ministry, without valid excuse, shall attend the cabinet councils, and no action shall be taken when not more than half of the members are present. No action shall be taken in those Norwegian affairs, disposed of in Sweden, pursuant to Article 15, unless the Norwegian Minister of State and one of the Norwegian Secretaries of State, or both of the Secretaries, be present.

Article 28. Communications concerning appointments to office and other matters of importance, except diplomatic affairs and military commands, shall be presented for consideration to the Ministry by the member thereof in whose department the business belongs, and he shall dispose of the same conformable to the resolve of the Ministry.

Article 29. In case a member of the Ministry is unable, for valid cause, to attend and present for consideration the matters pertaining to his department, the same shall be presented by another member of the Ministry, appointed for that purpose by the King, if present, or, in his absence, by the presiding member of the Ministry, in conjunction with the other members of the Ministry. If, for valid cause, so many are absent that not more than half of the regular members are in attendance, then other officials shall be appointed, in the mode aforesaid, to sit in the Ministry, in which case a report thereof shall at once be made to the King, who shall determine whether the officials thus appointed shall continue to serve.

Article 30. The Ministry shall keep a record of all business transacted. It shall be the duty of every person who has a seat in the Ministry to express his opinion fearlessly, to which the King shall listen, but he may resolve according to his own judgment. In case any member of the Ministry finds that the resolve of the King is in conflict with the form of government or the laws of the realm, or is manifestly detrimental to the country, then it is his duty to vigorously protest against the same, and to enter his objections in the record. He who does not thus protest, shall be deemed to have concurred with the King, and shall be accountable therefor, as subsequently determined, and may be impeached by the Odelsthing in the Court of Impeachment.

Article 31. All decrees issued by the King himself, except military commands, shall be countersigned by one of the Ministers of State.

Article 32. Resolutions taken by the Ministry in Norway, during the absence of the King, shall be issued in his name, and attested by the Ministry.

Article 33. All communications relative to Norwegian affairs, as well as the expedition of the same, shall be in the Norwegian language.

Article 34. The heir apparent, if son of the reigning King, shall bear the title of Crown Prince. The other royal heirs shall be known as Princes, and the royal daughters as Princesses.

Article 35. As soon as the heir apparent has filled his eighteenth year, he shall be entitled to take his seat in the Ministry, but without vote or accountability.

Article 36. No Prince of the blood shall marry without the consent of the King. If he violates this rule he shall forfeit his right to the crown of Norway.

Article 37. The royal Princes and Princesses shall personally only be answerable to the King, or to such judge as he may ordain for them.

Article 38. The Norwegian Minister of State, as well as the two Norwegian Secretaries of State, remaining with the King, shall have a seat and deliberative voice in the Swedish Ministry when matters affecting both kingdoms are there considered. The views of the Ministry in Norway shall also be obtained, in such cases, unless the urgency for immediate action is so great that there is no time therefor.

Article 39. If the King dies and his successor is still under age, the Norwegian and Swedish Ministries shall immediately assemble, and jointly issue a call convening the Storthing in Norway and the Rigsdag in Sweden.

Article 40. Until the legislative bodies of both realms are convened and have provided for the government during the minority of the King, the administration of the kingdoms, conformable to their respective Constitutions, shall be conducted by a Ministry composed of an equal number of Norwegian and Swedish members. The Norwegian and Swedish Ministers of State, having a seat in this Ministry, shall determine, by lot, who shall preside.

Article 41. The provisions of Articles 39 and 40, aforesaid, shall also be complied with in all those cases in which, under the Constitution of Sweden, the Swedish Ministry, as such, is entitled to conduct the government. When, however, the King, by reason of travels abroad or sickness, is unable to conduct the administration, the Prince, entitled to the succession, if of age, shall conduct the administration as the temporary representative of the King, with the same power as belongs to an ad interim government.

Article 42. The King shall submit to the next Storthing in Norway and the next Rigsdag in Sweden a bill, based on the principles of perfect equality between both kingdoms, to carry out the provisions of Articles 39, 40 and 41, aforesaid.

Article 43. The election of a Regency, to conduct the administration for the King during his minority, shall take place according to the same rules and in the same manner prescribed in Article 7, aforesaid, for the election of a successor to the Crown.

Article 44. The Norwegian members of the joint Ministry, to conduct the administration in the cases provided for in Articles 40 and 41, aforesaid, shall take the following oath before the Storthing:

"I promise and depose that I will conduct the administration of the government conformable to the Constitution and the laws, so help me God and His Holy Writ," and the Swedish members shall take an oath before the Legislative Assembly of Sweden. If the Storthing or Rigsdag is not at that time in session, the oath shall be deposited, with the Ministry, in writing, and shall be renewed before the next Storthing or Rigsdag.

Article 45. As soon as the administration of the joint Ministry shall cease, they shall render an account of the same to the King and the Storthing.

Article 46. If those, on whom it is incumbent, pursuant to Articles 39 and 41, fail to immediately convene the Storthing, it shall be the peremptory duty of the Supreme Court, after a lapse of four weeks, to convene the same.

Article 47. The management of the education of the King, under age, shall, if his father has left no written directions concerning the same, be provided for in the manner prescribed in Articles 7 and 43. It shall be the invariable rule to give the King, during his minority, ample instructions in the Norwegian language.

Article 48. If the royal male line be extinct, and no successor has been selected, a new line of kings shall be chosen in the manner prescribed in Article 7; and in the meantime provision shall be made for the executive power as prescribed in Article 43 (40).

C. CITIZENSHIP AND THE LAW-MAKING POWER:

Article 49. The people shall exercise the legislative power through a Storthing, composed of two bodies, a Lagthing and an Odelsthing.

Article 50. All Norwegian citizens, dwelling within the realm, who have attained the age of twenty-five years, and have been residents of the country for five years, shall be qualified voters.

Article 51. All qualified voters shall be registered, in every city by the magistrate, and in every rural parish by the parson and tax collector. Changes that in the course of time may occur shall immediately be noted in the registry. Every voter shall, before he is registered, publicly in court, take an oath of fealty to the Constitution.

Article 52. The right of suffrage shall be suspended by:

(*a*) Indictment for an offence subject to the punishment described in Article 53; by

(*b*) Being placed under guardianship; by

(*c*) Assignment or bankruptcy, not caused by loss of fire or other evident misfortune, until the debtor, through full liquidation or composition, shall again regain control over his estate; and by

(*d*) Being supported, or having during the year immediately preceding the election been supported, as a public pauper.

Article 53. The right of suffrage shall be forfeited by:

(*a*) Having been sentenced to hard labor, removal from office, or imprisonment for an offence described in any of the chapters of the Criminal Code, relating to perjury, larceny, robbery or fraud; by (*b*) Entering the service of a foreign power, without the consent of the government; by

(*c*) Acquiring citizenship in a foreign country; and by

(*d*) Being convicted of buying votes, or selling one's own vote, or of voting in more than one election precinct.

Article 54. Elections and electoral meetings shall be held every third year. They shall be concluded before the end of the month of December.

Article 55. Elections shall be held, at the chief church of the parish, in the rural districts, and at a church, the town hall, or other suitable place, in the towns. The parish priest and his vestrymen shall be the judges of election in the rural districts, the magistrate and selectmen in the towns. The vote shall be taken in the order the names appear on the registry. Controversies about the right to vote shall be determined by the judges of election, whose decision may be appealed from to the Storthing.

Article 56. The Constitution shall be audibly read, in the towns by the chief magistrate, and in the rural districts by the priest, before the polls are opened.

Article 57. In the towns, one elector shall be chosen for every fifty inhabitants qualified to vote. Within eight days after their election, the electors shall assemble at the place designated therefor by the magistracy, and shall elect, either from their own number or from the other qualified voters in their electoral district, thirty-eight representatives, to meet and sit in the Storthing. Of this number, unless otherwise constitutionally provided, one shall be elected from Aalesund and Molde combined, one from Arendal and Grimstad combined, four from Bergen, one from Brevig, four from Christiania, Hónefas and Kongsvinger combined, two from Christianssand, one from Christianssund, two from Drammen, one from Flekkefjord, one from Frederickshald, one from Fredericksstad, one from Hammerfest, Vardó and Vadsó combined, one from Holmestrand, one from Kongsberg, one from Krageró, one from Laurvig and Sandefjord combined, one from Lillehammer, Hamer and Gjóvik combined, one from Moss and Dróbak combined, one from Porsgrund, one from Sarpsborg, one from Skien, two from Stavanger and Haugesund combined, one from Tromsö, four from Throndhjem and Levanger combined, one from Tunsberg, and one from Osterrisór. When a town, not herein named, shall have fifty or more inhabitants, who are qualified voters, it shall be attached to the nearest town-electoral district. The same rule shall apply to towns that may hereafter be founded. A town attached to a town-electoral district shall choose one elector, even though the number of inhabitants qualified to vote shall become less than fifty. In no case shall less than three electors be chosen in a town which, by itself alone, constitutes one representative district.

Article 58. In every parish in the rural districts, the inhabitants qualified to vote shall choose, in proportion to their numbers, electors as follows: One hundred or less shall choose one; from one hundred to two hundred, two; from two hundred to three hundred, three, and so on in the same proportion. The electors shall, within a month after their election, assemble at a place designated therefor by the high sheriff of the county, and shall then elect, either from their own number or from the other qualified voters in their county, seventy-six Representatives, to meet and sit in the Storthing, of whom five shall be chosen from the county of Agershus, five from the county of Nordre Bergenhus, five from the county of Sóndre Bergenhus, five from the county of Christians, two from the county of Finmarken, five from the county of Hedemarken, five from the county of Nordland, five from the county of Romsdalen, five from the county of Stavanger, two from the county of Tromsö, and four from each of the other eight counties of the kingdom. Ex-Ministers or ex-Secretaries of State shall be eligible for Representatives in any electoral district, if, barring residence, they are qualified voters and have not already been elected in some other district. But no district shall elect more than one non-resident Representative.

Article 59. (Repealed.)

Article 60. Qualified voters, being within the country, who, by reason of sickness, military service, or other valid excuse, are unable to attend the polls, may, in writing, transmit their votes to the judges of election before the polls are closed.

Article 61. No one shall be elected Representative unless he is thirty years of age and has resided ten years within the realm.

Article 62. Members of the Ministry, the officials employed in its bureaus, and the officials and pensionaries of the Court, are all ineligible for Representatives.

Article 63. Whoever is elected Representative, except ex-members of the Ministry elected under the last clause in Article 58, shall be required to accept the office, unless prevented by an excuse deemed valid by the electors, whose decision may be reviewed by the Storthing. Whoever has served as a Representative in three regular sessions of the Storthing succeeding the same election, shall not be bound to accept election to the next Storthing. If a Representative is prevented by valid excuse from attending the Storthing, the person receiving the next highest vote shall take his place, unless an alternate was elected at the district electoral meeting, in which case he shall take the place of the Representative.

Article 64. Immediately after their election, the Representatives shall be furnished with certificates of election, subscribed in the rural districts by the magistracy, in the towns by the chief magistrate, and in both cases by several electors, as evidence that they have been elected in the manner prescribed in the Constitution. The validity of these credentials shall be passed upon by the Storthing.

Article 65. Each Representative shall be entitled to compensation, from the State Treasury, for expenses of travel to and from the Storthing, and for subsistence during attendance.

Article 66. Representatives shall, except when apprehended in public offences, be privileged from arrest during their attendance at the Storthing, and in going to and returning from the same; and they shall not be answerable, outside of the sessions of the Storthing, for the expression of their views therein; but every Representative shall conform to the established rules of procedure.

Article 67. The Representatives, elected in the manner aforesaid, shall constitute the Storthing of the Kingdom of Norway.

Article 68. The Storthing shall, as a rule, convene on the first week-day in the month of February in each year, at the capital of the Kingdom, except when the King, on account of extraordinary circumstances, such as hostile invasion or contagious disease, shall designate another town in the realm therefor. Timely notice of such designation shall, in such case, be published.

Article 89. The King may, on extraordinary occasions, convene the Storthing at other than the usual time. In such case the King shall issue a proclamation, which shall be read in all the churches of the Episcopal towns at least fourteen days before the members of the Storthing shall assemble at the place prescribed.

Article 70. Such special Storthing may be adjourned by the King at his pleasure.

Article 71. The members of the Storthing shall serve as such for three successive years, as well at all special, as at all regular, sessions that may in the meantime be held.

Article 72. If a special Storthing be in session at the time a regular Storthing convenes, the former shall adjourn before the latter assembles.

Article 73. The Storthing shall select from its members one-fourth who shall constitute the Lagthing; the other three-fourths shall constitute the Odelsthing. The selection shall be made at the first regular Storthing which convenes after an election, and thereafter the Lagthing shall remain unchanged in all Storthings assembled after the same election, except in cases of vacancy, which shall be filled by special election. Each Thing shall hold its sessions separately, and appoint its own President and Secretary. Neither Thing shall be in session unless two-thirds of its members are present.

Article 74. As soon as the Storthing has organized, the King, or whoever he may appoint therefor, shall open its proceedings with a speech from the throne, wherein he shall give information touching the condition of the kingdom and the matters to which he especially desires to direct the Storthing's attention. No deliberation shall take place in the presence of the King. After the session of the Storthing has been opened, the Minister of State and the Secretaries of State shall be entitled to sit in the Storthing and both branches thereof, and to participate in its proceedings, without the right to vote, in open session on a footing of equality with the members, and in secret session only to the extent permitted by the Thing.

Article 75. The Storthing shall have power:

(*a*) To enact and repeal laws; to levy taxes, imposts, duties, and other public assessments, but such levy shall not remain in force beyond the first day of July in the year in which the next regular Storthing convenes, unless expressly revived by the latter;

(*b*) To borrow money on the credit of the Kingdom;

(*c*) To regulate the currency of the Kingdom;

(*d*) To appropriate the money necessary for the expenditures of the government;

(*e*) To determine the amount which shall yearly be paid the King for the maintenance of his royal household, and to settle the appanage of the royal family, which shall not, however, consist of landed estates;

(*f*) To cause to be laid before them the Journal of the Ministry in Norway and all official reports and documents, not pertaining to exclusive military commands, then on file, together with verified copies and extracts of the Journals, on file with the King, kept by the Norwegian Minister of State and the two Norwegian Secretaries of State remaining in Sweden, as well as the public documents on file with them;

(*g*) To cause to be communicated to them the Alliances and Treaties, which the King, on behalf of the state, has entered into with foreign powers, except secret articles, which must not, however, conflict with those that are public;

(*h*) To require any person to appear before them, in state affairs, except the King and royal family; but this exception shall not apply to royal princes holding office;

(*i*) To revise temporary salary and pension lists, and to make such changes therein as they find necessary;

(*k*) To appoint five auditors who shall yearly audit the accounts of the state and publish printed extracts of the same; and for this purpose the accounts shall be submitted to the auditors within six months from the expiration of the year for which the appropriations of the Storthing has been made; and

(*l*) To naturalize foreigners.

Article 76. Every bill shall first be introduced in the Odelsthing, either by a member thereof or by the Ministry, through one of its members. If the bill is there passed, it shall be sent to the Lagthing, which may concur in or reject it; in the latter case it shall be returned with objections appended, and the same shall be considered by the Odelsthing, which may either indefinitely postpone the bill or return it to the Lagthing with or without amendment. When a bill, from the Odelsthing, has been twice presented to the Lagthing and has been returned a second time rejected, the entire Storthing shall assemble in one body, and, by a two-thirds vote, dispose of the bill. At least three days must intervene between every such distinct consideration of the bill.

Article 77. When a measure, passed by the Odelsthing, has been concurred in by the Lagthing or the united Storthing, it shall be sent by a committee of both bodies of the Storthing to the King, if he is present, or if not present, to the Norwegian Ministry, with the request for the sanction of the King.

Article 78. If the King approve the measure, he shall affix his signature thereto, whereby it becomes a law. If he disapprove the same, he shall return it to the Odelsthing with the statement that, for the time being, he does not find it expedient to sanction the same.

Article 79. If a measure has been passed without amendment, by three regular Storthings, convened after three separate and successive elections, and separated from each other by not less than two intervening regular Storthings, and no measure in conflict therewith having, in the meantime, from the first to the last passage, been passed by any Storthing, and the measure is then presented to the King with the request that his Majesty will not refuse his sanction to a measure which the Storthing, after the most mature consideration, deem beneficial, it shall become a law, notwithstanding the King fails to sanction the same before the adjournment of the Storthing.

Article 80. The Storthing may remain in session so long as it deems necessary, not, however, over two months, without the permission of the King. When, after having finished its proceedings, or after having been in session the time limited, it is adjourned by the King, he shall communicate to it his action upon the measures passed, by approving or rejecting the same. All measures not expressly approved by him shall be deemed rejected.

Article 81. All laws shall be promulgated in the Norwegian language, and, except those passed pursuant to Article 79, in the name of the King, and under the seal of the Kingdom of Norway, in the following words:

"We—N. N.—make known that there has been presented to us an Act of the Storthing of the following tenor: (here follows the Act), which we have accepted and approved and hereby accept and approve, as law, under our hand and the seal of the realm."

Article 82. The sanction of the King shall not be required for those resolutions of the Storthing whereby:

(*a*) It declares itself convened as Storthing pursuant to the Constitution;

(*b*) It determines its own rules of procedure;

(*c*) It approves or rejects the credentials of the members present;

(*d*) It affirms or reverses decisions in election controversies;

(*e*) It naturalizes foreigners;

(*f*) And finally, not for the resolution whereby the Odelsthing shall impeach members of the Ministry, or others.

Article 83. The Storthing shall have the right to procure the opinion of the Supreme Court upon judicial subjects.

Article 84. The Storthing shall sit in open session and its proceedings shall be printed and published, except in cases where otherwise determined by a majority vote.

Article 85. Whoever shall obey a command, the purpose of which is to interfere with the freedom and safety of the Storthing, is guilty of treason against the Fatherland.

D. The Judicial Power:

Article 86. The members of the Lagthing, together with the Supreme Court, shall constitute the Court of Impeachment, which shall try, without appeal, cases instituted by the Odelsthing, against members of the Ministry and members of the Supreme Court for malfeasance in office, and against members of the Storthing for offences committed by them in their official capacity. The President of the Lagthing shall preside in the Court of Impeachment.

Article 87. The accused may, without cause, challenge as many as one-third of the members of the Court of Impeachment, but not so many, however, as to leave the Court with less than fifteen members.

Article 88. The Supreme Court shall be the tribunal of last resort. It shall consist of not less than one Chief-Justice and six associate judges. This article shall not prohibit the final disposal of criminal cases, pursuant to law, without appeal to the Supreme Court.

Article 89. In times of peace, the Supreme Court, together with two high military officers to be appointed by the King, shall constitute a court of appeal and of final resort in all court-martial cases, involving life, honor, or loss of liberty for a longer period than three months.

Article 90. The decisions of the Supreme Court shall in no case be appealed or reviewed.

Article 91. No one shall be appointed a member of the Supreme Court before he is thirty years of age.

E. GENERAL PROVISIONS:

Article 92. Public offices shall be filled only by Norwegian citizens who speak the language of the country and:

(*a*) Who are born within the realm of parents who are citizens of the country; or

(*b*) Who are born in foreign countries of Norwegian parents, not citizens of another nation; or

(*c*) Who shall hereafter reside ten years within the realm; or

(*d*) Who shall be naturalized by the Storthing. But persons without these qualifications may be appointed physicians, instructors in the university and grammar schools, and consuls in foreign places. No one shall be appointed a high magistrate before he is thirty years of age, nor an inferior judge, magistrate, or tax collector before he is twenty-five years of age. No one shall be a member of the Ministry unless he professes the established religion of the state; and the same rule shall apply to the other offices of the state, until otherwise provided by law.

Article 93. Norway shall not be liable for any other than its own national debt.

Article 94. Measures shall be taken to enact, at the next regular Storthing, or, if this is not possible, at the following one, a new general civil and criminal code. In the meantime the existing laws of the state shall remain in force so far as they are not in conflict with this Constitution or temporary ordinances meanwhile issued. Permanent taxes now existing shall continue as laid until the next Storthing.

Article 95. No dispensations, writs of protection, or letters of respite or reparation, shall be granted after the new general code takes effect.

Article 96. No one shall be tried except pursuant to law, nor punished except pursuant to judgment. Examination, by means of torture, is prohibited.

Article 97. No law shall be given retroactive effect.

Article 98. Fees paid to officials of Courts of Justice shall not be subject to any state tax.

Article 99. No one shall be arrested except in the case and manner prescribed by law. Whoever causes an unauthorized arrest, or unlawful detention, shall be answerable therefor to the person confined. The government shall have no right to employ military force against the citizens otherwise than pursuant to law, except in the case of an assembly disturbing the public peace and not immediately dispersing after the civil magistrate has thrice audibly read to them the articles in the public code relating to riot.

Article 100. The liberty of the press shall remain inviolate. No one shall be punished for any writing, printed or published, irrespective of its context, unless he has intentionally and clearly manifested, or urged others to manifest, disobedience to the laws, contempt for religion, morality, and the constitutional authorities, or resistance to the commands of the same, or has made false and defamatory charges against any person. Every person shall be permitted to express freely his opinion upon the administration of public affairs, or on any other subject whatsoever.

Article 101. New and permanent special privileges in industrial pursuits shall not be granted to any one hereafter.

Article 102. Domiciliary visits shall not be permitted except in criminal cases.

Article 103. No sanctuary shall be allowed to persons who hereafter become insolvent.

Article 104. Estates of inheritance, or distributive shares, shall in no case be subject to confiscation.

Article 105. If public necessity requires any person to relinquish his real or personal property for public use, he shall receive full compensation therefor from the State Treasury.

Article 106. The proceeds, as well as the income, of church estates, shall be devoted exclusively to the benefit of the church and the promotion of education. The property of charitable institutions shall be devoted exclusively to their use.

Article 107. Allodial tenure and statutory entailment shall not be abolished; but the conditions under which—for the good of the state and the advantages of the people—the same shall continue, shall be prescribed by the next or the following Storthing.

Article 108. No earldoms, baronies, or entailed manorial estates, shall hereafter be established.

Article 109. Every citizen, without regard to birth or fortune, shall, without exception, render military service to his country for a limited time. The application of this rule, the limitations to be placed on it, and whether it will be for the good of the country that liability to such service shall terminate with the twenty-fifth year, shall be left to the determination of the next regular Storthing, after a committee has obtained full information on the subject; and in the meantime all existing provisions in the premises shall remain in force.

Article 110. Norway shall have its own bank and its own currency and coinage, to be established by law.

Article 111. Norway shall be entitled to have its own Merchant Flag. Its naval ensign shall be a union flag.

Article 112. If experience demonstrates that any part of this Constitution of the Kingdom of Norway requires amendment, the proposition therefor shall be presented at a regular Storthing first succeeding an election, and notice thereof shall be given by publication; but no action shall be taken thereon until at one of the regular Storthings succeeding the next election. Such amendment shall not contravene the principles of this Constitution, and shall only relate to such modifications in single provisions as will not change the spirit of this Constitution, and shall be concurred in by two-thirds of the Storthing.

THE END

FOOTNOTES:

[1] Vendland, or Vindland, the country inhabited by the Vends, seems to have included Mecklenburg, Pomerania, and Prussia on the Baltic.

[2] The Swedes were then still heathens.

[3] Keelness (old Norse *Kjalarnes*) is supposed by the antiquaries to be the present Cape Cod, Massachusetts.

[4] Accounts of these journeys to Vinland are contained in the *Flateyar-bok*, or Flatey Codex, an Icelandic manuscript, which takes its name from the island Flatey, Iceland, where it was preserved. It was written by two priests between the years 1387 and 1395. The work is a collection of sagas transcribed from older manuscripts and arranged chronologically. The book is written on parchment, and is one of the most beautiful works of penmanship from that time in Europe. It is known that Christopher Columbus came to Iceland in 1477, on purpose to gain nautical information, and it would seem next to impossible that he should not have heard of the written accounts of the discoveries recorded in the Flatey Codex.

[5] A *Stallare* was a very influential officer, a kind of court marshal.

[6] The *Biarkemaal* is so called because it was composed and sung by Bodvar Biarke, a Norwegian, who, with Rolf Krake and others, was killed in battle. Rolf Krake was king in Seeland (Denmark); he had twelve powerful warriors called *Berserks* (*i.e.* dressed in bear skins); among them was Bodvar Biarke. Rolf and his men were attacked during the night, and the Biarkemaal was then sung to encourage Rolf's men to fight valiantly for their chief.

[7] "The Gray Goose," so called probably from the color of the parchment on which it is written, is one of the most curious relics of the Middle Ages, and gives us an unexpected view of the social condition of the Northmen in the eleventh century. Law appears to have been so far advanced among them that the forms were not merely established, but the slightest breach of the legal forms of proceeding involved the loss of the case. "The Gray Goose" embraces subjects not dealt with probably by any other code in Europe at that period. The provision for the poor, the equality of weights and measures, police of markets and of sea havens, provision for illegitimate children of the poor, inns for travellers, wages of servants and support of them in sickness, protection of pregnant women and even of domestic animals from injury, roads, bridges, vagrants, beggars, are subjects treated of in this code. (S. Laing.)

[8] From this union descended, in direct line, the royal house of Brunswick and Saxony, whose members until lately occupied the thrones of Hanover and Brunswick and still reign in England.

[9] The "guests" were one division of the king's men. They were of a lower rank than the *hird-men.*

[10] Ice-legs were skates made of sheep legs.

[11] Ski (pronounced she), the long snow-shoe used in the North.

[12] With this battle at Ree end the Sagas of the Norse Kings by Snorre Sturlason.

[13] The word *Edda* means great-grandmother.

[14] During the next twenty-five years Christian Frederick led an unnoticed life in Denmark and was soon forgotten by the Norwegian people. In 1839 he ascended the Danish throne as Christian VIII. He died in 1848.

[15] The word saga means a historical tale.

CPSIA information can be obtained
at www.ICGtesting.com
Printed in the USA
LVHW040957020323
740706LV00007B/734

9 789356 906198